Behavioral Science and the Manager's Role

SELECTED READINGS SERIES
NINE

Behavioral Science and the Manager's Role

Edited by

William B. Eddy

Director, Center for Management Development
School of Administration
University of Missouri at Kansas City

W. Warner Burke

Program Director
Center for Organization Studies
NTL Institute

Vladimir A. Dupré

Director, Regional and Metropolitan Activities
NTL Institute

Oron P. South

Director, Midwest Group for Human Resources
A Division of NTL Institute

NTL INSTITUTE FOR APPLIED BEHAVIORAL SCIENCE

G93-373 wak

Foreword

A major goal of the NTL Institute is to link theory and practice in the field of behavioral science. To help achieve that goal NTL's Organization Study Center has prepared this latest number in the Selected Reading Series, concerned with managerial behavior.

The articles were chosen because they have proven helpful to managers. Although many of the articles deal with the management process in the context of business organizations, their potential application is much broader. The material should be just as useful to the pastor, the YMCA secretary, the university president, or the classroom teacher as to the business executive, since each of these non-business persons has roles and functions which are clearly managerial.

The editors have had a wide variety of research, consulting and training experience in the field of applied behavioral science. In addition, all have been responsible, at one time or another, for "meeting a payroll."

The NTL Institute is pleased to add this volume to its series.

JERRY HARVEY, Deputy Director
NTL Institute

THE SELECTED READINGS SERIES

This series was initiated in 1961 to bring together papers bearing on major concerns in human relations training. Previous numbers in the series are listed below.

ONE Group Development
     edited by Leland P. Bradford

TWO Leadership in Action
     edited by Gordon L. Lippitt

THREE Human Forces in Teaching and Learning
     edited by Leland P. Bradford

FOUR Forces in Community Development
     edited by Dorothy and H. Curtis Mial

FIVE Issues in Training
     edited by Irving R. Wechsler and Edgar H. Schein

SIX Conference Planning
     edited by Richard Beckhard

SEVEN Citizen Participation in Urban Development——
     Concepts and Issues
     edited by Hans B.C. Spiegel

EIGHT Citizen Participation in Urban Development——
     Cases and Programs
     edited by Hans B.C. Spiegel

Contents

Contributors

ROBERT C. ALLBROOK

Associate Editor
Fortune Magazine

CHRIS ARGYRIS

Professor of Administrative
  Sciences
Yale University

HOWARD BAUMGARTEL

Professor of Psychology
University of Kansas

WARREN BENNIS

Vice president for Academic
  Development
State University of New York,
  Buffalo

ALVIN C. BIDWELL

Consultant in Communication
  and Training
Humble Oil and Refining Co.

ROBERT R. BLAKE

Scientific Methods, Inc.
Austin, Texas

PAUL J. BROUWER

Management Psychologist
Cleveland, Ohio

GILBERT BURCK

Member, Board of Editors
Fortune Magazine

W. WARNER BURKE

Program Director, Center for
  Organization Studies
NTL Institute

JAMES V. CLARK

Vice chairman, Graduate School
  of Business Administration
UCLA

SHELDON A. DAVIS

Vice president, Director of
  Industrial Relations
TRW Systems

WILLIAM B. EDDY

Associate Professor of
  Administration
University of Missouri at
  Kansas City

JACK R. GIBB

Consulting Psychologist
La Jolla, California

ROGER HARRISON

Consultant
London, England

GORDON L. LIPPITT

Professor of Behavioral Sciences
George Washington University

DOUGLAS M. McGREGOR*

formerly Sloan Professor of
   Management
Massachusetts Institute of
   Technology

JANE S. MOUTON

Scientific Methods, Inc.
Austin, Texas

M. SCOTT MYERS

Development Director
Texas Instruments, Inc.

BARRY OSHRY

Consultant
Boston, Massachusetts

CARL R. ROGERS

Resident Fellow, Center for
   Studies of the Person
La Jolla, California

JAMES V. SPOTTS

Assistant Professor of Psychology
University School of Medicine
University of Missouri at
   Kansas City

ROBERT TANNENBAUM

Professor of Behavioral Science
Graduate School of Business
   Administration
UCLA

RICHARD W. WALLEN*

formerly of Nevis-Wallen
   Associates
Cleveland, Ohio

* Deceased

Preface

Researchers, consultants, educators and practitioners working in the various disciplines of the social and administrative sciences are contributing to a growing body of knowledge and technique which we label "applied behavioral science." The literature in this relatively new field combines scientific theory and data from social psychology, industrial sociology and psychology, administrative science, and related disciplines, with methods of application developed by managers, consultants, teachers, and others acting as change agents.

The ideas and theories of applied behavioral science are not viewed as finalized and complete. The field is in a relatively early stage of development, and the hypotheses need further testing. The general point of view described in these articles, while well accepted, does not represent the thinking of all social scientists and administrators; there are other schools of thought. Indeed, the authors would probably disagree among themselves on several points.

These articles have been drawn together to help managers and students gain insight into this approach. They have particularly to do with that portion of organizational life which involves human behavior, and they deal in various ways with the interaction between people and the system, and the impact of each upon the other. The collection is slanted toward application as well as analysis and understanding. Hopefully, the reader will be stimulated to try out some of the ideas discussed.

The material is organized to represent the major foci of the field. Following some discussion of the relation of behavioral science to business, attention is paid to the individual—his characteristics and self-understanding. The focus then shifts to leadership as an interpersonal process and to the organizational social system. The next section examines approaches to changing and developing the organization. Our intention was not to encompass the entire management process, but rather to explore in some depth those aspects involving human interaction variables.

There is some overlapping in the content of the articles because of the wide variety of sources from which they were taken. This has also made it difficult in some cases to preserve the original format of certain charts and tables.

It goes without saying that the major credit for this book belongs to the authors of the original articles. We are grateful to our friends and colleagues in the field for stimulating our thinking about organizations and introducing us to many of the issues discussed herein. Howard Baumgartel, Seymour Levy, and Howard Trier made helpful suggestions about articles to be included. The assistance provided by Gladys Mullen was invaluable.

William B. Eddy
W. Warner Burke
Vladimir A. Dupré
Oron P. South

Kansas City, Missouri
July 1969

Behavioral Science
and Business

Two behavioral scientists, one a manager, the other an academician, discuss the changing value system they see emerging from new approaches to management and employee relations. The second article reveals common misunderstandings of behavioral science approaches on the part of the business community.

Values, Man, and Organizations

ROBERT TANNENBAUM and
SHELDON A. DAVIS

"... we are today in a period when the development of theory
within the social sciences will permit innovations which are at present
inconceivable. Among these will be dramatic changes in the organization and management of economic enterprise. The capacities of the
average human being for creativity, for growth, for collaboration, for
productivity (in the full sense of the term) are far greater than we have
recognized ... it is possible that the next half century will bring the
most dramatic social changes in human history." [1]

For those concerned with organization theory and with organizational development work, this is an exciting and challenging time.
Probably never before have the issues at the interface between changing
organizations and maturing man been so apparent, so compelling, and
of such potentially critical relevance to both. And to a considerable
extent, the sparks at the interface reflect differences in values both
within organizations and within man—human values which are coming
loose from their moorings, whose functional relevance is being re-
examined and tested, and which are without question in transition.

Many organizations today, particularly those at the leading edge of
technology, are faced with ferment and flux. In increasing instances,
the bureaucratic model—with its emphasis on relatively rigid structure,
well-defined functional specialization, direction and control exercised
through a formal hierarchy of authority, fixed systems of rights, duties,
and procedures, and relative impersonality of human relationships—is
responding inadequately to the demands placed upon it from the outside and from within the organization. There is increasing need for
experimentation, for learning from experience, for flexibility and
adaptability, and for growth. There is a need for greater inventiveness

1. McGregor, D. M., *The Professional Manager*. New York, McGraw-Hill, 1967.
p. 244.

Reprinted by permission from *Industrial Management Review*, Vol. 10, No. 2
(Winter 1969) pp. 67-83. Copyright by the Alfred P. Sloan School of Management, Massachusetts Institute of Technology.

and creativity, and a need for collaboration among individuals and groups. Greater job mobility and the effective use of temporary systems seem essential. An environment must be created in which people will be more fully utilized and challenged and in which people can grow as human beings.

In his recent book, *Changing Organizations,* Warren Bennis has pointed out that the bureaucratic form of organization "is becoming less and less effective, that it is hopelessly out of joint with contemporary realities, and that new shapes, patterns, and models . . . are emerging which promise drastic changes in the conduct of the corporation and in managerial practices in general."[2] At least one of the newer models, the one with which our recent experience is most closely connected, is organic and systems-oriented. We feel that, for the present at least, this model is one which can suggest highly useful responses to the newer demands facing organizations.

At this historical juncture, it is not just organizations which are in flux. Man, perhaps to an extent greater than ever before, is coming alive; he is ceasing to be an object to be used, and is increasingly asserting himself, his complexity, and his importance. Not quite understanding why or how, he is moving slowly but ever closer to the center of the universe.

The factors underlying man's emergence are complex and interrelated. They include higher levels of educational attainment, an increased availability of technology which both frees man from the burdens of physical and routine labor and makes him more dependent on society, an increasing rate of change affecting his environment which both threatens and challenges him, and higher levels of affluence which open up opportunities for a variety and depth of experiences never before so generally available.

The evidences of this trend are many. They are to be found, for example, in the gropings within many religions for more viable modes and values. They are to be found in the potent thrusts for independence of minorities everywhere, and in the challenges of our youth who find our values phony and often materialistically centered. They are to be found in the involvement of so many people in psychotherapy, in sensitivity training, and in self-expression activities in the arts and elsewhere. They are also to be found in the continuing and growing interest in writings and ideas in the general direction of the humanistic-existential orientation to man.

2. Bennis, W. G., *Changing Organizations*, New York, McGraw-Hill, 1966, p. 4.

Organizations are questioning and moving away from the bureaucratic model, in part because man is asserting his individuality and his
centrality, in part because of growing dissatisfaction with the personally
constraining impact of bureaucracies. In this flux, organizations and
man must find a way with each other. In our view, this way will be
found through changing values—values which can hopefully serve the
needs for effectiveness and survival of organizations and the needs for
individuality and growth of emergent man. Those concerned with
organization theory and with organizational development have, in our
judgment, a most important role to play in this quest.

Values in Transition

Deeply impressed with the managerial and organizational implications of the increasing accumulation of knowledge about human
behavior, Professor Douglas McGregor formulated his assumptions of
Theory Y. [3] According to him, these assumptions were essentially his
interpretations, based upon the newer knowledge and on his extensive
experience, of the nature of man and of man's motivation. In our view,
McGregor was overly cautious and tentative in calling the Theory Y
tenets "assumptions" and in limiting them to being his "interpretations." In trying to be "scientific," he seemed reluctant in his writing to
assert explicity as *values* those elements (including the Theory Y
assumptions) which so much affected his organizational theory and
practice. He was not alone in his reluctance. Perhaps the most pervasive
common characteristic among people in laboratory training and in
organizational development work is their values, and yet, while organizational development academicians and practitioners are generally
aware of their shared values and while these values implicitly guide
much of what they do, they too have usually been reluctant to make
them explicit.

We want here not only to own our values but also to state them
openly. These values are consistent with McGregor's assumptions and in
some instances go beyond his. They are not scientifically derived nor
are they new, but they are compatible with relevant "findings" emerging in the behavioral sciences. They are deeply rooted in the nature of
man and are therefore basically humanistic. As previously suggested,
many of the values underlying the bureaucratic model and its typical

3. See p. 157.

implementation have been inconsistent with the nature of man, with the result that he has not been fully utilized, his motivation has been reduced, his growth as a person stunted, and his spirit deadened. These outcomes sorely trouble us, for we believe organizations can in the fullest sense serve man as well as themselves.

Growing evidence strongly suggests that humanistic values not only resonate with an increasing number of people in today's world, but also are highly consistent with the effective functioning of organizations built on the newer organic model. As we discuss a number of these values, we will provide some face validity for their viability by illustrating them with cases or experiences taken from our involvements with or knowledge of a number of organizations which recently have been experimenting with the interface between the organizational and humanistic frontiers described above. The illustrations come primarily from TRW Systems, with which we have had a continuing collaboration for more than four years. Other organizations with which one or both of us have been involved include Aluminum Company of Canada, Ltd., U.S. Department of State, and the Organizational Behavior Group of Case Institute of Technology.

We clearly recognize that the values to which we hold are not absolutes, that they represent directions rather than final goals. We also recognize that the degree of their short-run application often depends upon the people and other variables involved. We feel that we are now in a period of transition, sometimes slow and sometimes rapid, involving a movement away from older, less personally meaningful and organizationally relevant values toward these newer values.

Away from a View of Man as Essentially Bad Toward a View of Him as Basically Good—At his core, man is not inherently evil, lazy, destructive, hurtful, irresponsible, narrowly self-centered, and the like. The life experiences which he has, including his relationships with other people and the impact on him of the organizations with which he associates, can and often do move him in these directions. On the other hand, his more central inclination toward the good is reflected in his behavior as an infant, in his centuries-long evolution of ethical and religious precepts, and in the directions of his strivings and growth as a result of experiences such as those in psychotherapy and sensitivity training. Essentially man is internally motivated toward positive personal and social ends; the extent to which he is not motivated results from a process of demotivation generated by his relationships and/or environment.

We have been impressed with the degree to which the fairly pervasive cultural assumption of man's badness has led to organizational forms and practices designed to control, limit, push, check upon, inhibit, and punish. We are also increasingly challenged by the changes in behavior resulting from a growing number of experiments with organizational forms and practices rooted in the view of man as basically good. Within an organization it is readily apparent to both members and perceptive visitors whether or not there is, in general, an atmosphere of respect for the individual as a person. Are people treated arbitrarily? Are there sinister coups taking place? How much of the time and energy of the members of the organization is devoted to constructive problem solving rather than to playing games with each other, back-biting, politicking, destructive competition, and other dysfunctional behavior? How does management handle problems such as the keeping of time records? (Some organizations do not have time clocks and yet report that employees generally do not abuse this kind of a system.) One of the authors can remember a chain of retail stores which fired a stock clerk because he had shifty eyes, although he was one of the best stock boys in that chain. There are all kinds of negative assumptions about man behind such an incredible action.

For a long period of time, two senior engineers, Taylor and Durant, had real difficulty in working together. Each had a negative view of the other; mutual respect was lacking. Such attitudes resulted in their avoiding each other even though their technical disciplines were closely related. A point in time was reached when Taylor sorely needed help from Durant. Caught up in his own negative feelings, however, he clearly was not about to ask Durant for help. Fortunately, two of Taylor's colleagues who did not share his feelings prodded him into asking Durant to work with him on the problem. Durant responded most positively, and brought along two of his colleagues the next day to study the problem in detail. He then continued to remain involved with Taylor until the latter's problem was solved. Only a stereotype had kept these men apart; Taylor's eventual willingness to approach Durant opened the door to constructive problem solving.

Away from Avoidance or Negative Evaluation of Individuals Toward Confirming Them as Human Beings—One desire frequently expressed by people with whom we consult is: "I wish I knew where I stand with my boss (with this organization) (with my colleagues) (with my subordinates). I'd really like to know what they think of me personally." We are not referring to the excessively neurotic needs of some persons for attention and response, but rather to the much more pervasive and basic need to know that one's existence makes a difference to others.

Feedback that is given is generally negative in character and often destructive of the individual instead of being focused on the perceived shortcomings of a given performance. It seems to be exceedingly difficult for most of us to give positive feedback to others—and, more specifically, to express genuine feelings of affection and caring.

When people are seen as bad, they need to be disciplined and cor-rected on the issue only; when they are seen as good, they need to be confirmed. Avoidance and negative evaluation can lead individuals to be cautious, guarded, defensive. Confirmation can lead to personal release, confidence, and enhancement.

A senior executive reported to one of us that he did not get nearly as much feedback as he wanted about how people thought about him as a person and whether or not they cared for him. He reported that one of the most meaningful things that had happened to him in this regard occurred when the person he reported to put his arm around him briefly at the end of a working session, patted him on the shoulder, and said, "Keep up the good work," communicating a great deal of warmth and positive feelings towards the person through this behavior. This event had taken place two years ago and lasted about five seconds, yet it was still fresh in the senior executive's memory and obviously has had a great deal of personal meaning for him. In our culture, most of us are grossly undernourished and have strong need for the personal caring of others.

Away from a View of Individuals as Fixed, Toward Seeing Them as Being in Process—The traditional view of individuals is that they can be defined in terms of given interests, knowledge, skills, and personality characteristics: they can gain new knowledge, acquire additional skills, and even at times change their interests, but it is rare that people really change. This view, when buttressed by related organizational attitudes and modes, insures a relative fixity of individuals, with crippling effects. The value to which we hold is that people can constantly be in flux, groping, questing, testing, experimenting, and growing. We are struck by the tremendous untapped potential in most individuals yearning for discovery and release. Individuals may rarely change in core attributes, but the range of alternatives for choice can be widened, and the ability to learn how to learn more about self can be enhanced.

Organizations at times question whether it is their responsibility to foster individual growth. Whether or not it is, we believe that for most organizations, especially those desiring long-term survival through adaptability, innovation, and change, it is an increasing necessity. Further, evidence suggests that to have people in process requires a growth-enhancing environment. Personal growth requires healthy organizations. This value, then, carries with it great implications for work in organizational development. In organizations, people continuously experience interpersonal difficulties in relating to the other people with whom they must work. Some reasons for the difficulties are that people listen very badly to each other, attribute things of a negative nature to another person, and make all kinds of paranoid assumptions, with the result that communication breaks down rather severely.

There have been many instances within TRW Systems of people, who, in the eyes of others around them, produce some fairly significant changes in their own behavior. Most of these changes have been reported quite positively. In some cases there have been rather dramatic changes with respect to how a person faces certain kinds of problems— how he handles conflicts, how he conducts staff meetings. In those cases an individual who is perceived as having changed quite often reports that these changes are personally rewarding, that he feels better about himself and more optimistic and expansive about life.

TRW Systems is committed to a continuation and improvement of its Career Development program, which places considerable emphasis on the personal and professional growth of its members. Although the original commitment was perhaps largely based on faith, experience gained in recent years strongly suggests that one of the most productive investments the organization can make is in the continuing growth of its members and in the health of the environment in which they work.

Away From Resisting and Fearing Individual Differences Toward Accepting and Utilizing Them—The pervasive and long-standing view of man as bad takes on even more serious implications when individual differences among men appear—differences in race, religion, personality (including personal style), specialties, and personal perceptions (definitions of truth or reality). A bad man poses sufficient problems but a strange bad man often becomes impossible.

Organizations and individuals are frequently threatened by what they consider questioning of or challenge to their existing values and modes, represented by the presence of alternative possibilities. And they choose to avoid the challenge and the related and expected conflicts, discomforts, and the like, which might follow. As a result, they achieve drabness, a lack of creativity, and a false sense of peace and security. We firmly believe that the existence of differences can be highly functional. There is no single truth, no one right way, no chosen people. It is at the interface of differences that ferment occurs and that the potential for creativity exists. Furthermore, for an organization to deny to itself (in the name of "harmony" or some similar shibboleth) the availability of productive resources simply because they do not conform to an irrelevant criterion is nothing short of madness. To utilize differences creatively is rarely easy, but our experience tells us that the gains far outweigh the costs.

In the play "Right You Are," Pirandello makes the point that truth in a particular human situation is a collection of what each individual in the situation sees. Each person will see different facets of the same event. In a positive sense, this would lead us to value seeing all the various facets of an issue or problem as they unfold in the eyes of all the beholders and to place a positive value on our interdependence with others, particularly in situations where each of us can have only part of the answer or see part of the reality.

An organization recently faced the problem of filling a key position. The man whose responsibility it was to fill the position sat down with five or six people who, due to their various functional roles, would have a great deal of interaction with the person in that position and with his organization. The man asked them to help him identify logical candidates. The group very quickly identified a number of people who ought to be considered and the two or three who were the most logical candidates. Then the group went beyond the stated agenda and came up with a rather creative new organizational notion, which was subsequently implemented and proved to be very desirable. After this took place, the executive, who had called the meeting in order to get the help for the decision he had to make, reported that it was very clear to him that doing the job became much easier by getting everyone together to share their varying perceptions. This meant that he had more relevant data available to him in making his decision. Furthermore, the creative organizational concept only came about as a result of the meeting's having taken place.

In most organizations persons and groups with markedly different training, experience, points of view, and modes of operating frequently bump into each other. Project managers face functional performers, mechanical engineers face electrical engineers, designers face hardware specialists, basic researchers face action-oriented engineers, financial specialists face starry-eyed innovators. Each needs to understand and respect the world of the other, and organizations should place a high value upon and do much to facilitate the working through of the differences which come into sharp focus at interfaces such as these.

Away from Utilizing an Individual Primarily with Reference to his Job Description Toward Viewing Him as a Whole Person—People get pigeon-holed very easily, with job description (or expectations of job performance) typically becoming the pigeon hole. A cost accountant is hired, and from then on he is seen and dealt with as a cost accountant. Our view is that people generally have much more to contribute and to develop than just what is expected of them in their specific positions. Whole persons, not parts of persons, are hired and available for contribution. The organizational challenge is to recognize this fact and discover ways to provide outlets for the rich, varied, and often untapped resources available to them.

One of many personal examples that could be cited within TRW Systems is that of a person trained as a theoretical physicist. Having pursued this profession for many years, he is now effectively serving also as a part-time behavioral science consultant (a third-party process facilitator) to the personnel organization within the company. This is an activity for which he had no previous formal training until a new-found interest began asserting itself. The organization has supported him in this interest, has made a relevant learning opportunity available to him, and has opened the door to his performing an additional function within the organization.

An organizational example involves the question of charters that are defined for particular sub-elements of the organization: divisions, staffs, labs, etc. What are their functions? What are they supposed to do? To state the extreme, an organizational unit can have very sharply defined charters so that each person in it knows exactly what he is supposed to do and not do. This can lead to very clean functional relationships. Another approach, however, is to say that the *core* of the charter will be very clear with discrete responsibilities identified, but the outer edges (where one charter interacts with others) will not be sharply defined and will deliberately overlap and interweave with other charters. The latter approach assumes that there is a potential synergy within an organization which people can move toward fully actualizing if they can be constructive and creative in their interpersonal and intergroup relations. Very different charters are produced in this case, with very different outcomes. Such charters must, by definition, not be clean and sharply described, or the innovative and coordinated outcomes that might come about by having people working across charter boundaries will not occur.

Away from Walling-Off the Expression of Feelings Toward Making Possible Both Appropriate Expression and Effective Use—In our culture, there is a pervasive fear of feelings. From early childhood, children are taught to hide, repress, or deny the existence of their feelings, and their learnings are reinforced as they grow older. People are concerned about "losing control," and organizations seek rational, proper, task-oriented behavior, which emphasizes head-level as opposed to gut-level behavior. But organizations also seek high motivation, high morale, loyalty, team work, commitment, and creativity, all of which, if they are more than words, stem from personal feelings. Further, an individual cannot be a whole person if he is prevented from using or divorced from his feelings. And the energy dissipated in repression of feelings is lost to more productive endeavors.

We appreciate and are not afraid of feelings, and strongly believe that organizations will increasingly discover that they have a reservoir of untapped resources available to them in the feelings of their members, that the repression of feelings in the past has been more costly, both to them and to their members, than they ever thought possible.

One of the relevant questions to ask within an organization is how well problems stay solved once they are apparently solved. If the feelings involved in such problems are not directly dealt with and worked through, the problem usually does not remain solved for very long. For example, if two subordinates are fighting about something, their supervisor can either intervene and make the decision for them or arbitrate. Both methods can solve the immediate difficulty, but the fundamental problem will most likely again occur in some other situation or at some other time. The supervisor has dealt only with the symptoms of the real problem.

The direct expression of feelings, no matter what they are, does typically take place somewhere along the line, but usually not in the relevant face-to-face relationship. A person will attend a staff meeting and experience a great deal of frustration with the meeting as a whole or with the behavior of one or more persons in it. He will then talk about his feelings with another colleague outside the meeting or bring them home and discuss them with or displace them on his wife or children, rather than talking about them in the meeting where such behavior might make an important difference. To aid communication of feelings, participants at a given staff meeting could decide that one of the agenda items will be: "How do we feel about this meeting; how is it going; how can it be improved?" They could then talk face-to-face with each other while the feeling is immediately relevant to the effective functioning of the staff group. The outcomes of the face-to-face confrontation can be far more constructive than the "dealing-with symptoms" approach.

Away from Maskmanship and Game-Playing Toward Authentic Behavior—Deeply rooted in existing organizational lore is a belief in the necessity or efficacy of being what one is not, both as an individual and as a group. Strategy and out-maneuvering are valued. Using diplomacy, wearing masks, not saying what one thinks or expressing what one feels, creating an image—these and other deceptive modes are widely utilized. As a result, in many interpersonal and intergroup relations, mask faces mask, image faces image, and much energy is employed in dealing with the other person's game. That which is much more basically relevant to the given relationship is often completely avoided in the transaction.

To be that which one (individual or group) truly is—to be authentic—is a central value to us. Honesty, directness, and congruence, if widely practiced, create an organizational atmosphere in which energies get focused on the real problems rather than on game-playing and in which individuals and groups can genuinely and meaningfully encounter each other.

Recently, two supervisors of separate units within an organization got together to resolve a problem that affected both of them. At one point in their discussion, which had gone on for some time and was proving not to be very fruitful, one of them happened to mention that he had recently attended a sensitivity training laboratory conducted by the company. At that point, the other one mentioned that sometime back he had also attended a laboratory. They both quickly decided "to cut out the crap," stop the game they were playing, and really try to solve the problem they had come to face. Within a very short period of time, they dramatically went from a very typical organizational mode of being very closed, wearing masks, and trying to outmaneuver each other, to a mode of being open and direct. They found that the second mode took less energy and that they solved the problem in much less time and were able to keep it solved. But, somehow, at least one of them had not felt safe in taking off his mask until he learned that the other one had also gone through a T Group.

When people experience difficulty with others in organizations, they quite often attribute the difficulty to the fact that the other person or group is not trustworthy. This attitude, of course, justifies their behavior in dealing with the other. On numerous occasions within TRW Systems, groups or individuals who are experiencing distrust are brought together and helped to articulate how they feel about each other. When the fact that "I do not trust you" is out on the table, and only then, can it be dealt with. Interestingly, it turns out that when the feeling is exposed and worked through, there are not really very many fundamentally untrustworthy people. There certainly are all kinds of people continuously doing things that create feelings of mistrust in others. But these feelings and the behavior that triggers them are rarely explored in an effort to work them through. Instead, the mistrust escalates, continues to influence the behavior of both parties, and becomes self-fulfilling. Once the locked-in situation is broken through and the people involved really start talking to each other authentically, however, trust issues, about which people can be very pessimistic, become quite workable. This has happened many, many times in organizational development efforts at TRW Systems.

Away from Use of Status for Maintaining Power and Personal Prestige Toward Use of Status for Organizationally Relevant Purposes—In organizations, particularly large ones, status and symbols of status can play an important role. In too many instances, however, they are used for narrowly personal ends, both to hide behind and to maintain the aura of power and prestige. One result is that dysfunctional walls are built and communication flow suffers.

We believe that status must always be organizationally (functionally) relevant. Some people know more than others, some can do things others cannot do, some carry more responsibility than others. It is often useful for status to be attached to these differences, but such status must be used by its holder to further rather than to wall off the performance of the function out of which the status arises. An organization must be constantly alert to the role that status plays in its functioning.

It is relatively easy to perceive how status symbols are used within an organization, how relatively functional or dysfunctional they are. In some organizations, name-dropping is one of the primary weapons for accomplishing something. A person can go to a colleague with whom he is having a quarrel about what should be done and mention that he had a chat with the president of the organization yesterday. He then gets agreement. He may or may not have talked with the president, he may or may not have quoted him correctly; but he is begging the question by using a power figure in order to convince the other person to do it his way. In other organizations, we have observed that people very rarely work a problem by invoking the name of a senior executive, and that, in fact, those who do name-drop are quickly and openly called to task.

At TRW Systems, with only minor exceptions, middle- and top-level executives, as well as key scientists and engineers, are typically available for consultation with anyone in the organization on matters of functional relevance to the organization. There is no need to use titles, to "follow the organization chart," to obtain permission for the consultation from one's boss or to report the results to him afterwards. As a result, those who can really help are sought out, and problems tend to get worked at the point of interface between need on the one hand and knowledge, experience, and expertise on the other.

Away from Distrusting People Toward Trusting Them—A corollary of the view that man is basically bad is the view that he cannot be trusted. And if he cannot be trusted, he must be carefully watched. In our judgment, many traditional organizational forms exist, at least in part, because of distrust. Close supervision, managerial controls, guarding, security, sign-outs, carry with them to some extent the implication of distrust.

The increasing evidence available to us strongly suggests that distrusting people often becomes a self-confirming hypothesis—distrusting another leads to behavior consciously or unconsciously designed by the person or group not trusted to "prove" the validity of the distrust. Distrust begets distrust. On the other hand, the evidence also suggests that trust begets trust; when people are trusted, they often respond in ways to merit or justify that trust.

Where distrust exists, people are usually seen as having to be motivated "from the outside in," as being responsive only to outside pressure. But when trust exists, people are seen as being motivated "from the inside out," as being at least potentially self-directing entities. One motivational device often used in the outside-in approach involves the inculcation of guilt. Rooted in the Protestant ethic, this device confronts the individual with "shoulds," "oughts," or "musts" as reasons for behaving in a given way. Failure to comply means some external standard has not been met. The individual has thus done wrong, and he is made to feel guilty. The more trustful, inside-out approach makes it possible for the individual to do things because they make sense to him, because they have functional relevance. If the behavior does not succeed, the experience is viewed in positive terms as an opportunity to learn rather than negatively as a reason for punishment and guilt.

Organizations which trust go far to provide individuals and groups with considerable freedom for self-directed action backed up by the experience-based belief that this managerial value will generate the assumption of responsibility for the exercise of that freedom.

In California, going back about 27 years, a forward-looking director of one of our state prisons got the idea of a "prison without walls." He developed and received support for an experiment that involved bringing prisoners to the institution where correctional officers, at that time called guards, carried no guns or billy clubs. There were no guards in the towers or on the walls. The incoming prisoners were shown that the gate was not locked. Under this newer organizational behavior, escape rates decreased, and the experiment has become a model for many prisons in this country and abroad.

An organizational family embarked upon a two-day team-development lab shortly after the conclusion was reached from assessment data that the partial failure of a space vehicle had resulted from the non-functioning of a subsystem developed by this team. At the outset of the lab, an aura of depression was present but there was no evidence that the team had been chastised by higher management for the failure. Further, in strong contrast with what most likely would have been the case if they had faced a load of guilt generated from the outside, there was no evidence of mutual destructive criticism and recriminations. Instead, the team was able in time to turn its attention to a diagnosis of possible reasons for the failure and to action steps which might be taken to avoid a similar outcome in the future.

During a discussion which took place between the head of an organization and one of his subordinates (relating to goals and objectives for that subordinate for the coming year), the supervisor said that one of the things he felt very positive about with respect to that particular subordinate was the way he seemed to be defining his own set of responsibilities. This comment demonstrated the large degree of trust that was placed in the subordinates of this particular supervisor. While the supervisor certainly made it clear to this individual that there were some specific things expected of him, he consciously created a large degree of freedom within which the subordinate would be able to determine for himself how he should spend his time, what priorities he ought to have, what his function should be. This is in great contrast to other organizations which define very clearly and elaborately what they expect from people. Two very different sets of assumptions about people underlie these two approaches.

Away from Avoiding Facing Others with Relevant Data Toward Making Appropriate Confrontation—This value trend is closely related to the one of "from maskmanship toward authenticity," and its implementation is often tied to moving "from distrust toward trust."

In many organizations today there is an unwillingness to "level" with people, particularly with respect to matters which have personal implications. In merit reviews, the "touchy" matters are avoided. Often, incompetent or unneeded employees are retained much longer than is justified either from the organization's or their own point of view. Feelings toward another accumulate and at times fester, but they remain unexpressed. "Even one's best friends won't tell him."

Confrontation fails to take place because "I don't want to hurt Joe," although in fact the non-confronter may be concerned about being hurt himself. We feel that a real absurdity is involved here. While it is widely believed that to "level" is to hurt and, at times, destroy the other, the opposite may often be the case. Being left to live in a "fool's paradise" or being permitted to continue with false illusions about self is often highly hurtful and even destructive. Being honestly confronted in a context of mutual trust and caring is an essential requirement for personal growth. In an organizational setting, it is also an important aspect of "working the problem."

A quite dramatic example of confrontation and its impact occurred in a sensitivity training laboratory when one executive giving feedback to a colleague said to him that he and others within the organization perceived him as being ruthless. This came as a tremendous jolt to the person receiving the feedback. He had absolutely no perception of himself as ruthless and no idea that he was doing things which would cause others to feel that way about him. The confrontation was an upending experience for him. As a result, he later began to explore with many people in the organization what their relationship with him was like and made some quite marked changes in his behavior after getting additional data which tended to confirm what he had recently heard. In the absence of these data (previously withheld because people might not want to hurt him), he was indeed living in a fool's paradise. A great deal of energy was expended by other people in dealing with his "ruthlessness," and a considerable amount of avoidance took place, greatly influencing the productivity of everyone. Once this problem was exposed and worked through, this energy became available for more productive purposes.

Away from Avoidance of Risk-Taking Toward Willingness to Risk— A widely discernible attribute of large numbers of individuals and groups in organizations today is the unwillingness to risk, to put one's self or the group on the line. Much of this reluctance stems from not being trusted, with the resulting fear of the consequences expected to follow close upon the making of an error. It often seems that only a reasonable guarantee of success will free an individual or group to take a chance. Such a stance leads to conformity, to a repetition of the past, to excessive caution and defensiveness. We feel that risk-taking is an essential quality in adaptable, growthful organizations; taking a chance is necessary for creativity and change. Also, individuals and groups do learn by making mistakes. Risk-taking involves being willing "to take the monkey on my back," and it takes courage to do so. It also takes courage and ingenuity on the part of the organization to foster such behavior.

At TRW Systems, the president and many of the senior executives were until recently located on the fifth floor of one of the organization's buildings, and part of the language of the organization was "the fifth floor," meaning that place where many of the power figures resided. This phrase was used quite often in discussion: "The fifth floor feels that we should—." In working with groups one or two levels below the top executives to explore what they might do about some of the frustrations they were experiencing in getting their jobs done, one of the things that dominated the early discussions was the wish that somehow "the fifth floor" would straighten things out. For example, a group of engineers of one division was having problems with a group of engineers of another division, and they stated that "the fifth floor" (or at least one of its executives) ought to go over to the people in the other division and somehow "give them the word." After a while, however, they began to realize that it really was not very fruitful or productive to talk about what they wished someone else would do, and they began to face the problem of what they could do about the situation directly.

The discussion then became quite constructive and creative, and a number of new action items were developed and later successfully implemented—even though there was no assurance of successful outcomes at the time the action items were decided upon.

Away from a View of Process Work as Being Unproductive Effort Toward Seeing it as Essential to Effective Task Accomplishment—In the past and often in the present, productive effort has been seen as that which focused directly on the production of goods and services. Little attention has been paid to the processes by which such effort takes place; to do so has often been viewed as a waste of time. Increasingly, however, the relevance to task accomplishment of such activities as team maintenance and development, diagnosis and working through of interpersonal and intergroup communication barriers, confrontation efforts for resolution of organizationally dysfunctional personal and interpersonal hangups, and assessment and improvement of existing modes of decision making is being recognized. And, in fact, we harbor growing doubts with respect to the continued usefulness of the notion of a task-process dichotomy. It seems to us that there are many activities which can make contributions to task accomplishment and that the choice from among these is essentially an economic one.

Within TRW Systems, proposals are constantly being written in the hope of obtaining new projects from the Department of Defense, NASA, and others. These proposals are done under very tight time constraints. What quite often happens is that the request for the proposal is received from the customer and read very quickly by the principals involved. Everybody then charges off and starts working on the proposal because of the keenly felt time pressure. Recently, on a very major proposal, the proposal manager decided that the first thing he should do was spend a couple of days (out of a three-month period of available time) meeting with the principals involved. In this meeting, they wrould not do any writing of the proposal but would talk about how they were going to proceed, make sure they were all making the same assumptions about who would be working on which subsystem, how they would handle critical interfaces, how they would handle critical choice points during the proposal period, and so on. Many of the principals went to the meeting with a great deal of skepticism, if not impatience. They wanted to get "on with the job," which to them meant writing the proposal. Spend ng a couple of days talking about "how we're going to do things" was not defi ed by them as productive work. After the meeting, and after the proposal had be n written and delivered to the customer, a critique was held on the process used. Those involved in general reported very favorably on the effects of the meeting which took place at the beginning of the proposal-writing cycle. They reported things such as: "The effect of having spent a couple of days as we did meant that at that point when we then charged off and started actually writing the proposal, we were able to function as if we had already been working together for perhaps two months. We were much more effective with each other and much more efficient, so that in the final analysis, it was time well spent." By giving attention to their ways of getting work done, they clearly had facilitated their ability to function well as a team.

Away from a Primary Emphasis on Competition Toward a Much Greater Emphasis on Collaboration—A pervasive value in the organizational milieu is competition. Competition is based on the assumption that desirable resources are limited in quantity and that individuals or groups can be effectively motivated through competing against one another for the possession of these resources. But competition can often set man against man and group against group in dysfunctional behavior, including a shift of objectives from obtaining the limited resource to blocking or destroying the competitor. Competition inevitably results in winners and losers, and at least some of the hidden costs of losing can be rather high in systemic terms.

Collaboration, on the other hand, is based on the assumption that the desirable limited resources can be shared among the participants in a mutually satisfactory manner and, even more important, that it is possible to increase the quantity of the resources themselves.

As organizational work becomes more highly specialized and complex, with its accomplishment depending more and more on the effective interaction of individuals and groups, and as the organic or systems views of organizational functioning become more widely understood, the viability of collaboration as an organizational mode becomes ever clearer. Individuals and groups are often highly interdependent, and such interdependency needs to be facilitated through collaborative behavior rather than walled off through competition. At the same time, collaborative behavior must come to be viewed as reflecting strength rather than weakness.

In organizations which have a high degree of interdependency, one of the problems people run into regarding the handling of this interdependency is that they look for simple solutions to complex problems. Simple solutions do not produce very good results because they deal with the symptoms rather than with the real problems.

A major reorganization recently took place within TRW Systems. The president of the organization sketched out the broad, general directions of the reorganization, specifying details only in one or two instances. He assigned to a large number of working committees the development of the details of the new organization. The initial reaction of some people was that these were things that the president himself should be deciding. The president, however, did not feel he had enough detailed understanding and knowledge to come up with many of the appropriate answers. He felt strongly that those who had the knowledge should develop the answers. This was an explicit, conscious recognition on his part of the fact that he did indeed need very important inputs from other people in order to effect the changes he was interested in making. These working committees turned out to be very effective. As a result of the president's approach, the reorganization proceeded with far less disruption and resistance than is typically the case in major reorganizations.

Another example involved a major staff function which was experiencing a great deal of difficulty with other parts of the organization. The unit having the trouble made the initial decision to conduct briefings throughout the organization to explain what they were really trying to accomplish, how they were organized, what requirements they had to meet for outside customers, and so on. They felt that their job would be easier if they could solicit better understanding. What actually took place was quite different. Instead of conducting briefings to convince the "heathen," the people in this unit revised their plan and met with some key people from other parts of the company who had to deal with them to ask what the unit was doing that was creating problems at the interface. After receiving a great deal of fairly specific data, the unit and the people with whom they consulted developed joint collaborative action items for dealing with the problems. This way of approaching the problem quickly turned interfaces that had been very negative and very hostile into ones that were relatively cooperative. The change in attitude on both sides of the interface provided a positive base for working toward satisfactory solutions to the problems.

Some Implications of These Values in Transition

Many people would agree with the value trends stated in this paper and indeed claim that they use these guidelines in running their own organizations. However, there is often quite a gap between saying that you believe in these values and actually practicing them in meaningful, important ways. In many organizations, for example, there is a management-by-objectives process which has been installed and used for several years—an approach which can involve the implementation of some of the values stated earlier in this paper. If, however, one closely examines how this process takes place in many organizations, it is in fact a very mechanical one, one which is used very defensively in some cases. What emerges is a statement of objectives which has obtained for the boss what he really wants, and, at the end of the year, protects the subordinate if he does not do everything that his boss thought he might do. It becomes a "Pearl Harbor file." The point that needs emphasis is that the payoff in implementing these values by techniques is not in the techniques themselves but in how they are applied and in what meaning their use has for the people involved.

To us, the implementation of these values clearly involves a bias regarding organizational development efforts. Believing that people have vast amounts of untapped potential and the capability and desire to grow, to engage in meaningful collaborative relationships, to be creative in organizational contexts, and to be more authentic, we feel that the most effective change interventions are therapeutic in nature. Such interventions focus directly on the hangups, both personal and organizational, that block a person from realizing his potential. We are referring to interventions which assist a person in breaking through the neurotic barriers in himself, in others around him, and in the ongoing culture.

We place a strong emphasis on increasing the sanity of the individuals in the organization and of the organization itself. By this we mean putting the individuals and the organization more in touch with the realities existing within themselves and around them. With respect to the individual, this involves his understanding the consequences of his behavior. How do people feel about him? How do they react to him? Do they trust him? With respect to the organization, it involves a critical examination of its culture and what that culture produces: the norms, the values, the decision-making processes, the general environment that it has created and maintained over a period of time.

There are obviously other biases and alternatives available to someone approaching organizational development work. One could concentrate on structural interventions: How should we organize? What kind of charters should people in various functional units have? The bias we are stating does not mean that structure, function, and charters are irrelevant, but that they are less important and have considerably less leverage in the early stages of organizational development efforts than working with the individuals and groups in a therapeutic manner. Furthermore, as an individual becomes more authentic and interpersonally competent, he becomes far more capable of creative problem-solving. He and his associates have within them more resources for dealing with questions of structure, charters, and operating procedures, in more relevant and creative ways, than does someone from outside their system. Such therapeutic devices include the full range of laboratory methods usually identified with the NTL Institute: sensitivity training, team building, intergroup relationship building, and so on. They also include individual and group counseling within the organization, and the voluntary involvement of individuals in various forms of psychotherapy outside the organization.

In order to achieve a movement towards authenticity, focus must be placed on developing the whole person and in doing this in an organic way. The program cannot be something you crank people through; it must be tailored in a variety of ways to individual needs as they are expressed and identified. In time, therapy and individual growth (becoming more in touch with your own realities) become values in and of themselves. And as people become less demotivated and move toward authenticity, they clearly demonstrate that they have the ability to be creative about organization matters, and this too becomes a value shared within the organization. Once these values are introduced and people move towards them, the movement in and of itself will contain many forces that make for change and open up new possibilities in an organization. For example, as relationships become more trustworthy, as people are given more responsibility, as competition gives way to collaboration, people experience a freeing up. They are more apt to challenge all the given surroundings, to test the limits, to try new solutions, and to rock the boat. This can be an exciting and productive change, but it can also be troublesome, and a variety of responses to it must be expected.

Therapeutic efforts are long-term efforts. Movement towards greater authenticity, which leads to an organization's culture becoming more positive, creative, and growthful, is something that takes a great deal of time and a great deal of energy. In this kind of approach to organizational development, there is more ambiguity and less stability than in other approaches that might be taken. Patience, persistence, and confidence are essential through time if significant change is to occur and be maintained.

For the organizational development effort to have some kind of permanency, it is very important that it becomes an integral part of the line organization and its mode of operating. Many of the people involved in introducing change in organizations are in staff positions, typically in personnel. If, over time, the effort continues to be mainly one carried out by staff people, it is that much more tenuous. Somehow the total organization must be involved, particularly those people with line responsibility for the organization's success and for its future. They must assimilate the effort and make it a part of their own behavior within the organization. In other words, those people who have the greatest direct impact on and responsibility for creating, maintaining, and changing the culture of an organization must assume direct ownership of the change effort.

In the transition and beyond it, these changes can produce problems for the organization in confronting the outside world with its traditional values. For example, do you tell the truth to your customers when you are experiencing problems building a product for them, or do you continue to tell them that everything is going along fine? For the individual, there can be problems in other relationships around him, such as within his family at home. We do not as yet have good methods developed for dealing with these conflicts, but we can certainly say that they will take place and will have to be worked out.

As previously stated, the Career Development program at TRW Systems, now in its fifth year of operation, is an effort in which both authors have been deeply involved. We feel it is one of the more promising examples of large-scale, long-term, systematic efforts to help people move toward the values we have outlined.

One question that is constantly raised about efforts such as the Career Development program at TRW Systems relates to assessing their impact. How does one know there has been a real payoff for the organization and its members? Some behavioral scientists have devised rather elaborate, mechanical tools in order to answer this question. We feel that the values themselves suggest the most relevant kind of measurement. The people involved have the capacity to determine the relevance and significance to them and to their organizational units of what they are doing. Within TRW Systems, a very pragmatic approach is taken. Questions are asked such as: Do we feel this has been useful? Are these kinds of problems easier to resolve? Are there less hidden agenda now? Do we deal more quickly and effectively with troublesome intergroup problems? The payoff is primarily discussed in qualitative terms, and we feel this is appropriate. It does not mean that quantitative judgments are not possible, but to insist on reducing the human condition to numbers, or to believe that it can be done, is madness.

The role of the person introducing change (whether he is staff or in the line) is a very tough, difficult, and, at times, lonely one. He personally must be as congruent as he can with the values we have discussed. If people perceive him to be outside the system of change, they should and will reject him. He must be willing and able to become involved as a person, not merely as the expert who will fix everybody else up. He, too, must be in process. This is rewarding, but also very difficult.

Introducing change into a social system almost always involves some level of resistance to that change. Accepting the values we have described means that one will not be fully satisfied with the here and now because the limits of man's potential have certainly not been reached. All we know for sure is that the potential is vast. Never accepting the status quo is a rather lonely position to take. In effect, as one of our colleagues has put it, you are constantly saying to yourself, "Fifty million Frenchmen are wrong!" From our own experience we know that this attitude can produce moments when one doubts one's sanity: "How come nobody else seems to feel the way I do, or to care about making things better, or to believe that it is possible to seek improvements?" Somehow, these moments must be worked through, courage must be drawn upon, and new actions must follow.

We are struck with and saddened by the large amounts of frustration, feelings of inadequacy, insecurity, and fear that seem to permeate groups of behavioral science practitioners when they meet for seminars or workshops. Belief in these values must lead to a bias towards optimism about the human condition. "Man does have the potential to create a better world, and I have the potential to contribute to that effort." But in addition to this bias towards optimism, there has to be a recognition of the fundamental fact that we will continuously have to deal with resistance to change, including resistances within ourselves. People are not standing in line outside our doors asking to be freed up, liberated, and upended. Cultures are not saying: "Change us, we can no longer cope, we are unstable." Commitment to trying to implement these values as well as we can is not commitment to an easy, safe existence. At times, we can be bone weary of confrontation, questioning, probing, and devil's-advocating. We can have delightful fantasies of copping out on the whole mess and living on some island. We can be fed up with and frightened by facing someone's anger when we are confronting him with what is going on around him. We can be worn out from the continuous effort to stretch ourselves as we try to move towards living these values to the fullest.

On the other hand, the rewards we experience can be precious, real, and profound. They can have important meaning for us individually, for those with whom we work, and for our organizations. Ultimately, what we stand for can make for a better world—and we deeply know that this is what keeps us going.

This paper was prepared for the McGregor Conference on Organizational Development, sponsored by the Organizational Studies Group, Sloan School of Management, MIT, October 1967.

Distortions of Behavioral Science

JAMES V. CLARK

Schools of business administration and in-company training programs are spending more and more money and time on education in the behavioral sciences. Carnegie Tech, Chicago, Harvard, MIT, Stanford, UCLA, and Yale, to name only a few, all have substantial organizational behavior, human relations, anthropology, psychology, and sociology course offerings in their business schools—at the undergraduate, graduate, and executive program levels. Away from the ivory towers, the American Management Association, Alcan, ESSO, Pacific Finance, and many other firms and industrial organizations have major residential training programs devoted exclusively to theory and practice in the behavioral sciences.

As a teacher and student of behavior in formal organizations, I spend much of my time in these programs. I view my task there as bringing to students some of the findings and methods of the behavioral sciences which have been found relevant to their practice as administrators. Briefly, these findings and methods highlight aspects of the administrator's "territory" which he typically overlooks, due to his background and/or the pressures under which he operates. Given this modest aim, however, the most extraordinary things generally happen in these programs. I very early learned, for example, that it was next to impossible for me to say, "Here is something you are overlooking" without being heard as saying, "Behavioral science knows everything—the average administrator knows nothing."

First in astonishment, then in anger, and lately from scientific curiosity (or more accurately from a mixture of all three), I have become intrigued by this kind of misunderstanding. Again and again, simple findings and basic methods of scientific investigators become shockingly distorted by intelligent listeners. And most training programs are set up for such short periods of time that the teacher can scarcely hope to deal with more than a few of these confusions. Consequently, they spread.

As my experience in this educational adventure extended, I began to notice a consistency in the distortions. The same mistaken impressions were turning up again and again, whether I was teaching in a university or an industry and whether I was teaching twenty-, forty-, or sixty-year-olds, top management or first line foremen, management, or union personnel. And conversations with colleagues convinced me these particular misunderstandings were not encountered only in my classes —they were endemic.

As I informally collected and sorted these confusions, I thought I saw a pattern in them and a plausible explanation for their prevalence. In the hope that it might contribute to an improved understanding of some of the communication problems between businessmen and social and psychological investigators of business, I will list some of the more frequently heard distortions and advance a few ideas about what might be behind them.

Black or White Magic?

The misunderstanding of what teachers of behavioral science, human relations, organizational behavior, or call it what you will, are trying to say takes two major forms. People either believe that the behavioral scientists believe a distortion, or they themselves believe it. That is, people take a tentative or partial statement of ours, magnify it out of all proportion, and then conclude either that we are fools or that we are wizards who have the answers to everything. Fritz Roethlisberger once said in a classroom lecture that businessmen take behavioral scientists for either black magicians or white magicians. As his remark suggests, and as I shall try to show, these superficially different perceptions are variations on the same viewing dynamic.

But first, let us look at some of the distortions themselves. Here is a list of assertions commonly advanced by many business-oriented behavioral scientists, followed by oversimplified representations of the distortions which often crop up in their presence. Recall that a distortion can take two forms: the listener either thinks behavioral scientists believe it, or he believes it.

Since these confusions arise around different topics, I have grouped them accordingly.

Organizational Behavior

Statement: Knowledge exists about organizational behavior.
Distortion: If you know enough, you can solve any administrative problem.

Statement: Much data has been collected on social and nonlogical behavior at the work group level, but little concerning top management groups.
Distortion: People on the bottom of a formal organizational chart are illogical. People above the bottom are logical.
Statement: There are nonlogical aspects to people's behavior.
Distortion: Nobody is logical.

Individual Behavior

Statement: Psychological determinants of behavior are important.
Distortion: One's behavior is entirely determined by his psychological makeup.

Small Workgroup Behavior

Statement: Social determinants of behavior are important.
Distortion: One's behavior is determined by his membership in social groups.
Statement: It is helpful to realize that people's aspirations at work have many aspects; they seek membership, self-esteem, economic security, prestige, and so on.
Distortion: Pay--even incentive pay--isn't of much importance anymore.
Statement: Social behavior and individual need satisfaction are related in some significant fashion to productivity.
Distortion: You ought to give workers whatever they want. If they're happy, they'll produce more.
Statement: Social subsystems in organizations exert much control over their members. Consequently, an administrator's control is limited.
Distortion: Nobody can really be a boss, only a follower. We should all be soft and tender-minded.

Intergroup Behavior

Statement: It is helpful if an administrator has a way of thinking that helps him account for conflict between groups.
Distortion: You should always get along with everybody and not have conflicts.
Statement: Shared goals are important for collaboration between groups.
Distortion: Everybody should think alike so they can work together as a group.

Administration

Statement: It is helpful for an administrator to have a way of thinking about collecting information and learning about problems in organizational behavior.
Distortion: Administrators should be research types, studying things but not acting on them.
Statement: Thinking about organizational behavior as occurring in a sociotechnical system helps in dealing with specific administrative problems.

Distortion:	You ought to be a social scientist if you're going to be an administrator.
Statement:	Sometimes the interactive process involved in understanding an administrative problem alleviates the problem.
Distortion:	If you're a nondirective leader all your problems take care of themselves.
Statement:	Appropriate and useful administrative behavior often involves an administrator in responding flexibly to different situations.
Distortion:	Consistency of values is neither desirable nor useful.
Statment:	Top management often exerts considerable influence on the social system of an organization.
Distortion:	Unless you're top management, you're stymied and can't change anything.
Statement:	It is important for an administrator to pay attention to the internal processes of his organization.
Distortion:	If you pay attention to human relations, you don't need to know anything about the business.
Statement:	Some of the methods and findings of psychotherapy have relevance to the administrator's understanding and skill in communication.
Distortion:	An administrator has to practically be a psychiatrist in order to communicate.
Statement:	An administrator should know his own limits.
Distortion:	Administrators should put others ahead of themselves.
Statement:	Administrators should be able to accept feelings of inadequacy.
Distortion:	Administrators should be introspective all the time.

In my experience, most businessmen and many professors of business agree with a dozen or more of the distortions. Anyone agreeing with only eight or nine of them has probably done considerable reading in the area. If one agrees with five or less, he may well have spent the equivalent of a full-time year studying and discussing these matters. It takes between two and five years of full-time work before people believe none of the distortions and know that very few behavioral scientists believe them either.

Why are these distortions so prevalent? Clearly, this is a complicated question, and no small part of its answer is suggested by the old adage that when the pupil hasn't learned, the teacher hasn't taught. But these midunderstandings are encountered by such a variety of teachers and in such a range of teaching contexts that some more general force seems likely to be an underlying contributing factor.

Progressive or Stubborn?

I believe that much of the problem stems from the fact that, for the most part, behavioral scientists and businessmen have recently been concerned with different aspects of human behavior. The great discoveries of the behavioral scientists over the last fifty to seventy-five years, for example, have been around the stubborn, recalcitrant nature of human personality, alone or in groups. Of course, man has known for thousands of years that behavior does not change easily, but not with the depth of understanding of contemporary social science. The extent to which the human organism reacts so as to maintain equilibrium and resist change, therefore, has occupied perhaps the most prominent part of social science inquiry since it began in earnest around the latter part of the nineteenth century.

Businessmen, on the other hand, have experienced the last sixty-odd years as the golden age of economic expansion, development, change, and progress. They have created vast organizations in which great technological and distributive inventions have produced economic developments beyond anyone's dreams. And still today, ten new horizons open up for every one crossed. The fruits of these labors are obvious; we do have a different economic situation today than we had sixty years ago, and the businessman has been spending his time working to bring it about.

It is important here to note that both groups may be in a stage of reacting against what they are beginning to feel are excesses. Behavioral scientists, for example, are becoming increasingly interested in rationality and growth. At the very root of the postwar existential school of psychoanalysis now being regarded so seriously by American psychotherapists, for instance, lies the exercise of will, choice, and commitment. Meanwhile, business is beginning to rediscover the complexity of human needs. Sheer technological or economic improvement is wearing thin for many, and a worried discussion of national goals is replacing the breast-beating which has characterized the American businessman during much of this century. Moreover, he is reading books, taking courses in behavioral science and human relations, and hiring Ph.D.'s at an ever-increasing rate and with an ever-increasing seriousness.

Regardless of the historical antecedents or future possibilities for reconciliation, however, a different orientation toward human behavior has existed for the past sixty years between social scientists and most businessmen. During this period, these two groups seem to have picked out and focused on different aspects of human behavior. I say these two *groups* because there have been individuals in each whose interest was wider than that of his co-workers. Many behavioral scientists (and particularly many who have been based in schools of business administration) have been interested in the growthful, willful, "open-ended" aspects of human personality and groups. And many businessmen have been profoundly aware—in theory and in practice—that their organization's members had more needs than economic theory alone might suggest.

Nevertheless, a number of social and psychological investigators have appeared to focus on one side of human behavior, while the businessmen centered their attention on the other. It appears to some observers, however, that human behavior in fact always includes *both* the aspect in which the behavioral scientists have been interested *and* the facet on which the businessmen have concentrated. It is possible we have been struggling with a choice when none was logically necessary. Many writers now think that all individuals and groups exhibit, on the one hand, a tendency and capacity to *maintain* themselves in something like a steady state and, on the other hand, a tendency and capacity to *differentiate* and elaborate themselves internally and externally.

The psychologist Gordon Allport believes that both these tendencies are requirements for open, mature personalities. But, he observes, "Most current theories of personality . . . emphasize stability rather than growth, permanence rather than change, 'uncertainty reduction' (information theory) and 'coding' (cognitive theory) rather than creativity. In short, they emphasize *being* rather than *becoming*." [1]

Allport conducted an informal investigation to reveal the underlying preference of his psychologist colleagues as to whether they conceived the human personality to be essentially equilibrium-seeking or forward-pushing. His findings are interesting. Studying *Psychological Abstracts* issues over the past thirty years, and randomly sampling five-page excerpts in current journals, Allport discovered the ratio of the former to the latter to be five-to-one. As he put it, the psychologist's vocabulary is "five times richer in terms like *reaction, response, reinforcement, reflex, respondent, retroaction, recognition, regression, repression, reminiscence* than in terms like *production, proceeding, proficiency, problem-solving, propriate,* and *programming*." [2] To an outsider, these terms of—let us call them for shorthand purposes "reaction" and "pro-action"—seem innocuous enough, being almost sheer description. But there is considerable debate brewing here in psychological circles. Many writers are contending that behavioral science needs to take fuller

1. Allport, Gordon, "The Open System in Personality Theory." *Personality and Social Encounter*, Beacon Press, Boston, 1960.

2. *Ibid*.

account of growth, will, and the forward-thrusting aspects of people. Their critics maintain that such tendencies are not observable in the strict sense.

The Reactive — Pro-active Dimension

Well, isn't this a problem we should leave to the psychologists to iron out? Maybe so, but we haven't. The psychologists are just one group among many in this discussion. Profound feelings are evoked around it far beyond the confines of the psychology department. This can be seen if we let our mind's eye roam over the images called up by the following set of terms, each of which has been used in place of "reactive" and "pro-active" to point to similar phenomena. Think of "reactionary—liberal," or "passive—active," and "maintenance oriented —task oriented," "equilibrium—growth," "realism—mysticism," "nonlogical—logical," "emotion—will," "intellectual—anti-intellectual," "tough-minded—tender-minded," "devil—angel," "masculine— feminine." And there are others.

Even whole cultures line up on either side of these hyphens. For example, the Hindus, anticipating certain modern psychologists by two or three millennia, stated that man's needs were, in ascendant order, for pleasure, success, duty, and to search for meaning or to know. Clearly, our Western value system tends to emphasize the lower levels of this need hierarchy. We do not venerate our philosophers; we idolize our movie stars, sports heroes, "wheelers and dealers," and political leaders.

At any rate, I hope our list has been sufficient to underscore the fact that feelings run deep around this reactive-pro-active business. This is an area where people's taste is very much a matter of dispute.

It shouldn't surprise us, therefore, that social scientists and businessmen align themselves on one side or the other of this discussion. While Allport's study shows where the choices of many of his colleagues lie, no one has done a similar study in journals of business, but I believe it would show the opposite. I am almost certain that in business publications *progress, problem solving, production, proficiency,* and the like squeeze out *resistance to change, reaction, regression,* and so forth, by at least the five-to-one Allport found for the opposite direction among psychologists. Another indication of the same preference is the high percentage of "How to" books and articles published for businessmen. All carry the same implication and feed the same underlying preference: The world can—and should—be improved rationally, fixed up.

It is possible that this difference between business and management writers on the one hand and social and psychological writers on the other may help us understand some of the problems they have had in communicating with each other. Each, defending and justifying the work and progress of themselves and their fellows, often confuses an aspect of reality with reality itself. It seems to me, for example, that the famous critic of behavioral science education, Malcolm McNair, Professor of Retailing at Harvard, shows a strong preference for the pro-active side of reality which he does not realize is a preference. He writes incisively as he asks "What Price Human Relations?",[3] but he writes with the incision of one who is defending a position against onslaught. Professor McNair and other pioneers in business education were dedicated to the value of improving business practice rationally. They were—and remain—vigorous pro-actives. But in their efforts to resist, or at least to contain, the advances of the social scientists who point to the existence of reactive behaviors, they appear to be fighting a battle of values which has some meaning for them above and beyond trying to understand behavior from the scientific point of view. It's as if they would be letting their side down by admitting any truth for the "opposition." In their defense, however, let us not forget that this works two ways: the social science invasion into schools of management often appears to be flying a banner which reads, "Give me nonlogical, emotional behavior or give me death!" Of course, the final and almost impenetrable confusion in this continuing debate is that the pro-actives often find themselves defending against the attacking reactives. And does not this somewhat absurd situation, with its reactive pro-actives paired off against the pro-active reactives, suggest to us that a false dichotomy is producing more heat than light?

Keeping the World Safe for Progress

In the shadow of this discussion, turn back briefly to the distortions listed earlier. Notice that all except one or two caricature the image of the pro-active's opposite. Think of everything the typical vigorous, progressive businessman does not believe himself to think or be, and you have the list of distortions we saw there. That is, businessmen many times think behavioral scientists believe that knowledge is everything, people are completely nonlogical, pay isn't important, executives ought to make workers happy, ought never to have conflict, never pay atten-

3. McNair, Malcolm, "Thinking Ahead: What Price Human Relations?" *Harvard Business Review*, XXXV (2).

tion to the business of the business, and act like nondirective therapists. Clearly, none of these describes the image of the firm, tough, pro-active businessman dutifully and powerfully improving his business (and hence the world) through the use of rationality and consciousness.

Of course, what a businessman can get out of manufacturing these distorted statements—statements which he can resist in such good conscience—is the comforting belief that he is keeping the world safe for progress. Notice that he can thus actually defend himself against new knowledge (much of which points to realistic aspects of organizational behavior which in fact limits his control as executive) by using words of offense. He thus uses pro-active-sounding *talk* in order to *behave* reactively.

So much for the resisting kind of distortions. The other type of listeners, you will remember, themselves believe the distortions we looked at earlier. Thus, a student sitting in a classroom or an executive listening to a consultant's report, suddenly believes that enough scientific knowledge will solve all labor problems, workers can be influenced if enough is known of their illogicality, other enticements can always be extended instead of pay, workers will produce more if they are made happy, and communication problems will dissolve if all managers are taught how to be "nondirective." Clearly, what is involved in these distortions is that the listener has so convinced himself that the end of science is to improve technology that he grasps at the behavioral scientist's assertions as new and powerful tools of manipulation. Unfortunately, many of the commercial motivation research organizations, executive selection firms, and similar concerns have cruelly played on this oversimplified hope and given it some credence.

In summary, then, these distortions come from those people who share the culturally supported value that an executive's duty is to firmly and toughly improve the world technologically, through science and business. Given this deep-seated belief, then, most listeners find the partial, limited statements of the behavioral scientists—as often as not pointing to reactive aspects of behavior—as either antimanagment or supermanagement. Thus, behavioral science, to many businessmen, is either against him or a secret weapon on his side. Either way, of course, the basic misunderstandings remain.

An issue buried this deep cannot, of course, be cured easily. But it seems to me that some understanding of its nature can be helpful. Having seen the distortions listed here, for example, businessmen, students, administrators of training programs and the like can perhaps spot them better next time—in themselves and in others. Then, too, they can see that behavioral science should not be evaluated on its popularity alone. Given this analysis, any good educational program in this area will predictably encounter—and produce—resistances. Teachers of this material need special training and much experience before they can begin to help people clarify some of these distortions. Teaching psychology or sociology to liberal arts students with one set of values and to present or future businessmen with another set are very different experiences. Also, much time needs to be given to such education. High expectations for short-term programs must be tempered by some insight into the vast nature of the undertaking.

Then, too, behavioral scientists reading these remarks can ask themselves whether they favor stable, closed theories and disregard the forward-pushing, growing aspects of behavior. If the answer is "yes," they might further ask themselves what they are getting out of such a preference? What does it protect them from?

I find these implications easy to write, since they all involve other people. The implication which emerges for us teachers I pass on humbly, for I have firsthand knowledge of how profoundly hard it is: to be patient. We spend much time showing our businessmen, students, or clients how little control they often have over the behavior of their subordinates and what this fact means for themselves and for their administrative practice. Is not this good medicine for us? How much of what happens in our classrooms have we control over? How much control do we have, for example, over such beliefs as the basic cultural value discussed in this article that the duty of man is to improve the world rationally? Are not the implications of this fact for ourselves and our teaching practice at least as profound as those we pass on to our students? I think so, but this is another subject, and one which awaits an essay similar to this, but on the misunderstanding of businessmen by behavioral scientists, and preferably written by a businessman and former student!

The Manager as a Person

One of the basic tenets of applied behavioral science is that self-awareness is a crucial factor in interpersonal competence. No manager can have a really viable theory of or approach to management unless he has an accurate sub-theory of himself. This section contains some ideas for the manager to use in gaining greater understanding of himself.

The Power to
See Ourselves

PAUL J. BROUWER

A psychological fact is that manager development means change in the manager's self-concept. Each of us, whether we realize it or not, has a self-image. We see ourselves in some way — smart, slow, kindly, well-intentioned, lazy, misunderstood, meticulous, or shrewd; we all can pick adjectives that describe ourselves. This is the "I" behind the face in the mirror, the "I" that thinks, dreams, talks, feels, and believes, the "I" that no one knows fully. In this article we will explore the meaning of the self-image, particularly in relation to changing behavior in the growing manager, and how changes in self-concept come about.

One reason this self-concept is crucial is that it has a great deal to do with manager development — with being a growing person and eventually realizing one's self-potential. Note the term *manager* development rather than *management* development; the purpose of such development is to help individual managers to grow. After all, they have to do most of the job themselves. As a member of a firm of consulting psychologists to management, I can report that fact from experience — and add the further observation that no one can tell a manager exactly how to grow. Rather, the most one can do is to help the manager understand himself in his own situation, and then trust him to find the best direction himself.

In the first place, the self-concept is important because everything we do or say, everything we hear, feel, or otherwise perceive, is influenced by how we see ourselves. For example:

A businessman, who had traveled in many parts of the world, was incorrigibly curious about the customs, speech, local places of interest, history and traditions of any place he visited. However, on a one-week visit to London – his first – on a delicate mission for his company, he might just as well have been in Indianapolis for all he learned of English ways of life. Being on a business trip, he saw himself as a businessman, and actually perceived little of what was around him. But as a

Editor's note: This article was also printed as a chapter in *Managers for Tomorrow*, New American Library of World Literature, New York, 1965.

vacationer in London he would have seen England in depth, because he would have seen himself coming to London for that purpose.

Filters for Reality

Photographers often slip a reddish filter over the lens when snapping pictures of clouds on black and white film. The filter prevents some of the light rays from reaching the film, so that the final picture shows much darker skies and more sharply whitened clouds. The self-concept is like a filter that screens out what we do not want to hear and see, passes through what we do want to see and hear. In the reverse direction, it gives an idiosyncratic flavor to our behavior. Who among us doesn't usually pick his name out of a jumble of words on a page? Or hear his name announced at an airport amidst all of the other announcements that he fails to hear? This is called selective listening, and it is a function of our self-concept. Thus, how we see ourselves determines generally what we react to, what we perceive, and, in broad terms, how we behave in general.

And this shows up in business situations too. Imagine two executives, A and B, in identical situations. Each calls in a subordinate and delegates an assignment. The italicized words below give partial indications of their self-concepts. Executive A says:

"Tom, I'm *concerned* about our relations with the XYZ Company. Its *purchases* from us have fallen off lately and *rather abruptly*. You know our history with it. *Will* you *investigate* and find out the cause of the reduced volume? *Let me know* if you run into anything you don't understand."

Executive A is confident of his ability to handle the situation. He sees himself as unthreatened, able to cope with whatever Tom's investigation discloses, and willing to delay action until the facts are gathered and studied.

Executive B, on the other hand, says:

"George, the XYZ Company has cut back its purchases from us for the third month in a row. *We've got to get on this and quick*. Now, you go visit it. *I wish I could but I'm tied down here*. Talk to the purchasing agent – uh, what's his name again? Uh . . . (shuffling papers) . . . here it is . . . Bailey. *See* Bailey. Oh . . . and you'd better see the chief engineer, a nice guy . . . named . . . uh . . . his name slips me *for the moment* . . . you can get it from Bailey. But don't go near Sam Awful – he'll cover up whatever's happening anyway, and might use your visit as a sign we're scared of old XYZ. *I've got to have some answers on this one, George*. The boss is on my neck but good. So. . . ."

Executive B is obviously less confident. He feels threatened by the situation. He doesn't trust George to use his own common sense – as indicated by his explicit "do"s and "don't"s – probably because he himself lacks confidence.

Although the self-concept is important in understanding human behavior *generally*, it becomes critically so in understanding *manager development*, where changes in behavior are the objective. As a matter of cold, hard, psychological fact, a change in behavior on the job, for better or worse, means a change in self-concept. Thus, we are dealing with an immensely and immediately practical consideration.

Continuing Change

Human beings constantly change their behavior, as we see if we examine ourselves (and others) critically enough. It is a superficial observation to say that so-and-so is the same person he was five years ago. Technically, he isn't exactly the same today as he was even yesterday. For one thing, he is one day older. He has learned something new, however negligible, that becomes incorporated in his apperceptive mass. As a result, his perception of today's events is different, however slightly and undetectably, from what it was yesterday. He may have had nothing "significant" happen to him — no promotion, no accident, no soul-searching upset — but he will be different, even though only a person with Solomon's wisdom would know it. Change in behavior is constant.

The difficulties managers have in thinking about changes in behavior come from their inability to detect change, and from fuzzy thinking behind such comforting, though fallacious, notions as, "You can't teach an old dog new tricks," "He was born that way," or "He's been like that ever since I've known him."

On the other hand, sometimes superficial behavior changes are erroneously thought to be basic. For example, consider the simplest level of change in behavior, which is brought about by increased knowledge or skill:

The newly appointed foreman learns his new duties, dons a white shirt, delegates jobs he used to do himself, and learns to participate in his superintendent's meetings. His company provides him with instruction through manuals, books, conferences, sessions with his boss, and management training courses. He joins the National Foremen's Association, attends lectures, and may even be sent to a two-week seminar at the local university. He learns much and becomes suitably skillful in discharging his new functions. This new way of life changes the foreman's behavior, of course; but only peripherally, just as living in a new house does not basically alter the marriage relation. He knows more, sees more, has more and better skills.

If companies do want such "simple-level" changes, and only these, then management training is called for. The girl learns to type; the boy learns how to sell; the new zone manager learns the policy manual; and the new vice president of manufacturing learns how the company's controller figures costs. These specific learnings are the objectives of training, and can become changes in behavior produced by training.

Self-Development

If, however, a company wants growth in the *deeper* sense, then something more subtle and basic in its impact is called for in the manager development effort. Such deeper growth is, of course, a change in self-concept. The manager who once was unreliable in his judgment or who lacked drive *grows* toward reliability in judgment or toward stronger drive. Growth in this sense brings observable changes in outward behavior, because each person is now inwardly different — different, for example, in his perception of himself, in his attitude toward his job and his company as both relate to his own life, or in his feeling of responsibility for others.

But experience shows that such growth is as difficult to achieve as it is desirable. It demands the full-fledged participation of the manager. Actually the trite expression, "Management development is self-development," is psychologically sound. The growing manager changes because he wants to and because he has to in response to new insights and understandings that he gains on the job. He does not change because he is told to, exhorted to, or because it is the thing to do.

Such growth implies changes in the man himself — in how he uses his knowledge, in the ends to which he applies his skills, and, in short, in his view of himself. The point is clear that the growing person examines himself; and as he does so, he emerges with new depths of motivation, a sharper sense of direction, and a more vital awareness of how he wants to live on the job. Growth in this sense is personalized and vital. And such growth in self-concept is at the heart of a real manager development effort.

But growth in self-concept is not always simple and clear.

Each human being is several selves. He lives comfortably in the role of father, husband, businessman, president, golfer, bridge player, the life of the party, and so on. But if there are conflicts among any of these roles, then discomfort arises. And such conflict brings with it such dynamics as tension, guilt feelings, and compensation. Let us illustrate with a familiar example:

A man sees himself both as a good father and as a good businessman. As a father, he spends time with his children; but as a businessman, he finds the demands on his time overwhelming. Now what does he do? He obviously cannot be home most evenings with his family and also be out of town on necessary business trips. He cannot realize both self-concepts simultaneously. So what happens? He compromises by giving his business his time Monday through Friday, and his family the weekend.

This seems like an easy resolution. What, then, is the problem? The man in our example has had to modify both self-concepts and may feel deeply dissatisfied with such a necessity. So his dissatisfaction, his psychological discomfort, his basic conflict in self-concepts, may show in his behavior. He may be unduly critical of business associates (or subordinates) who will not follow his example and give up their family life during the week. Or he may resent his children, who blithely go about their own activities on the weekend, ignoring him. And if by chance his teen-age son develops any emotional problems which are ascribed to "parental neglect," our man really hits the ceiling! "Neglect? How can that be? Haven't I given my boy every weekend?" he asks.

In the deeper sense, conflicts lie behind many self-concepts, but it is beyond our scope to explore them. In an individual case, this is a matter for professional study and expert handling. By definition, effective, consistent behavior is integrated behavior, while unintegrated behavior is the behavior of conflict.

Unrealism in Self-Concept

In addition to conflicts between self-concepts as a cause of ineffective behavior, there is the crucial matter of disparity between "how I see myself" and "how others see me." Unrealistic self-appraisal has cost many a manager his job. Think of men you know who have been fired, eased out, or moved laterally because they no longer "seemed up to the job." Has there not been in many such cases the subtle flavor of unadaptability, of a rigid inability in a manager to adjust his sights to a new role as times have changed?

Most familiar are the unnecessarily tragic cases of men who cannot grow old gracefully. Next are those uncounted misfits who fail through lack of realistic insight into their true worth. For example, take the good vice president who flunks as president because he never realized his inability to endure the rigors of being top man. There are endless instances of failures owing to a disparity between "who I am" and "who I think I am." Unfortunately, it is not only outright failure that may come from disparities in self-concept; more insidious is a partial or fuzzy self-appraisal. In fact, if the proposition is right that realism in the individual's view of himself has a one-to-one relationship with effectiveness on the job, then it surely follows that all of us can improve our effectiveness by the simple expedient of developing a more realistic, more accurate self-concept!

In short, the more realistic one's view of himself, the more is personal effectiveness guaranteed. Here is an example that underscores this point:

George H., the vice president of sales for a $50-million company with a staff of 250 sales and service men, was in serious organizational trouble. The group had increased in size so rapidly that it had long since outgrown its organizational pattern. There were constant complaints such as: "Whom do I work for?" "Nobody knows whether I'm doing well or poorly." "We haven't any system to follow in service to customers." The executives under George tried manfully to do two and three times as much as they had always done. The situation was, frankly, a mess.

George as a person was well liked and respected. He was democratic, attentive to others, soft-spoken, unlikely to "order," always likely to "suggest," and unsure of himself as an administrator. In general he was a man who saw himself as a stimulator and coordinator of his men, an excellent personal salesman, but not a supervisor. Somehow he had completely missed sensing that his men waited for directions from him. He felt that a sensible district sales manager should know what to do. His own perception of himself and his men's perception of him as vice president of sales were poles apart.

The impasse was breached when an outsider on whom George relied heavily (and who also had the confidence of the top men in the department) finally told him bluntly, "George, your people are waiting for you to clear the air. They'll follow any organizational plan you want them to. This step only you can take. They respect you and want your leadership. They value you. Don't ask them; tell them, for goodness' sake, how you're going to organize their activities."

George tried to integrate this new dimension into his self-concept. At first, he swung to one extreme and "got tough:" He made explicit, directive demands; he swore; he told everybody, in effect, "I want what I want when I want it – and that's right now!" But soon he abandoned his pretense and absorbed into his self-concept the new "take-charge" aspect of his functioning. He defined an organizational plan, set up policies and procedures which sorted out sales and service duties, discussed them fully with all involved, and said, in effect, "This is it. Let's go."

This example is, of course, an oversimplification; it highlights the fact that disparity in perception can reduce managerial effectiveness. What George saw himself to be in the office of vice president of sales precluded his seeing the needs of his men. And this blind spot nearly cost him prolonged chaos, if not his job.

Finally, it is manifestly clear that change in self-concept as a function of executive growth has a payoff. Recall situations where a critical appointment has to be made. Who gets the nod? Usually it is the man who *as a person* is thought to have potential and who is able through his style of life on the job to make a contribution to the "mix" of key executives. Consequently, many companies, in selecting their hand-picked future executives, feed in "trainees" with liberal arts degrees. They are looking for the *man,* not his knowledge or special skills. By the same token, as the young man grows, it is his self-concept that will change and come more into line with what he is becoming in relation to his potential. It is on the basis of his self-concept that he emerges as a top executive. To twist an old adage, it isn't what you know that finally counts; it's who you *are*.

Natural Resistance

But there is still one big question to answer. If changes in the self-concept of the executive are desirable, just what brings them about? In fact, are changes in self-concept possible? Of course changes are possible, but there is one obvious block to growth.

Even when executives want to change, the lurking suspicion that such effort is futile tends to vitiate the process of change. Faint mutterings of self-discontent tend to get quashed by the notion that "an old dog can't learn new tricks." And the basic comfort of the status quo seems to outweigh the value of the new mode of behavior.

One reason for such feelings of resistance is that, psychologically, the mature person resists change. By definition, the self-concept is an organization or patterning of attitudes, habits, knowledge, drives, and the like. And also, by definition, the fact of organization means a cementing together of all these complex components.

For example, the man who for many years has been highly and aggressively competitive cannot, except with difficulty, either suddenly or gradually become insightfully cooperative; he will still tend to see himself as needing to surpass the other fellow. The individual retains his pattern, his consistency, his basic characteristics; and in this sense resists change. Indeed, this is a good thing, or we still would all be going through the throes of "finding ourselves" as we did as adolescents.

When the mature person changes, therefore, he does so against a natural resistance; but whether this resistance is a deeply stabilizing influence that helps him to retain his basic direction and character, or whether it is a cocoon that makes him unreachable, is a moot question. Resistance, though built in, may thus be either a roadblock or a gyroscope.

We have noted that changes in the self-concept of the executive are "gut-level," not peripheral. They are changes in perception and attitude and understanding, not changes in knowledge or experience or skills. So our exploration of how change occurs must include those factors which seem to operate more deeply within the individual and which polarize new directions and behaviors. We are looking for those basic, vital factors which, as they operate, really change the person beyond his power of dissimulation or pretense. This is change in the fundamental makeup of the person, not change in his apparel. When such changes occur, the man is different.

STEPS TO MATURITY

Let us be clear about one point. Growth does not proceed in clear-cut, discrete, logical steps. Sometimes it occurs in inexplicable spurts; at other times with agonizing slowness. There are cases where real learning is so deeply unconscious that no overt behavioral change shows up for a long time. Even regressions will occur, as when an adolescent girl, perhaps troubled by her day's activities, will sleep with a doll as she did at age six. The process of growth is a nebulous, multifactored, fluid, dynamic process, often astounding, and usually only partially controllable.

But for the sake of discussion, and understanding, we can postulate a sequence of steps.

Self-Examination

If we were to attempt a systematic analysis of what happens when growth in a manager occurs, we would need to begin with self-examination. For here the individual first knows he *doesn't know* or first gets an inkling that he wishes his behavior were different in some respect. He is forced, either by circumstance or his own conscious introspection, to look at himself critically. This is what happens when a golfer sees movies of his swing, or when a mother scolds her child by saying, "Just look at yourself — all dirty." Or when the supervisor's thinly veiled anger over a subordinate's sloppy work finally becomes known. Every man sees himself each time he shaves, but does he really examine what he sees? Does he appraise and evaluate and study what manner of man he is?

The function of self-examination is to lay the groundwork for insight, without which no growth can occur. Insight is the "Oh, I see now!" feeling which must, consciously or unconsciously, precede change in behavior. Insights — real, genuine glimpses of ourselves as we really are — are reached only with difficulty and sometimes with real psychic pain. But they are the building blocks of growth. Thus self-examination is a preparation for insight, a groundbreaking for the seeds of self-understanding which gradually bloom into changed behavior.

Self-Expectation

As an individual raises his sights for himself, as he gets an insight into the direction in which he wants to grow, as he "sees" himself in a particular respect that he does not like, then he is changing his self-expectation. New demands on himself are set up, not by anyone else, just by himself. This is another way of saying what the theologians insist on, that a conviction of sin precedes salvation. Or, as the psychologists put it, first accept the fact that *you* have the problem — not anyone else — and then you are ready to find a solution. Here are two cases that illustrate the importance of self-expectation through insight:

John P. was a chronic complainer. Nothing was ever his fault. He frequently and self-pityingly inveighed against his boss, his subordinates, his peers, and the competition. He was capable, knowledgeable, a hard worker, critical. And never once, when he sang the old refrain, "Why does this always happen to me?" did an inner voice whisper back, "It's no different for you, old boy, than for anyone else. It's just the way you take it."

Efforts by his boss and his friends to develop some insight in John seemed wasted. Logical explanations, patiently made, were of course futile. Anger toward him only proved to him he was picked on. Gentle tolerance only gave him a bigger pool to wallow in.

One day in a meeting of executives to find answers to a particular crisis that had hit everyone (an unexpected price slash by a major competitor), he held forth at length on the uselessness of market research, on the futility of keeping a "pipeline" on the competitor's situation, on how his department (sales) couldn't be blamed for not anticipating the vagaries of the competition's pricing policy, and so on. He finally stopped. And, as though by prearrangement, the whole group, perhaps in complete disgust at his immaturity and irrelevance, sat in stony silence.

At length the silence became so oppressive that it suddenly dawned on the complainer that he was just that — an immature complainer. He recalled the words of his colleagues and his own dim awareness that he did complain a lot. Insight finally occurred.

At long last he was ready to begin to grow out of his immaturity. He saw (and disliked) himself at this point. Now his growth could become self-directed; he could easily find many opportunities to quash feelings of self-pity and to face reality in a more statesmanlike fashion, because now he expected more statesmanlike attitudes of himself.

Pete B., age 58, was vice president of engineering of a company that made fine-quality capital goods equipment. He had been with his company 35 years. He was a good engineer, who knew the product inside out; and through the years he had learned to know the customers, too. He felt proud of and personally involved in each installation of the product. It was not unusual to see him on an evening, coatless and with his tie loose, perched on a stool before a drafting board, surrounded by young engineers, digging at a tough installation problem. While some thought Pete did too much himself, others felt that with him on the job the customer would be satisfied.

About four years ago, however, the president, whose family owned the company, sold it to a large corporation, and the company became a wholly owned subsidiary. One allied product line was acquired, then another. Finally Pete's department was asked to do the engineering work for several subsidiaries that were not set up to do their own.

Now Pete's job had changed, subtly but surely, and trouble began to brew for Pete because he couldn't seem to change with the situation.

Psychologically, Pete saw himself as a one-man department (with assistants as trainees) who personally engineered the product for the customer, his friend. He resisted the impersonality of working on engineering problems of "sister companies" whose customers and products he barely knew and cared less about. The new-fangled system of a "home office" engineering vice president who was "staff" seemed to him just another unnecessary complication. Nothing worked the way it used to. He saw himself bypassed by progress and change.

So, unconsciously, he began to resist and to fight. His yearning for the "good old days" subconsciously forced him to run faster and faster in order to know more customers and more product lines; to work more evenings; to press new systems into the form of old procedures. And, of course, he began to slip, and badly. Gradually, Pete was viewed by his superiors as "good old Pete, but let's not get him in on this matter or he'll have to take it over himself and we'll get bogged down," and by his subordinates as a fine fellow, but stodgy and old-fashioned.

Fortunately, before the situation compelled a major organizational shift, Pete took stock of his situation, and really saw himself as he was. He got the insight that his self-image of a kind of personal engineer was no longer applicable to the corporation's greatly expanded needs. And right then, with this new glimpse of himself (and the courage and self-honesty to face it), he began to change. He started by focusing on how his years of experience could be applied to the coaching of his subordinates. He put himself in the shoes of the staff vice president and could then see how to mesh gears better. Then he stopped resisting the new-fangled data processing and automation procedures. His growth began with a new self-expectation.

Change in Self-Expectation

How does one get a new self-demand, a new self-expectation? How does one find out that his present self-concept is inadequate? How does one know not only that he can be different but should be as well? Unfortunately for those who like recipes or formulas, such questions are perennially bothersome because there is no one best way.

What can be done to stimulate change in self-expectation besides honest, realistic, self-appraising introspection? In the business context, the constructive pointing up of an executive's needs for growth by his superior is a tremendous source of insight. The emphasis, of course, is on the word *constructive,* which means helpful, insightful ideas from the superior and not, as so often happens, a ceremonial, judgmental, "I'll tell you what I think about you" appraisal.

A further source of insight is wives – the perceptive ones, that is. Perceptive wives have unique ways of jerking husbands up short when their self-images become distorted.

In fact, anything which enables the man to get a new perception – reading, observing, studying, going to conferences, attending meetings, and participating in clubs — can provide insight into himself. *Out of insight comes change in self-expectation.*

And, of course, life situations which are kaleidoscopic always enable the perceptive person to see himself in a new light. Here is another example:

Paul W. was acutely self-critical, often to the point where his fear of failure immobilized him. He delayed decisions, fussed endlessly with details, and generally strained to be perfect. In time his relation with the psychologist, who genuinely accepted him without criticism, praise, blame, or hostility, enabled him to see how his self-critical attitudes really stemmed from his self-pride. He felt he had to be perfect because it was "safer" to be free from criticism and failure. But he finally "rejoined the human race" and demanded of himself only that he do his best. The insight that he was human after all freed him to change his self-expectations.

Self-Direction

A man is master of his own destiny in the sense that he takes charge of his own development if he wants to grow. Nothing can be done to him to make him grow; he grows only as he wants to and as his own insights enable him to.

The change in self-concept that an executive undergoes must continue primarily through his own self-direction. It is clear that many development programs miss their mark badly at this point. They make the naive assumption that exposure to experiences or people or books or courses is enough to produce growth. Not so. They effect change in the participant only as he reaches out and appropriates something — a bit of wisdom, a new idea, or a new concept — that stretches him, and gives him an answer to his own self-generated problem.

Put another way, we might say that, just as learning is impossible without motivation, so real executive development is impossible unless the executive seeks it. Furthermore, his desire is infinitely stronger if he seeks development because he wants to develop than if he is merely trying to please his boss or do what is expected of him. As any teacher knows, the pupils who listen and learn merely in order to pass the course are far poorer learners than those who want to learn.

Fundamentally, this is the age-old problem of motivation, of keeping steam up in the boiler. The maintenance of a growing edge, as an executive emerges from insight to insight to realize his potential, is a consequence of intrinsic motivation. He is driven toward unrealized objectives, perhaps toward unrealizable goals; this is what keeps the executive honing his growing edge.

After he develops insight into himself *in relation to what he wants to be,* the power that keeps him growing is the veritable necessity of doing something that to him is intrinsically, basically, and lastingly worthwhile. Growing executives are so because they derive their strength and desire and drive from inner, unachieved goals; and their satisfactions from self-realization. This is intrinsic motivation as it relates to self-concept.

Broadened Perceptions

The dynamics of this factor of growth are very clear: anyone must see himself in relation to his environment, both personal and impersonal, and must develop his image of himself partly in response to what he sees around him. So if he sees a very small world (as a child does), his concept of himself must necessarily be narrow; if he sees himself as a citizen of the world (as a world traveler might), his self-concept embraces the world. This is the difference between the real provincial, such as a hillbilly, and the true sophisticate.

A most common complaint of superiors is that a subordinate is too narrow in his outlook. For example, the sales manager promoted to vice president of sales irritates his peers in manufacturing or research by having "only a salesman's point of view." The former production supervisor, now a vice president, is derided by the people in sales for his attitude of "We'll make it at low cost; it's up to you to sell it, and don't bother me with special runs for special customers or model changes — sell 'em." Both men suffer from constraint of the self-concept: they perceive their jobs (and themselves) too narrowly.

A vice president of sales was brought in from outside the company to gear up the effort of merchandising a new line of products. He did a magnificent job, old pro that he was, of shaping up and vitalizing a sales force. Volume of sales picked up excellently, and he was the hero of the hour.

But after a year, when he felt on top of his job, some of his attitudes and habits reasserted themselves, annoying others and stalling progress. For instance, he persisted in making frequent references to his former (and larger) company. He climbed on manufacturing for delivery delays, and on research and engineering for perfectionism before releasing the specifications for what he felt were needed product changes. The time it took to explain to him, pacify him, and argue with him was ill-spent and futile. He was rapidly becoming a block in the path of progress.

One day the president approached him directly. "George," said the president, "what's your title?"

"Why," said George, puzzled, "vice president of sales."

"Right. And what does vice president mean to you?"

George paused. What was the president getting at? "Well," he said, "it means lots of things, I guess. Responsibility for sales, building a . . . ."

"Stop right there," interrupted the president. "Responsibility for sales, you say. True in a way. But the sales manager also has this responsibility, doesn't he?"

"Well, yes."

"Then what does the word *vice president* mean in your title?"

"Oh, I see . . . . Well, I guess it means seeing or having responsibility for the sales function of the company from the point of view of the company . . . that part of your office."

"You got my point before I mentioned it, George," said the president. "A vice president speaks from the company point of view, not just that of his department. He tries to keep the overall good of the company in mind."

George thought this conversation over. He got the point. He realized the narrowness of his own view. He had been thinking of himself as "on loan" from his former employer to straighten things out here. As he pondered the president's comments, he broadened his perception of his job − and of himself. And sometime later he began to act as an officer of the total company.

SELF-REALIZATION POWER

It is not enough, however, just to see ourselves as we are now. Such understanding is a necessary starting point, or basis on which to build. But we must also see what our real selves *could* be, and grow into that.

The strong men of history have had one psychological characteristic in common: they seem always to have been themselves as persons − Michelangelo, fighting against odds for a change to sculpt; Beethoven, continuing to compose after he became deaf; Milton, who didn't allow blindness to interfere with his writing. Such men have given meaning to the phrase, "fulfilling one's destiny."

In less dramatic form, any strong executive fulfills himself as he lives a life that is an unfolding of his potential. He must be himself. In this sense, the self-concept of the strong executive is a constantly evolving, changing thing as he continuously realizes himself. This is, indeed, genuine growth and the kind that continues until senescence sets in.

Can all men aspire to be this strong − to accomplish such self-realization? Of course not. But a growing person (by definition) has unrealized power if his self-concept, his self-expectation, his self-direction, and his constantly broadening perceptions (wisdom) allow him to find it. The difference between a strong man and a weak man may not be a difference in ability, for many clerks have keen intelligence; or in drive, for many ambitious men get nowhere; or in opportunity, for somehow, strong men *make* opportunity. No, the difference lies in self-concept. How much do I value my life? What do I want to do with it? What must I do to be myself? Strong men have emerged with clear-cut answers to such questions; weak men equivocate and temporize and never dare.

Thus growth, finally, is the evolvement of personal goals and the sense of venture in pursuing them. This is the meaning of the dedicated man. His personal goals, his company goals, and his job goals have coincidence to a great extent; and his personal power is directed single-mindedly toward seeing himself in relation to the fulfillment of his executive potential.

Toward Becoming a Fully Functioning Person

CARL R. ROGERS

I am sure that each of us has puzzled from time to time as to his own goals, and the goals which he believes would be desirable for others. "What is my purpose in life?" "What am I striving for?" "What do I want to be?" These are questions which every individual asks himself at one time or another, sometimes calmly and meditatively, sometimes in agonizing uncertainty or despair. They are old, old questions which have been asked and answered in every century of history. Yet they are also questions which every individual must ask and answer for himself, in his own way. They are questions which I, as a therapist, hear expressed in many differing ways as men and women in personal distress try to learn, or understand, or choose the directions which their lives are taking.

THE PROBLEM

As I have worked for many years with troubled individuals, I believe that I can discern a pattern, a trend, a direction, an orderliness, a commonality, in the tentative answers to these questions which these people have found for themselves. And so I would like to share with the reader the picture of the optimum human person, as I have formed this picture from my experience with my clients. It is my perception of what human beings appear to be striving for, when they feel free to choose their own direction. It is also my picture of what constitutes personal or psychological health.

The Background from Which the Problem is Approached

I shall have to make it clear at the outset that my observations are made from a background of client-centered therapy. Quite possibly all

From Perceiving, Behaving, Becoming: A New Focus for Education. 1962 Yearbook, Washington, D.C.: Association for Supervision and Curriculum Development, 1962. pp. 21-33. Reprinted with permission of the Association for Supervision and Curriculum Development and the author. ©1962.

successful psychotherapy has a similar personality outcome, but I am less sure of that than formerly, and hence wish it to be clear that I speak from a particular perspective. The trends I have observed have occurred in a relationship which, when it is at its best, partakes of these characteristics. The therapist has been willing to *be* his real feelings, has been willing to be genuine, in the relationship with the client. He has been able to enter into an intensely personal and subjective relationship with the client—relating not as a scientist to an object of study, not as a physician expecting to diagnose and cure, but as a person to a person.

The therapist feels this client to be a person of unconditional self-worth; of value no matter what his condition, his behavior, or his feelings. The therapist is able to let himself go in understanding this person; no inner barriers keep him from sensing what it feels like to be the client at each moment of the relationship, and he has been able to convey to the client something of this empathic understanding. It means that the therapist has been comfortable in entering this relationship fully, without knowing cognitively where it will lead, satisfied with providing a climate which will free the client to become himself.

For the client, this optimal therapy has meant an exploration of increasingly strange and unknown and dangerous feelings in himself; the exploration proving possible only because he is gradually realizing that he is accepted unconditionally. Thus, he becomes acquainted with elements of his experience which have in the past been denied to awareness as too threatening, too damaging to the structure of the self. He finds himself experiencing these feelings fully, completely, in the relationship, so that for the moment he *is* his fear, or his anger, or his tenderness, or his strength. And as he lives and accepts these widely varied feelings, in all their degrees of intensity, he discovers that he has experienced *himself,* that he *is* all these feelings. He finds his behavior changing in constructive fashion in accordance with his newly experienced and newly accepted self. He approaches the realization that he no longer needs to fear what experience may hold, but can welcome it freely as a part of his changing and developing self.

This is a thumbnail sketch of what client-centered therapy might be at its optimum. I give it here to suggest the kind of situation in which I have observed certain trends occurring in clients who have participated in such therapy. I would like now to proceed to my main concern: what are these directions, and what personality characteristics appear to develop in the client as a result of this kind of experience?

CHARACTERISTIC DIRECTIONS

What follows is based both upon clinical observation and upon research. It tries to present the trends I have seen in our clients, but it also pushes these trends to the limit, as it were, in order better to see the kind of person who would emerge if therapy were optimal, the kind of person who might be said to be the goal which individuals discover they are aiming toward.

An Increasing Openness to Experience

A major observation is that the individual moves toward being open to his experience. This is a phrase which has come to have increasingly definite meaning for me. It is the polar opposite of defensiveness. Defensiveness I have described in the past as being the organism's response to experiences which are perceived or anticipated as incongruent with the structure of the self. In order to maintain the self-structure, such experiences are given a distorted symbolization in awareness, which reduces the incongruity. Thus, the individual defends himself against any threat of alteration in the concept of self by not perceiving those meanings in his experience which contradict his present self-picture.

In the person who is open to his experience, however, every stimulus, whether originating within the organism or in the environment, would be freely relayed through the nervous system without being distorted by a defensive mechanism. There would be no need of the mechanism of "subception"[1] whereby the organism is forewarned of any experience threatening to the self. On the contrary, whether the stimulus was the impact of a configuration of form, color or sound in the environment on the sensory nerves, or a memory trace from the past, or a visceral sensation of fear or pleasure or disgust, the person would be "living it," would have it completely available to awareness.

Perhaps I can give this concept a more vivid meaning if I illustrate it from a recorded interview. A young professional man reports in the forty-eighth interview the way in which he has become more open to some of his bodily sensations, as well as other feelings.

Client: It doesn't seem to me that it would be possible for anybody to relate all the changes that you feel. But I certainly have felt recently that I have more

1. A term used by R. S. Lazarus and R. A. McCleary in "Autonomic Discrimination without Awareness: A Study of Subception." *Psychological Review* 58: 113-22, 1951.

respect for, more objectivity toward, my physical make-up. I mean I don't expect too much of myself. This is how it works out: It feels to me that in the past I used to fight a certain tiredness that I felt after supper. Well now I feel pretty sure that I really am *tired*—that I am not making myself tired—that I am just physiologically lower. It seemed that I was just constantly criticizing my tiredness.

Therapist: So you can let yourself *be* tired, instead of feeling along with it a kind of criticism of it.

Client: Yes, that I shouldn't be tired or something. And it seems in a way to be pretty profound that I can just not fight this tiredness, and along with it goes a real feeling of *I've* got to slow down, too, so that being tired isn't such an awful thing. I think I can also kind of pick up a thread here of why I should be that way in the way my father is and the way he looks at some of these things. For instance, say that I was sick, and I would report this, and it would seem that overtly he would want to do something about it, but he would also communicate, "Oh, my gosh, more trouble." You know, something like that.

Therapist: As though there were something quite annoying really about being physically ill.

Client: Yeah, I am sure that my father has the same disrespect for his own physiology that I have had. Now last summer I twisted my back; I wrenched it; I heard it snap and everything. There was real pain there all the time at first, real sharp. And I had the doctor look at it and he said it wasn't serious; it should heal by itself as long as I didn't bend too much. Well this was months ago—and I have been noticing recently that—hell, this is a real pain and it's still there—and it's not my fault, I mean it's—

Therapist: It doesn't prove something bad about you—

Client: No—and one of the reasons I seem to get more tired than I should maybe is because of this constant strain and so on. I have already made an appointment with one of the doctors at the hospital that he would look at it and take an X-ray or something. In a way I guess you could say that I am just more accurately sensitive—or objectively sensitive to this kind of thing. I can say with certainty that this has also spread to what I eat and how much I eat. And this is really a profound change, as I say, and of course my relationship with my wife and the two children is—well you just wouldn't recognize it if you could see me inside—as you have—I mean—there just doesn't seem to be anything more wonderful than really and genuinely—really *feeling* love for your own children and at the same time *receiving* it. I don't know how to put this. We have such an increased respect—both of us—for Judy, and we've noticed just—as we participated in this—we have noticed such a tremendous change in her—it seems to be a pretty deep kind of thing.

Therapist: It seems to me you are saying that you can listen more accurately to yourself. If your body says it's tired, you listen to it and believe it, instead of criticizing it, if it's in pain you can listen to that, if the feeling is really loving your wife or children, you can *feel* that, and it seems to show up in the differences in them, too.

Here, in a relatively minor but symbolically important excerpt, can be seen much of what I have been trying to say about openness to experience. Formerly he could not freely feel pain or illness, because being ill meant being unacceptable. Neither could he feel tenderness and love for his child, because such feelings meant being weak, and he had to maintain his facade of being strong. But now he can be genuinely open to the experience of his organism—he can be tired when he is tired, he can feel pain when his organism is in pain, he can freely experience the love he feels for his daughter, and he can also feel and express annoyance toward her, as he goes on to say in the next portion of the interview. He can fully live the experiences of his total organism, rather than shutting them out of awareness.

I have used this concept of availability to awareness to try to make clear what I mean by openness to experience. This might be misunderstood. I do not mean that this individual would be self-consciously aware of all that was going on within himself, like the centipede who became aware of all his legs. On the contrary, he would be free to live a feeling subjectively, as well as be aware of it. He might experience love, or pain, or fear, living in this attitude subjectively. Or he might abstract himself from this subjectivity and realize in awareness, "I am in pain"; "I am afraid"; "I do love." The crucial point is that there would be no barriers, no inhibitions, which would prevent the full experiencing of whatever was organismically present, and availability to awareness is a good measure of this absence of barriers.

Openness to experience is not a construct which is easy to measure with our present instruments, but such research as exists tends to support the notion that it is characteristic of those who are coping effectively with life. Chodorkoff (1954), for example, found in a very careful study that the better adjusted subjects perceived themselves more accurately. They were, that is, more open to the facts of their experience and thus perceived themselves in much the same way as they were seen by a group of competent and unbiased observers. Even more interestingly, they tended accurately to recognize threatening experiences (in this case tachistoscopically presented threatening words) more quickly than they recognized neutral experiences. They thus seemed very open even to stimuli which were threatening. The poorly adjusted group showed the reverse trend, and seemed to have a set toward keeping threatening experiences inadequately differentiated and inadequately symbolized.

Toward Becoming a Process

A second major trend which I have observed is that the individual moves toward more acceptantly being a process, a fluidity, a changing. He lives in a more existential fashion, living fully in each moment. Let me see if I can explain what I mean.

I believe it would be evident that for the person who was fully open to his experience, completely without defensiveness, each moment would be new. The complex configuration of inner and outer stimuli which exists in this moment has never existed before in just this fashion. Consequently, such a hypothetical person would realize that, "What I will be in the next moment, and what I will do, grow out of that moment, and cannot be predicted in advance either by me or by others." Not infrequently we find clients expressing this sort of feeling. Thus one, at the end of therapy, says in rather puzzled fashion, "I haven't finished the job of integrating and reorganizing myself, but that's only confusing, not discouraging, now that I realize this is a continuing process . . . . It is exciting, sometimes upsetting, but deeply encouraging to feel yourself in action and apparently knowing where you are going even though you don't always consciously know where that is."

One way of expressing the fluidity which is present in such existential living is to say that the self and personality emerge *from* experience, rather than experience being translated or twisted to fit a preconceived self-structure. It means that one becomes a participant in and an observer of the ongoing process of organismic experience, rather than being in control of it. As one client put it: "I have a feeling that what I have to do is to take more the position of passenger, rather than driver. See how things go when they're left alone. It's awful kind of scary—feeling that nobody's at the wheel. Of course it's a tremendously challenging feeling, too. Perhaps *this* is the key to freedom."

Or again, the same client, a bit later: "I'm not changing from *me* into something else, I'm changing from *me* to *me*. More like being an amoeba than a caterpillar-butterfly. The amoeba changes shape, but it's still an amoeba. In a way that's sort of a relief. I can keep the parts of me I really like. I don't have to chuck the whole thing, and start all over again."

Such living in the moment, then, means an absence of rigidity, of tight organization, of the imposition of structure on experience. It means instead a maximum of adaptability, a discovery of structure *in* experience, a flowing, changing organization of self and personality.

It is this tendency toward existential living which appears to me very evident in people who are involved in the process of psychological health. It means discovering the structure of experience in the process of living the experience. Most of us, on the other hand, bring a preformed structure and evaluation to our experience and never relinquish it, but cram and twist the experience to fit our preconceptions, annoyed at the fluid qualities which make it so unruly in fitting our carefully constructed pigeonholes. To open one's self to what is going on *now,* and to discover in that present process whatever structure it appears to have—this to me is one of the qualities of the healthy life, the mature life, as I see clients approach it.

An Increasing Trust in His Organism

Still another characteristic of the person who is living the process of health appears to be an increasing trust in his organism as a means of arriving at the most satisfying behavior in each existential situation. Again let me try to explain what I mean.

In choosing what course of action to take in any situation, many people rely upon guiding principles, upon a code of action laid down by some group or institution, upon the judgment of others (from wife and friends to Emily Post), or upon the way they behaved in some similar past situation. Yet as I observe the clients whose experiences in living have taught me so much, I find that increasingly such individuals are able to trust their total organismic reaction to a new situation because they discover to an ever-increasing degree that if they are open to their experience, doing what "feels right" proves to be a competent and trustworthy guide to behavior which is truly satisfying.

As I try to understand the reason for this, I find myself following this line of thought: The hypothetical person who is fully open to his experience would have access to all of the available data in the situation, on which to base his behavior—the social demands; his own complex and possibly conflicting needs; his memories of similar situations; his perception of the uniqueness of this situation. The data would be very complex indeed. But he could permit his total organism, his consciousness participating, to consider each stimulus, need and demand, its relative intensity and importance, and out of this complex weighing and balancing, discover that course of action which would come closest to satisfying all his needs in the situation.

An analogy which might come close to a description would be to compare this person to a giant electronic computing machine. Since he is open to his experience, all of the data from his sense impressions, from his memory, from previous learning, from his visceral and internal states, are fed into the machine. The machine takes all of these multitudinous pulls and forces which are fed in as data, and quickly computes the course of action which would be the most economical vector of need satisfaction in this existential situation. This is the behavior of our hypothetical person.

The defects which in most of us make this process untrustworthy are the inclusion of information which does *not* belong to this present situation, or the exclusion of information which *does*. It is when memories and previous learnings are fed into the computations as if they were *this* reality, and not memories and learnings, that erroneous behavioral answers arise. Or when certain threatening experiences are inhibited from awareness, and hence are withheld from the computation or fed into it in distorted form, this too produces error. But our hypothetical person would find his organism thoroughly trustworthy, because all of the available data would be used, and it would be present in accurate rather than distorted form. Hence his behavior would come as close as possible to satisfying all his needs—for enhancement, for affiliation with others, and the like.

In this weighing, balancing and computation, his organism would not by any means be infallible. It would always give the best possible answer for the available data, but sometimes data would be missing. Because of the element of openness to experience, however, any errors, any following of behavior which was not satisfying, would be quickly corrected. The computations, as it were, would always be in process of being corrected, because they would be continually checked against their consequences.

Perhaps the reader will not like my analogy of an electronic computing machine. Let me put it in more human terms. The client I previously quoted found himself expressing annoyance to his daughter, as well as affection, when he "felt like it." Yet he found himself doing it in a way which not only released the tension in himself, but which freed this small girl to voice her annoyances. He describes the differences between communicating his annoyance and directing his feeling of anger at, or imposing it on, her: " 'Cause it just doesn't feel like I'm imposing my feelings on her, and it seems to me I must show it on my face. Maybe she sees it as 'Yes, daddy is angry, but I don't have to cower.' Because she never *does* cower. This in itself is a topic for a novel, it just feels that good." In this instance, being open to his experience, he selects, with astonishing intuitive skill, a subtly guided course of behavior which meets his need for release of angry tension, but also satisfies his need to be a good father and his need to find satisfaction in his daughter's healthy development. Yet he achieves all this by simply doing the thing that feels right to him.

Another way of saying this is that the individual guides his behavior by the meanings which he discovers in the immediate feeling process which is going on within him. Gendlin (1961) terms this immediately present feeling process "experiencing," and shows how the individual can turn again and again to his experiencing to discover further meanings in it. The experiencing is thus a referent by which the individual may guide his behavior.

Observation has shown that clients who appear to have gained the most from therapy come to trust their experiencing. They accept the realization that the meanings implicit in their experiencing of a situation constitute the wisest and most satisfying indication of appropriate behavior. I think of one client who, toward the close of therapy, when puzzled about an issue, would put his head in his hands and say, "Now what *is* it I'm feeling? I want to get next to it. I want to learn what it is." Then he would wait, quietly and patiently, until he could discern the exact flavor of the feelings occurring in him. Often I sense that the client is trying to listen to himself, is trying to hear the messages and meanings which are being communicated by his own physiological reactions. No longer is he so fearful of what he may find. He comes to realize that his own inner reactions and experiences, the messages of his senses and his viscera, are friendly. He comes to want to be close to his inner sources of information rather than closing them off.

Again there is a bit of research evidence to indicate that this trust of one's own experiencing is associated with the healthy personality. Crutchfield (1955), in a most interesting study, presented potential military leaders with a situation in which the individual's clear perception and experience of a given situation appeared to be at variance with the judgment of all the other members of the group. Should he now rely on the evidence of his own senses or defer to the judgment of the group? The evidence shows that those who trusted their own experiencing were better adjusted individuals, more mature, with greater leadership ability. Those who distrusted their own sensing of the situation and adopted the group judgment were the less mature, less well adjusted persons.

It seems to be this trust of his own experiencing which guided the scientific behavior of Einstein, holding him toward a given direction, long before he could give any completely conscious and rational basis for it. During this initial period he simply trusted his total organismic reaction. He says, "During all those years there was a feeling of direction, of going straight toward something concrete. It is, of course, very hard to express that feeling in words, but it was decidedly the case, and clearly to be distinguished from later considerations about the rational form of the solution." [2] This is the type of behavior which is also, I

2. Wertheimer, Max. *Productive Thinking*. New York, Harper & Brothers: 1945, pp. 183-84.

believe, characteristic of the person who has gained greatly from therapy.

SOME IMPLICATIONS

The three trends I have tried to describe—toward openness to experience, living as a process, and trust of one's own experiencing—add up to the fact that the person in whom they are observed is becoming a more fully functioning person. This picture of a more fully functioning individual has many implications, but I will restrict myself to pointing out three which I believe have special importance.

Integration

The trends I have presented describe an individual who is becoming integrated. He is unified within himself from the surface level to the level of depth. He is becoming "all of one piece." The distinctions between "role self" and "real self," between defensive facade and real feelings, between conscious and unconscious, are all growing less the further these trends continue. All that the individual experiences and is, within the envelope of his organism, is increasingly available to his conscious self, to himself as a person. There is a continuing growth of good communication between all the different aspects and facets of himself.

Creativity

Watching my clients, I have come to a much better understanding of creative people. El Greco, for example, must have realized, as he looked at some of his early work, that "good artists do not paint like that." But somehow he trusted sufficiently his own experiencing of life, the process of himself, so that he could go on expressing his own unique perceptions. It was as though he could say, "Good artists do not paint like this, but *I* paint like this." Or, to move to another field, Ernest Hemingway was surely aware that "good writers do not write like this." But fortunately he moved toward being Hemingway, being himself, rather than toward someone else's conception of a good writer.

Einstein seems to have been unusually oblivious to the fact that good physicists did not think his kind of thoughts. Rather than drawing back because of his inadequate academic preparation in physics, he simply moved toward being Einstein, toward thinking his own thoughts, toward being as truly and deeply himself as he could. This is not a phenomenon which occurs only in the artist or the genius. Time and again in my clients, I have seen simple people become significant and creative in their own spheres, as they have developed more trust of the processes going on within themselves, and have dared to feel their own feelings, live by values which they discover within, and express themselves in their own unique ways.

Such a person would, I believe, be recognized by the student of evolution as the type most likely to adapt and survive under changing environmental conditions. He would be able creatively to make sound adjustments to new as well as old conditions. He would be a fit vanguard of human evolution.

Trustworthiness of Human Nature

It will have been evident that one implication of the view presented here is that the basic nature of the human being, when functioning freely, is constructive and trustworthy. For me this is an inescapable conclusion from a quarter century of experience in psychotherapy. When we are able to free the individual from defensiveness, so that he is open to the wide range of his own needs, as well as to the wide range of environmental and social demands, his reactions may be trusted to be positive, forward-moving, constructive. We do not need to ask who will socialize him, for one of his own deepest needs is for affiliation and communication with others. When he is fully himself, he cannot help but be realistically socialized. We do not need to ask who will control his aggressive impulses, for when he is open to all of his impulses, his need to be liked by others and his tendency to give affection are as strong as his impulses to strike out or to seize for himself. He will be aggressive in situations in which aggression is realistically appropriate, but there will be no runaway need for aggression. His total behavior, in these and other areas, when he is open to all his experience, is balanced and realistic—behavior which is appropriate to the survival and enhancement of a highly social animal.

I have little sympathy with the rather prevalent concept that man is basically irrational, and that his impulses, if not controlled, would lead to destruction of others and self. Man's behavior is exquisitely rational, moving with subtle and ordered complexity toward the goals his organism is endeavoring to achieve. The tragedy for most of us is that our defenses keep us from being aware of this rationality, so that consciously we are moving in one direction, while organismically we are moving in another. But in our hypothetical person there would be no such barriers, and he would be a participant in the rationality of his organism. The only control of impulses which would exist or which would prove necessary is the natural and internal balancing of one need against another and the discovery of behaviors which follow the vector most closely approximating the satisfaction of all needs. The experience of extreme satisfaction of one need (for aggression, sex, etc.) in such a way as to do violence to the satisfaction of other needs (for companionship, tender relationship, etc.)—an experience very common in the defensively organized person—would simply be unknown in our hypothetical individual. He would participate in the vastly complex self-regulatory activities of his organism—the psychological as well as physiological thermostatic controls—in such a fashion as to live harmoniously, with himself and with others.

BECOMING A FULLY FUNCTIONING PERSON

Let me conclude by drawing together these observational threads into a more unified strand. As I have observed individuals who appear to have made important strides toward psychological health, I believe they may be thought of as moving toward an implicit goal—that of becoming a fully functioning person.

I find such a person to be a human being in flow, in process, rather than having achieved some state. Fluid change is central in the picture.

I find such a person to be sensitively open to all of his experience—sensitive to what is going on in his environment, sensitive to other individuals with whom he is in relationship, and sensitive perhaps most of all to the feelings, reactions, and emergent meanings which he discovers in himself. The fear of some aspects of his own experience continues to diminish, so that more and more of his life is available to him.

Such a person experiences in the present, with immediacy. He is able to live in his feelings and reactions of the moment. He is not bound by the structure of his past learnings, but these are a present resource for him, insofar as they relate to the experience of the moment. He lives freely, subjectively, in an existential confrontation of this moment of life.

Such a person is trustingly able to permit his total organism to function freely in all its complexity in selecting, from the multitude of possibilities, that behavior which in this moment of time will be most generally and genuinely satisfying. He thus is making use of all of the data his nervous system can supply, using this data in awareness, but recognizing that his total organism may be, and often is, wiser than his awareness.

Such a person is a creative person. With his sensitive openness to his world, and his trust of his own ability to form new relationships with his environment, he is the type of person from whom creative products and creative living emerge.

Finally, such a person lives a life which involves a wider range, a greater richness, than the constricted living in which most of us find ourselves. It seems to me that clients who have moved significantly in therapy live more intimately with their feelings of pain, but also more vividly with their feelings of ecstasy; that anger is more clearly felt, but so also is love; that fear is an experience they know more deeply, but so is courage; and the reason they can thus live fully in a wider range is that they have this underlying confidence in themselves as trustworthy instruments for encountering life.

I believe it will have become evident why, for me, adjectives such as happy, contented, enjoyable, do not seem quite appropriate to any general description of this process I have called psychological health, even though the person in this process would experience each one of these feelings at appropriate times. But the adjectives which seem more generally fitting are adjectives such as enriching, exciting, rewarding, challenging, meaningful. This process of healthy living is not, I am convinced, a life for the fainthearted. It involves the stretching and growing of becoming more and more of one's potentialities. It involves the courage to be. It means launching oneself fully into the stream of life. Yet the deeply exciting thing about human beings is that when the individual is inwardly free, he chooses this process of becoming.

REFERENCES

Chodorkoff, B., "Self-Perception, Perceptual Defense, and Adjustment." *Journal of Abnormal and Social Psychology* (1954) 49: 508-12.

Crutchfield, R. S., "Conformity and Character." *American Psychologist* (1955) 10: 191-98.

Gendlin, E., "Experiencing: A Variable in the Process of Therapeutic Change," *American Journal of Psychotherapy* (1961) 15: 233-45.

Defenses and
the Need to Know

ROGER HARRISON

The purpose of this paper is to discuss the ways we have of protecting our views of ourselves and others. Specifically, it is intended to rescue the concept of "defensive behavior" from the ostracism in which it is usually held, to restore it to its rightful place as a major tool of man in adapting to a changing world, and to consider how defenses may help and hinder us in profiting from a learning situation.

Let us consider how we understand the world we live in, and particularly those parts of it concerning ourselves and our relations with other people. First of all, we organize the world according to *concepts,* or categories. We say that things are warm or cold; good or bad; simple or complex. Each of these concepts may be considered a dimension along which we can place events in the world—some closer to one end of the dimension, some closer to the other.

Actually, we can't really think without using these categories or dimensions to organize our thoughts. Any time we consider the qualities of ourselves, other persons, or events in the inanimate world, we have to use categories to do it. We are dependent for our understanding of the world on the concepts and categories we have for organizing our experiences. If we lack a concept for something which occurs in the world, we either have to invent one or we cannot respond to the event in an organized fashion. How, for example, would a person explain his own and others' behavior without the concept of love and hate? Think how much behavior would simply puzzle or confuse him or, perhaps, just go on by without really being perceived at all, for lack of this one dimension.

Concepts do not exist in isolation; they are connected to one another by a network of relationships. Taken all together, the concepts we use to understand a situation, plus the relationships among the concepts, are called a *conceptual system.* For example, we may say, "People who are warm and friendly are usually trusting, and hence,

Reprinted from *Human Relations Training News,* Vol. 6, No. 4, Winter, 1962-1963, pp. 1-4.

they are often deceived by others." Here we have a conceptual system linking the concepts of *friendly warmth, trust in others,* and *ease of deception.* Because concepts are linked one to another, the location of an event on one concept usually implies something about where the event is located on each of a whole network of concepts. It is thus almost impossible to take in a small bit of information about a characteristic of a person or event without its having a whole host of implications about other characteristics.

Images and stereotypes operate this way: when we discover that a person is a Negro, or a PTA president, a social scientist, or a wife, the information on these concepts immediately calls up a whole network of expectations about other characteristics of the person. In the case of stereotypes, these expectations may even be so strong that we do not check to find out whether our conceptual system worked accurately this time, but may even go to the other extreme of ignoring or distorting information which doesn't fit the conceptual system, so that the system may remain quite unaffected by disconfirming experiences.

The study of defenses, like the study of stereotypes, is the study of the processes that protect the organization of conceptual systems in the face of information and experiences which, if accurately perceived, would tend to break down or change the relationships among concepts in the system.

Why should conceptual systems be resistant to change? Actually, if they were simply intellectual exercises, they probably would not. In real life, conceptual systems come to have *value* attached to them. The values seem to be of two kinds: one kind I will call *competence value.* By the competence value of a conceptual system I mean its value for helping us to be effective in the world. After all, the conceptual systems we have were developed because we needed some way of making sense of the world; of predicting what kinds of results would follow from what kinds of causes; of planning what kinds of actions we needed to take in order to accomplish some desired result.

People have the conceptual systems they have because in some important situations the systems proved *adaptive* for them; by seeing the world in just this way they were able to get along better, to be more effective, to prepare better for what was coming next. For human beings conceptual systems are, in a very real sense, very nearly the most important survival equipment we have. Animals have instinctual patterns of response: complex systems of behavior that are set off without thinking in response to fairly fixed patterns of stimulation. Human beings have to do it the hard way, by developing systems of concepts that make sense of the world and then using these systems to make decisions as to what to do in each situation. Those conceptual systems that pay off over and over again tend to become parts of our permanent equipment for understanding the world and for deciding what to do in it. If we were to lose these systems we would become like ships without rudders; we would have lost our control systems and, with them, our chances of acting in an organized, intelligent fashion to meet our needs. This is what I mean by the *competence value* of conceptual systems.

Unfortunately, no conceptual system fits the world perfectly. In the interests of economy we simplify and leave things out as being unimportant: for example, we act as though relationships which are *statistical* (they are only true most of the time) are *necessary,* and hence true all of the time. On the rare occasions when the relationships don't hold, we tend to overlook it, rather than trying to understand why things didn't go as expected. We may, for example, conceptualize the qualities of warmth, lovingness, and femininity as incompatible with a ready ability to express anger. This conceptual system may not change even in the face of strong anger on the part of a woman about whose warmth and femininity we have ample evidence in the past. We simply pass it off as, "She's not herself," or, "She's not really that mad," or even, "Deep down inside she isn't so warm and feminine as she appears to be." We go through a lot of mental gymnastics to avoid seriously questioning a conceptual system which has proved useful in the past. So, frequently, the *last* alternative explanation we consider is, "It is perfectly possible for a woman to express deep anger readily and still be warm, loving, and feminine." Such an alternative would mean the significant alteration of a conceptual system.

The trouble is, you can't just alter one little conceptual system at will, and let it go at that. Concepts are too closely and complexly linked to change one or two relationships in isolation. One change leads to another, and pretty soon a major reorganization is going on. It may be, of course, that the reorganization may lead to substantial improvement in the person's understanding and effectiveness in the world, but in the meantime there may be considerable turmoil and confusion as the person questions relationships that once seemed solidly established and before new ways of seeing the world have been adequately tested and confirmed.

Of course, the more important the particular conceptual system in question is in making it possible for the person to meet his needs, the more strain and upset is involved in changing it. For example, one might believe that heavy objects fall more rapidly than light ones. The disconfirmation that would follow upon learning that all objects fall at the same rate would perhaps be uncomfortable, but only moderately so. Consider, on the other hand, the anxiety and stress which could be produced by the discovery that complying with another's demands does not always make the other like you and may, indeed, have the opposite effect. For a person who has put much reliance in his interpersonal relations on the techniques associated with such a conceptual system, its disconfirmation may have the dimensions of a major crisis in life.

So, much of the time we hang on to our not-so-accurate conceptual systems because they work for us most of the time, and to give them up would plunge us into mild or severe confusion without any real promise of eventually attaining a more accurate, effective reorganization. The picture does not look so good for improvement, and before I finish, it will look even bleaker.

There is another kind of valuing that goes on in placing events into conceptual systems, and I will call it *evaluation*. This is the well-known process of saying that some states of affairs are better and some are worse. For most conceptual systems, there is an element of evaluation: most concepts have a good end and a bad end, and we would rather see events come out on the good ends than on the bad.

Again, it is less important to see events come out well in some areas than in others. The closer we get to conceptual systems that are concerned with our *self-perceptions* and our important relationships with others, the more important evaluation becomes, and the more uncomfortably responsible we feel when events don't fall on the valued ends of the concepts. Thus, if we value love as against hate, and intelligence against stupidity, it becomes important to protect conceptual systems that organize the events so that we can see ourselves as brilliant and loving. People may desperately protect quite maladaptive, ineffective conceptual systems in order to maintain a favorable perception of self or others.

Sometimes *competence value* and *evaluation* compete for influence on the conceptual system. For example, some persons have led such difficult childhoods that it is only by seeing themselves as bad, worthless people that they can seem to make sense out of the awful things that people they trusted have done to them; at the same time, they have normal needs for self-esteem, and for seeing themselves at the valued ends of concepts. These people may experience considerable conflict between these two motivational influences on their conceptual systems.

These, then, are the "defenses." They serve to keep us from becoming confused, upset, and rudderless every time something happens contrary to our expectations. Frequently, they protect our liking for ourselves and others when we and they fail to live up to our ideals. Defenses give life as it is experienced more stability and continuity than could ever be justified by reference to the contingency and complexity of real events alone. Defenses keep our relations with others more pleasant and satisfying, protecting us from our own and others' anger, and helping us to go on loving people who are usually less than perfect and sometimes less than human.

At the same time, these same defenses block our learning, often dooming us to make the same mistakes over and over again. They make us blind to faults of our own we could correct, as well as those we can do nothing about. Sometimes they make us turn the other cheek when a good clout in the nose would clear the air and establish a new and firmer footing for an honest relationship. They can, in extreme cases, make so many kinds of information dangerous to our conceptual systems that we narrow and constrict our experiences, our feelings, and our thoughts, becoming virtual prisoners of our own protection.

I believe there is in each of us a kind of counterforce which operates in the service of learning. Let's call it a *need to know*, or a drive toward competence. We are used to thinking about physiological needs, and we recognize there are probably social needs, such as needs for love; but we often overlook the need for competence and knowledge. Yet it is in operation all around us. We see it in the baby when he begins to explore as soon as he can crawl; we see it again in the "battle of the spoon," where the child actually gives up the certainty of getting the food into his mouth for the less effective but exciting experiment of "doing it himself." We see this need again as the adolescent struggles to carve out for himself a life that is uniquely his own; and we see it reflected in continuing efforts to understand and master the world as adults. People who read history for pleasure, who have creative hobbies, or who attend sensitivity training laboratories are all manifesting this drive to competence and knowledge.

The need to know is the enemy of comfort, stability, and a placid existence. For its sake we may risk the discomfort of examining and revising our assumptions about groups and people; we may expose ourselves to the anxiety-provoking experience of "personal feedback," in which we often learn others do not see us quite as we see ourselves; we place ourselves in groups where we know in advance we will be confused, challenged, and occasionally scared. Some of us expose ourselves to such situations more than once; to me, there could be no more convincing proof that the need to know is frequently stronger than the desire to maintain the comfort and stability of accustomed conceptual systems.

The sensitivity training laboratory thus frequently becomes a battleground between our desires to increase our competence and understanding, and our defenses. In this battle, we tend to take the side of the need to know and, like partisans everywhere, we malign, attack, and propagandize against the other side. Sometimes we forget that both sides are parts of a person, and that if either side destroys the other the person loses a valuable part of himself. This is particularly true in the case of defenses. We know from clinical practice and, I think, from personal experience and logic, that when a person's first line of defense becomes untenable, he drops back to another one, a sort of "second string" defense. Unfortunately, since we usually put our best and most adaptive defenses out in front, the second string is apt to be even less effective and reality-oriented than the first. To put it strongly, the destruction of defenses does not serve learning; instead, it increases the anxiety of the person that he will lose the more or less effective conceptual systems he has with which to understand and relate to the world, and he drops back to an even more desperate and perhaps unrealistic defense than the one destroyed. Though it may seem paradoxical, we cannot increase learning by destroying the defenses which block it.

What we can do is to create situations where people will not need to stay behind their defenses all the time. We can make it safe to sally forth from behind the moat, so to speak, secure in the knowledge that while we are exploring the countryside no one will sneak in and burn the castle.

People need their defenses most when they are most under threat and pressure. To make a mistake or become confused or admit to oneself that the world, ourselves, and others are not quite what we thought they were means that while we are revising or building new conceptual systems we will not be able to cope so well as before with the "slings and arrows" of a difficult situation. If we need every bit of competence we possess, we simply can't afford to give up conceptual systems which are tried but not perfect, in favor of exciting new ways of looking at things that are untested.

It is for this reason that I believe we cannot really begin to learn deeply from one another in a training group until we create relationships of mutual support, respect, and trust.

When we know that others will not place us in situations where we need every bit of our competence to cope with what is going on; when we know they will respect our own personal rate of growth and learning; when we know we have friends to help if we get into difficulties exploring new relationships, understandings, and behavior—then we can begin to look hard at the inadequacies in our ways of making sense of the world. We can examine those "exceptions to the rule" that we've always half expected might prove the rule inadequate; we can afford to really explore why ways of behaving that used to work fine are for some reason not producing satisfactions for us the way they used to, or why they seem to work with some people but not others; and we can really listen to the things people say that indicate they don't see us quite the way we see ourselves.

Out of this kind of exploration can come new and more effective conceptual systems, new ways of behaving that go along with them, and the excitement and pride that accompany increases in competence and knowledge. And when the excitement is over, and the new ways have been tested and integrated and have become habitual ways of seeing and behaving, I hope we will not be surprised to find that under conditions of stress we defend them against new learning just as strongly as we did the old. For these two partners go hand in hand: the need to explore and learn and the need to defend against disconfirmation and confusion. The challenge is to know how we can create conditions under which we can suspend one to enhance the other.

Interpersonal Communication

W. WARNER BURKE

Communication, by definition, involves at least two individuals, the sender and the receiver. Consider yourself, first of all, as the sender of some message. There are certain filters or barriers (internal) which determine whether or not the message is actually transmitted. These barriers may be categorized as follows: (1) Assumptions about yourself—Do I really have something to offer? Am I safe to offer suggestions? Do I really want to share the information? Will others really understand? How will the communication affect my self-esteem? (2) Attitudes about the message itself—Is the information valuable? Do I see the information correctly, or understand it well enough to describe it to others? (3) Sensing the receiver's reaction—Do I become aware of whether or not the receiver is actually understanding? Or in other words, can I "sense" from certain cues or reactions by the receiver whether or not we are communicating?

Now consider yourself as the receiver. As a receiver you may filter or not hear certain aspects (or any aspect for that matter) of a message. Why? Because the message may seem unimportant or too difficult. Moreover, you may be selective in your attention. For example, you may feel that the sender is being redundant, so you quit listening after the first few words. You may be preoccupied with something else. Or your filtering or lack of attention may be due to your past experience with the sender. You may feel that "this guy has never made a point in his life and never will!"

Many times the receiver never makes use of his "third ear." That is, trying to be sensitive to nonverbal communication. The sender's eyes, gestures, and sometimes his overall posture communicate messages that the insensitive listener never receives.

There may be barriers that exist *between* the sender and the receiver, e.g., cultural differences. Environmental conditions may also cause barriers, e.g., poor acoustics. More common, however, are the differences in frames of reference. For example, there may not be a common understanding of purpose in a certain communication. You may ask me how I'm feeling today. To you the phrase, "How ya doing?" is nothing more than a greeting. However, I may think that you really want to know and I may tell you—possibly at length.

Now that some of the problems in interpersonal communication have been mentioned, let us delve somewhat deeper into this process of transferring a message from the brain and emotion of one person to the brain and emotion of another human being.

Sending the Message

In communicating a message effectively to another person, there are several obvious factors which are beneficial. Such things as correct pronunciation, lack of distracting brogue, dialect, or accent, or a pleasant resonance in one's voice usually facilitate the sending of a message.

Assuming the sender of a message really has a desire to be heard and understood and not just speak for the sake of speaking, he wants some assurance that he has communicated. The key to effective communication on the part of the speaker, then, is to obtain some feedback, of one form or another, from his listener(s). Some bright persons who really have something to say are ineffective speakers, be it lecturing or speaking to someone at a cocktail party, because they are unable to tell or care whether their listener(s) is understanding, or they do not make any effort to check on their effectiveness as a communicator. For example, many lecturers in a classroom situation are often unaware of when a listener is sound asleep. Unless there is interaction of some type between the speaker and his listener, the speaker is susceptible to "losing" his listener. Often the speaker must take the initiative in order to receive any feedback regarding the effectiveness of his communication. When speaking before a large group, I often resort to the simple act of requesting my audience to shake their head "yes" they understand what I have just said, or "no" they did not understand. Even though this technique is simple, I usually get considerable feedback quickly and I know immediately what I must do at that point to make my speech more effective or whether to continue on with my next point.

Even when talking to just one other person the speaker must often take the initiative, in an interactive sense, to determine whether his message is being understood. Even though I sometimes take the risk of "bugging" my listener, I often stop and ask him if he understands what I mean, or I occasionally ask him to tell me what he thinks I meant in my message.

There is a fairly small percentage of people who speak articulately and clearly enough to be understood most of the time. Most of us have to work at it, especially when we are attempting to communicate a message which is fairly abstract or when we want to tell something which is quite personal or highly emotional. In sending the message effectively, we must do two things simultaneously, (1) work at finding the appropriate words and emotion to express what we want to say, and (2) continually look for cues from the listener to get some feedback even if we must *ask* our listener for some.

Receiving the Message

In considering interpersonal communication, we might, at first thought, think that listening is the easier of the two functions in the process. If we assume, however, that the listener really wants to understand what the speaker is saying, then the process is not all that easy. The basic problem that the listener faces is that he is capable of thinking faster than the speaker can talk. In their *Harvard Business Review* article, Nichols and Stevens state that the average rate of speech for most Americans is about 125 words per minute. Most of our thinking processes involve words, and our brains can handle many more words per minute than 125. As Nichols and Stevens point out, what this means is that, when we listen, our brains receive words at a very slow rate compared with the brain's capabilities.

As you have experienced many times, you know that you can listen to what someone is saying and think about something else at the same time. As the "cocktail party" phenomenon illustrates, the human brain is truly remarkable in its ability to process a considerable amount of input simultaneously. Sometimes, at a cocktail party, I want to hear not only what the person in my small gathering is saying, but also what that lovely creature is talking about in the group about six feet away. If the overall noise level is not too loud, I can hear and understand both conversations.

The problem with listening, then, is that we have "spare" time in our thinking processes. How we use that spare time determines the extent of our listening effectiveness. It is easy for us to be distracted in listening, especially if the speaker talks slowly or haltingly or if he says something that stimulates another thought. For example, suppose you are listening to a friend who is telling you about a problem he is having in his department. In the process of describing the problem, he mentions a person whom you know, whereupon you start thinking about the person at length. Later, when your friend asks you what you would do about his problem, you're apt to respond, "what problem?"

Thus, a fundamental problem the listener must consider in the communicative process is the fact that his brain is capable of responding to a speaker at several different levels simultaneously. Naturally, this can be an asset to the listener rather than a problem. For example, the listener can attend to nonverbal cues the speaker gives, e.g., facial expression, gesture, or tone of voice, as well as listen to the words themselves.

Besides a highly active brain, an effective listener has another factor to consider in the communicative process. This factor involves the process of trying to perceive what the speaker is saying from his point of view.

A Barrier and a Gateway

According to Carl Rogers, a leading psychotherapist and psychotherapy researcher, the major barrier to effective communication is the tendency to evaluate. That is, the barrier to mutual interpersonal communication is our very natural tendency to judge, to evaluate, to approve or disapprove the statement or opinion of the other person or group. Suppose someone says to you, "I didn't like what the lecturer had to say." Your typical response will be either agreement or disagreement. In other words, your primary reaction is to evaluate the statement from your point of view, from your own frame of reference.

Although the inclination to make evaluations is common, it is usually heightened in those situations where feelings and emotions are deeply involved. Thus, the stronger our feelings, the more likely it is that there will be no mutual element in the communication. There will be only two ideas, two feelings, two judgements, missing each other in the heat of the psychological battle.

If having a tendency to evaluate is the major barrier to communication, then the logical gateway to communication is to become an active listener, to listen with understanding. Don't let this simple statement fool you. Listening with understanding means to see the expressed idea and attitude from the other person's point of view, to see how it feels to him, to achieve his frame of reference concerning his subject. One word that summarizes this process of listening with understanding is "empathy."

In psychotherapy, for example, Carl Rogers and his associates have found from research that empathetic understanding—understanding *with* a person not about him—is such an effective approach that it can bring about major changes in personality.

Suppose that in your next committee meeting you were to conduct an experiment which would test the quality of each committee member's understanding. Institute this rule: "Each person can speak up for himself only after he has first related the ideas and feelings of the previous speaker accurately and to that speaker's satisfaction." This would mean that before presenting your own point of view, it would be necessary for you to achieve the other speaker's frame of reference—to understand his thoughts and feelings so well that you could summarize them for him.

Can you imagine what this kind of approach might mean if it were projected into larger areas, such as congressional debates or labor-management disputes? What would happen if labor, without necessarily agreeing, could accurately state management's point of view in a way that management could accept; and management, without necessarily approving labor's stand, could state labor's case in a way that labor agreed was accurate? It would mean that real communication was established, and conditions would be more conducive for reaching a workable solution.

Toward More Effective Listening

Some steps the listener can take to improve interpersonal communication have been stated. To summarize and be more explicit, let us consider these steps.

1. Effective listening must be an active process. To make certain that you are understanding what the speaker is saying, you, as the listener must interact with him. One way to do this is to paraphrase or summarize for the speaker what you think he has said.

2. Attending to nonverbal behavior that the speaker is communicating along with his verbal expression usually helps to understand the oral message more clearly. Often a facial expression or gesture will "tell" you that the speaker feels more strongly about his subject than his words would communicate.

3. The effective listener does not try to memorize every word or fact the speaker communicates, but, rather, he listens for the main thought or idea. Since your brain is such a highly effective processor of information, spending your listening time in more than just hearing the words of the speaker can lead to more effective listening. That is, while listening to the words, you can also be searching for the main idea of the message. Furthermore, you can attempt to find the frame of reference for the speaker's message as well as look at what he is saying from his perspective. This empathetic process also includes your

attempting to experience the same feeling about the subject as the speaker.

These three steps toward more effective listening seem fairly simple and obvious. But the fact remains that we don't practice these steps very often. Why don't we?

According to Carl Rogers, it takes courage. If you really understand another person in this way, if you are willing to enter his private world and see the way life appears to him without any attempt to make evaluative judgements, you run the risk of being changed yourself. This risk of being changed is one of the most frightening prospects many of us face.

Moreover, when we need to utilize these steps the most, we are likely to use them the least, that is, when the situation involves a considerable amount of emotion. For example, when we listen to a message that contradicts our most deeply held prejudices, opinions, or convictions, our brain becomes stimulated by many factors other than what the speaker is telling us. When we are arguing with someone, especially about something that is "near and dear" to us, what are we typically doing when the other person is making his point? It's certainly not listening empathetically! We're probably planning a rebuttal to what he is saying, or we're formulating a question which will embarrass the speaker. We may, of course, simply be "tuning him out." How often have you been arguing with someone for 30 minutes or so, and you make what you consider to be a major point for your point of view, and your "opponent" responds by saying, "But that's what I said 30 minutes ago!"

When emotions are strongest, then, it is most difficult to achieve the frame of reference of the other person or group. Yet it is then that empathy is most needed if communication is to be established. A third party, for example, who is able to lay aside his own feelings and evaluation, can assist greatly by listening with understanding to each person or group and clarifying the views and attitudes each holds.

When the parties to a dispute realize that they are being understood, that someone sees how the situation seems to them, the statements grow less exaggerated and less defensive, and it is no longer necessary to maintain the attitude, "I am 100% right and you are 100% wrong."

Summary

Effective communication, at least among human beings, is not a one-way street. It involves an interaction between the speaker and the listener. The responsibility for this interaction is assumed by both parties. You as the speaker can solicit feedback and adjust your message accordingly. As a listener, you can summarize for the speaker what you think he has said and continually practice the empathetic process.

One of the joys of life, at least for me, is to know that I have been heard and understood correctly and to know that someone cares enough to try to understand what I have said. I also get a great deal of satisfaction from seeing this same enjoyment on the face of a speaker when he knows I have understood him.

The Three Types of
Executive Personality

RICHARD W. WALLEN

For top management there can hardly be any more agonizing question than how to select the right man for the right job. It is a problem that is filled with far more pitfalls than the planning of a production line; a wrong choice in management selection can cost a company far more money than a misjudged financial investment and can do far more damage to a corporation's profit-and-loss statement than, say, a marketing program that unexpectedly backfires.

Yet in the selection of management men there is still far less precision than in any other area of business. This is understandable, since the complexities of human personalities are myriad compared to the intricacies of engineering, finance or marketing.

Nevertheless, it is a job that must be done. That being so, how can top executives attempt to judge the personality traits of the men whom they consider for promotion?

Some executives wash their hands of the problem entirely and turn the question over to trained personnel psychologists. And in many instances this is a sound decision, for the executive's role is to help drive the corporation forward, not to immerse himself in the practice of psychology. But there are scores of companies whose executives cannot afford either the money to keep a psychologist on a steady retainer or the time to permit a man to undergo the kind of thorough examination that a personnel psychologist must give him if the examination is to be made properly.

When the pressure is on to decide whether a man is capable of handling a new and bigger job, most businessmen rely heavily on the man's job history. Previous success, they feel, is the best indicator of future success.

This, however, is not always true. For when a man takes on a new job, it will almost always be found that there is only the most superficial resemblance between this position and the jobs he held earlier in his career. Clearly, then, a top executive must delve deeper if he is to gain any real assurance that the candidate he picks has not only the technical ability to master the new job but also the necessary personality traits.

Yet all too often these same top executives are confined by narrow and naive conceptions of human nature. They do not know how to interpret and systematically order their observations and information about a man. Some confidently trust to their intuition. Others struggle to classify "introverts" and "extroverts" among the job candidates. A few seek to base their selection on such fuzzily defined qualities as "initiative," "team spirit" and "will to win." But men cannot be graded usefully in these terms; human personality is far too complex for that.

Where, then, can a top executive turn for help in this difficult task? He can find at least a partial answer simply by organizing his observations and feelings about people and by learning how to interpret those observations. True, there are a host of factors other than personality that affect a man's decision on who to select for a particular job. But to understand a man's personality is at least a good part of the battle.

To gain that understanding we need to recognize that within all of us there are broad patterns of personality. These arise from the ways in which we handle two basic sets of emotions and impulses: the tender and the tough.

The tender emotions, of course, are those that express affection, sympathy and consideration for others. The tough emotions are those of aggression, pushing for action and struggling against obstacles. Both sets of emotions are within each of us. But many people, as they mature, reject or deny one or the other; though they cannot obliterate their tender or tough feelings altogether, they do seek to disguise these impulses and to alter the ways in which they express them.

Because of this, top executives can find three distinct personality types in the ranks of almost any corporation. To recognize these types is no mere academic exercise; it is, in fact, a major asset for the executive who must select men for management posts. The three:

- the "modest helper."
- the "strong achiever."
- the "detached critic."

Consider first, the type called the "modest helper." These are the people who, for one reason or another, have determined to reject or deny their capacities for aggression and toughness. They are modest, unassuming, and they find their greatest satisfaction in helping others. In cases where these people have gone to extreme lengths to deny their aggressive impulses, they have great difficulty in being firm or standing up for themselves at all. These are people who have gone so far as to reject even normal self-assertion, because they equate it with aggression.

Bias of an equal and opposite degree is the hallmark of the "strong achiever." He accepts his tough impulses and rejects his tender ones. He views life as highly competitive, believes deeply that the best defense is a good offense, and to him an obstacle is something to be beaten down as rapidly as possible. Such a man usually makes a poor listener and a bad corporate diplomat or bargainer.

More complex is the personality of the "detached critic," the man who rejects the display of both tender and tough emotions, who is determined to view all his associations coolly and logically. He seeks to be emotionally remote. Usually he has a passion for accuracy and order- liness, a dedication to facts and systems.

How effective are these personality types as executives? All three have, to an extent, some defects in their make-up. But this by no means disqualifies them from executive position. All three can be invaluable in running a corporation. But all three can also fail miserably and can damage a company's future if they are functioning in the wrong jobs.

The helper is a fellow who not only accepts his own affectionate tendencies, he also expects a good deal of consideration and affec- tionate goodwill from others. He seeks to win this by being agreeable and useful. At committee meetings, for instance, he will try to reconcile differences; if others' tempers begin to stir, he will try to relieve the tension with a joke or a diplomatic shift to a new topic.

Harmony, though, is of little interest to the achiever. He does not like the delays that stem from efforts to keep the peace and reconcile differences. His whole idea is to "get the job done," and when he is convinced that he is moving toward that goal, he will spend long hours at work if the task requires it. If he is not selected by a superior to take charge of a group, he will often elect himself to just that role, for the achiever typically likes to coordinate other people's activities and to make assignments.

In contrast, the critic is an orderly and systematic man. He likes to have plans that are thorough and detailed. And when he functions as a member of a committee, he will usually be well-prepared, with copious notes and valuable information, and so will usually be able to skillfully evaluate the ambitious proposals that might come from his more impetuous colleagues.

Basically different though they may be, there is no reason why men of these three varying personality types cannot work together effectively—so long as they are not called on to function in jobs that are essentially wrong for them and so long as the biases in their personalities are not extreme.

Each will, of course, try to exert an influence on the others, sometimes subtly, sometimes overtly and determinedly. Helpers usually take the indirect tack; sometimes they do not even like to think of themselves as seeking to exert their influence on others. They do favors willingly, for they want to build up a supply of good will and obligation on which they can draw later. Their use of praise and appreciation is unconsciously designed to enlist people in their service.

Achievers, unafraid of their own tough impulses, press their influence on others openly and directly. They will not only ask for what they want—they will, when they can, command it. True, they will not necessarily do this with a threat or a shout; power does not always shout, and the achievers are just as likely to make their demands while being smoothly polite and jovially informal.

The detached critics, in contrast, usually exert influence over others by their own degree of knowledge and the logic of their arguments. Ordinarily, they will take a stand only when they are well fortified with information—and once having taken that stand they are likely to be stubborn about maintaining it. If their stand is attacked, they are likely to resort to shrewd and analytical attacks on their opponents' positions.

In Others' Eyes

None of this means, though, that the three different types of men will necessarily or invariably have low opinions of each other. In the right situations they will often value highly the differences among them. The warm-hearted helper will look with admiration to the fearless and vigorous achiever and to the idealistic yet objective attitudes of the critic. The critic will admire the bold planning of the achiever and the intuitive understanding of the helper. And the achiever will equally admire the warmth of the helper's personality and the informed and analytical mind of the critic.

But if men like these are forced through faulty management selection into the wrong jobs or are put under severe strain in jobs that are only partially suited to their personalities, the whole situation can change for the worse. There is a strong chance that they will react violently to one another and will express this reaction either in bitterness to one another or in the administration of their departments.

The helper, under stress, will see only the ruthlessness of the achiever and the coldness and stubbornness of the critic. The achiever

The Rose-Colored Glasses . . .

Can three such diverse types as the achiever, the helper and the critic hope to work in harmony? When their differing patterns are not extreme, and their relationships pleasant as a result, they are apt to get along surprisingly well. In fact, this is the rosy light in which they would view each other:

The Perceiver		What He Sees	
	Helper	Achiever	Critic
Helper	_ _ _ _	Fearless, vigorous.	Faithful to ideals, controlled.
Achiever	Warm, supportive.	_ _ _ _	Informed, analytical.
Critic	Intuitive, understanding.	Enterprising, bold planner.	_ _ _ _

. . . and the Clash of Personality

But when their individual patterns are sharp and inflexible, the whole scene changes in the eye of the viewer. Rising frustrations and unsatisfied needs transform what have been virtues in the other types of executives to imagined vices of the worst sort:

The Perceiver		What He Sees	
	Helper	Achiever	Critic
Helper	_ _ _ _	Domineering, ruthless.	Cold, stubborn.
Achiever	Weak, sentimental.	_ _ _ _	"Nitpicker," impractical.
Critic	Subjective, demanding.	Unorganized, impulsive.	_ _ _ _

will write off the helper as a sentimental weakling and the critic as an impractical "nitpicker." And the critic himself will accuse the achiever of disorganized impulsiveness and the helper of irrational, sentimental demands.

Dangerous flaws can quickly appear, flaws that can wreck the effectiveness of a management group. Pushed to extremes, the helper might begin to feel that he is being martyred—that the burdens he suffers are not appreciated by anyone else—and make pathetic demands for assistance. The achiever's tough impulses might become disastrously exaggerated. And the critic is likely to withdraw into a state of silent sulking.

And these, of course, are all among the reasons why it is important that a man's personality traits—just as much as his past job performance—be judged in the selection of candidates for management responsibility. Yet that difficulty of selection remains. For rarely does a man fall into such neatly categorized slots as those drawn so far. And the fact is that few if any men can even be wholly described by these categories. The terms *helper, achiever* and *critic* are relatively narrow; each of us, as noted, has some of each of these strains in his character, and nobody can be fitted neatly into such arbitrary pigeonholes.

Each man has his own particular set of capabilities, and he tends to mold his job to fit those capabilities. There has long been a mutual attraction between the character of the modest helper and such jobs as teaching, counseling and the ministry. In such occupations, the helper is most likely to get the greatest reward—emotionally—for his desire to help others and to have the gratitude of others. Any corporation president knows that dozens of men on his staff are likely to have this trait in their personalities; these are the men who, in unguarded moments, will tell their associates that all their lives they have "really wanted to go into teaching."

The critics have their own particular best professions, too. These precise men, always wanting information, properly organized, at their fingertips, are often attracted to such fields as corporate law, scientific research, accounting and engineering.

For many decades, though, it is the achiever who has found his proper place in the field of corporate management. And at the same time, it is true that for just as long the rewards for men who excel in corporate management have been far greater than for those who can excel in science or teaching. And this, probably beyond all other reasons, is why corporate management contains in its ranks so many different personalities. Some men are always bound to head toward fields where the economic reward is greatest, no matter how stultified they might feel emotionally.

Yet it is not necessarily true that only the achiever is fit for corporate management. For management is increasingly a group operation, and if there is any value in the group, it lies in the diverse personalities it brings together. It is true that achievers cannot long tolerate being "assistant to" anyone—that they regard such a position as being no more than an intermediate training phase, necessary before they graduate to a job in which they can exert their will-power. Helpers, on the other hand, can be extremely useful as assistants to top corporate officers, for their devotion and their noncompetitiveness are assets that are sometimes extremely hard to find. And critics can be invaluable in jobs that do not, as a rule, require arbitrary policy decisions.

No man, though, is entirely unchangeable. A blend of all these characteristics probably makes the most valuable of men. Some men have this blend inherent in their personalities. Many, however, do not. And it is possible for men who are aware of the buried and sometimes rejected facets of their personalities to set about deliberately developing them.

The helper possibly has the best chance. He needs to re-integrate the lost aggressive trait into his personality. He needs to learn again how to stand up and defend himself. He needs to see that conflict can be a constructive and even creative force in human relations and that a constant effort to preserve outward harmony may well bury problems that are best aired.

Achievers need to learn patience—which is probably one of the most difficult of assets to acquire deliberately. They need, too, to learn the value of careful planning and compassion. There is no reason why they should not continue to be suspicious of sentimentality, but they need to learn that in some human situations, openly expressed affection is desirable.

Critics probably have the hardest task of all in attempting to transform their personality, for they have, in their past, rejected both compassion and aggression. They need to learn that emotion is not necessarily opposed to cool reason. They also need to learn that when they begin to express and share their feelings, they are likely to find a greater degree of acceptance from others and an increasing degree of tolerance in themselves.

A man who can master these needs reaches an end result that is worth the trouble: he becomes a whole and integrated person. He reacts to a situation according to the demands of the situation, not according to any inner bias built up in his personality. When a bell rings, he does not automatically salivate in the fashion of Pavlov's dogs. Nor does he react to a situation with a desperate struggle to control one or another exaggerated impulse. And because all his emotional resources are freely available to deal with whatever the next problem might be, he can sleep nights—even though he might have no idea just what that next problem might be.

Clearing The Air In Human Relations

BARRY I. OSHRY

When a manager begins to muse about his human relations skills in dealing with superiors, peers, subordinates, customers, clients, and so forth, he most frequently asks: "Am I too soft? Should I be rougher with people?" or "Am I too hardnosed? Should I be more kind and considerate of others?" I propose that the most relevant questions about work relationships center not around being hard or soft but around being *honest* or *dishonest.* Specifically, are strong feelings toward a person or group honestly expressed or are they dishonestly denied or ignored?

Feelings are part of the reality of organizational life. The pressure of too little time for too much work, the need to resolve differences of opinion, the necessity for meshing complexly different personality types—all of these elements inevitably leave their residues of anger, resentment, jealousy, frustration, helplessness, and hopelessness. What happens to these feelings in organizational life? What consequences does their expression or suppression have for organizational functioning, in particular for management development and group problem solving. Consider the following case:

Frank Maddox settled back in his chair. As the rest of the staff filed back to their places, he thought to himself, *"Maybe the coffee break will have helped us sort things out."* He glanced down at his note pad with two columns of phrases and figures headed "pro's" and "con's" and at the bottom a giant question mark absently doodled into an angrily frowning face. For three days the staff had been wrestling with a difficult decision and what had once seemed fairly clear-cut now was hopelessly muddled. *"It's a strange thing about this staff,"* he thought, *"how sharp and imaginative we are when we're working alone, but as soon as you bring us together to work on a common problem, we fall apart."*

Tom Burns had worked right through the coffee break and now was ready with a proposal. As Tom began, Maddox listened with forced concentration. He was drained, and from the looks on others' faces they were too. There was so much work waiting for him at his office—important work—but all was at a standstill until they could come to some agreement on this problem. Burns' analysis sounded pretty solid. There were lots of loopholes, but at least it looked liked a reasonable place to dig in.

Reprinted from *Business Horizons,* Graduate School of Business, Indiana University. Spring, 1966 by permission of the author and publisher.

Suddenly, from across the table, came Al Green's voice. *"Oh no!"* thought Maddox to himself. *"Ten to one we're in for a blow-by-blow discussion of how Green tried this when he was Barnes' assistant general manager at the Coast-X division."*

"You remember about five years ago," droned Green, "when Coast-X was having that big squabble about bringing out. . . ." Maddox slumped down in his chair; Burns leaned back, propped his feet up on the table, and stared blankly out the window. From across the table, knowing glances were exchanged. Some smiled; some glowered; some fidgeted trying to find more comfortable positions; some coughed; someone reached to pour himself a glass of water. No one looked at Al.

"Good grief!" thought Maddox. *"Is that man stupid? I must have heard this Coast-X story fifteen times, and I can't imagine it having any relevance to what we're doing. That man just irritates me. He's got one of the best sets of marketing brains in the country, but he can so exasperate you with those long, windy, off-beat tales that you just stop listening after a while. Who knows, he may be coming up with a top idea right now but I doubt if anyone is listening hard enough to recognize one if he did. Why on earth does he do it? Does he think we appreciate his humor? Does he think we're listening? Is it possible he just doesn't realize how much he exasperates us?"*

Tom Burns managed deftly to turn the discussion back to the point of his proposal by saying, "Al, what you've been saying checks out for the most part with my thinking. Let me see if I can build on some of the points you've been making." And with that he valiantly attempted to reorient the staff to the train of thought he had been developing. Within two minutes, Al Green was back at him. "Now hold it! That's exactly the tack Josh Barnes and I took at Coast-X. Josh Barnes," he said longingly, "now there was a manager. . . ." "That does it!" muttered Frank Maddox low enough for no one to hear.

Before proceeding, as an exercise, put yourself in Frank Maddox's position. Would you say anything at all or would you let the situation pass, hoping for the best? If you would say something, it will be useful for later reference to write on a slip of paper *not* what you would like to say, *not* what you think ought to be said, but *what you would say* were you in his position.

Many of the differences among individuals, groups, and organizations, with regard to climate of group meetings, interpersonal relationships, productivity and creativity, and styles of managerial development, revolve around the norms developed for handling situations such as those described above. In essence, we are talking about a situation in which a manager is working toward some short- or long-range goal. He has some task to do, some problem to solve, some decision to make. In order to reach this goal, he must either enlist the cooperation of or avoid interference from some other person or persons. These people seem to block the manager's path by being resentful or uncooperative, by exercising poor judgment, or by being insensitive to the needs of the manager or others. At this point, the manager experiences certain feelings, which, in varying intensity, combine impatience, annoyance, hopelessness, and helplessness. He also can describe the other person's behavior. He has seen the other's actions and with varying degrees of clarity can specify what aspect of that behavior triggered his feelings. It may be the other's persistent failure to listen to other people; it may be his insensitivity, his tendency to make light of everything, or his tendency to side with the boss regardless of the position the boss takes. Whatever the specific behavior, the manager is able to make some connections between what the other does and how he himself feels.

What does the manager then do with these feelings and perceptions? In this paper, we describe two styles by which managers react to their own feelings. The first, the *avoidance pattern,* will be recognized as the typical organizational style, based on the assumption that feelings are either irrelevant or disruptive of smooth organizational functioning. The second style, *problem-oriented feedback,* more atypical of organizational life, is based on the assumption that managerial development and group problem solving deteriorate in climates of suppressed feelings.

THE AVOIDANCE PATTERN

As part of a training activity, forty-eight management participants in a human relations training program were presented an abbreviated version of the Frank Maddox incident. They were asked how they would respond were they in Maddox's position. For the purpose of the exercise, the participants were not allowed to let the situation pass without commenting on it. The following are typical responses:

"All right, Al, now that we've heard from you, do you suppose we could explore Tom's proposal in a little more detail?"

"Will you please shut up and give someone else a chance to talk!"

"Al, that was quite a speech. Well done! Now I think we're much clearer about your thoughts on this matter as well as Tom's. Why don't we leave it up to the group to decide whom they want to hear from next?"

"Good point, Al, but why don't we give Tom some more time to discuss his proposal?"

"Dammit, Al, shuddup!"

Although the reactions vary greatly, they share a number of characteristics of the avoidance pattern.

Emotional content is latent in all of them. Not one of the forty-eight managers made any direct statement of personal feeling. No one mentioned that he was angry with Al. Although it might be argued that such feelings are easily read into these statements and that they are likely to be communicated to Al, it is equally possible to misread this latent emotionality in a number of ways.

Moreover, the responses avoid dealing with the underlying problem. None of the responses indicated a direct invitation to discuss the general nature of Green's communications within the group. The goal seems to be to get on with work immediately, by quieting Al without placing this particular situation in the perspective of the feelings and reactions he has generated in the past and is likely to generate in the future.

The avoidance pattern also retards management development. Although managerial development and training activities are often relegated to outside programs or to special activities within the organization, the most fertile ground for such learning is the normal daily work for interactions among managers. One way the manager can improve his effectiveness is to reduce the gap between what he *intends* to accomplish and what he in fact does accomplish. At issue here is the role played by the avoidance pattern in either promoting or interfering with managerial growth. For example, what has Al Green learned about his effects on this group, which will have consequences for his future performance?

Learning and change of managerial style require that one recognize the feelings evoked in others, the specific behavior leading to these feelings, and the fact that the specific incident is part of a larger time sequence in which these same behaviors have repeatedly evoked similar emotions in others. In the Maddox case, for example, it is unlikely that Al will realize that others are irritated and exasperated, that their feelings stem from his windy off-target monologues, and that this pattern has been recurring in his past associations with this staff. It is more likely that distortions and denials such as those described in succeeding passages will occur.

Overgeneralized Negative

Another aspect of the avoidance pattern is sensitivity to unspoken, latent negative feelings. This response assumes that these feelings are associated with one's whole person rather than to specific actions. Consider the following example from a management training program:

Bob Jay had served as "manager" during an organization exercise in which his group was competing with another at a production task. At the completion of the exercise, Jay's group was feeding back to him their impressions of the effectiveness of his managerial style. Their reactions clearly fitted the avoidance pattern. To the trainer, the group appeared annoyed with Jay's autocratic performance and his failure to make use of others' resources during the exercise, yet in a fifteen-minute barrage of statements aimed at Jay, not a single direct expression of feeling was heard. In fact, when the trainer asked how people felt about Jay's behavior—whether they were annoyed or irritated by it—the undisputed response of one member was: "We don't have any strong feelings about what he did, it's just that we feel he would be more effective if he handled it differently." Despite the group's elaborate attempts to keep feelings out of the discussion and to frame their comments within the context of constructive criticism, Jay, when asked what he thought others were trying to tell him, said simply, "They don't like *me*."

Two elements of the overgeneralized negative reaction are (1) that the individual accurately detects the latent negative feeling (although he may fail to discriminate fine nuances such as dislike and annoyance), and (2) that he attributes these feelings to his whole self rather than to specific pieces of his behavior. Sensing only the feeling and not its cause, his choice is either to stop talking or to continue in his usual way. Neither alternative is likely to produce very satisfactory results for him or those with whom he interacts. Most important, the polite, face-saving intentions of the avoidance pattern are wholly violated in practice. If the intention was to avoid *awkward* discussion of feelings, only the awkwardness is avoided while the feelings are communicated. If the intention was to avoid personality attacks, personality has been attacked in the most brutal way, that is, as a whole rather than in parts. For the overgeneralized negative, all the pains of direct feeling confrontation are present with few of the possibilities for constructive learning.

Selective Positive Feedback

The ambiguity of the avoidance pattern also makes it easier to "not hear" latent negative feelings, and to be sensitive only to signs of acceptance or positive praise. Managers frequently describe their version of the avoidance pattern as the velvet glove treatment. An over-generalized negative reaction is to attend only to the iron fist, whereas a selective positive reaction is to experience only the velvet glove. In the Maddox case, all Al might selectively learn is that he is an accepted and sometimes respected member of this group. His ideas may or may not be accepted as best, but they are always welcome. When this is the reaction, it is clear that the learning and development goals have been lost completely.

No Feedback

It is also possible to learn nothing from the avoidance pattern. Perhaps Al learned neither that he was liked nor disliked in whole or in part. He reacted in a way characteristic for him, and the responses evoked may not affect at all the chances of his responding similarly in the future. In our training experience we are often surprised at how little feedback managers receive in their day-to-day work lives. As participants become more aware of the scope and extent of their impact on others, some begin to wonder: "Why hasn't anyone told me?" Although, in fact, no one has told him, we also suspect that, in the face of such an ambiguous feedback model, *some men do not hear even when told repeatedly.* Thus, if one goal of the avoidance pattern is to help a manager grow in order to improve his effectiveness, then it fails dismally. Because of its ambiguity and closed character, this pattern allows the receiver to distort it in many ways—hearing it as support, hearing it as an attack on his personality, or not hearing it at all. In most cases, however, this pattern is not intended as a learning experience; it merely enables the manager to avoid facing uncomfortable feelings in himself—reactions which he feels he ought not have or which he ought not show to others. It serves as a diversionary move to eliminate a temporary inconvenience and get on with the task.

> Recently a high-ranking member of a large industrial organization told me that one of his colleagues would be attending our next management conference. "Give him plenty of feedback," he said. "He really needs it!" When I asked him to explain, he replied, "This fellow has risen fast in our organization, and is now slated to become general manager of one of our most important divisions. This new position is going to stretch to the limit his ability to work with others. He'll be dealing with a bright, aggressive, and competitive bunch of men, and from what I've seen of him, his ability to work with others leaves a lot to be desired. In meeting after meeting I've seen him alienate a whole group, antagonize people, and stifle creativity. He pushes his own ideas and rolls over or ignores the ideas of others. This aggravates people and they don't put out as much for him as they would for someone else. Up to this point he has been bright enough and aggressive enough to go it alone, but as divisional general manager he will need these other people."
>
> I asked, "Then why send him to the program? The next time you see this pattern in a staff meeting, why not tell him about it and discuss it right there?" It became clear from his answer that action was not appropriate in his organization and that the management development program was a legitimate means of accomplishing a job considered too "dirty" for the organization itself.

In our daily interactions with our superiors, peers, and subordinates, we are continually confronted with the opportunities to contribute to others' managerial development. When the avoidance pattern is chosen, no contribution is made to this development process. Human relations training programs such as those sponsored by the National Training Laboratories may provide powerful confrontations for managers unaccustomed to more direct feedback, but in terms of organizationally relevant management development, these experiences pale in contrast to the possibilities of day-to-day confrontation in the work itself.

THE AVOIDANCE PATTERN
AND GROUP PROBLEM SOLVING

A major dilemma for problem-solving groups is the separate but unequal treatment generally accorded to ideas and feelings. In a recent organizational study, we asked 100 managers to describe how often they observed twenty different aspects of problem-solving behavior in their work meetings and how important they thought each of these was for the effective functioning of these meetings. Two findings stand out:

1. Ideas are more highly valued than feelings. These managers place relatively high value on the abilities to express and be receptive to ideas, and relatively low value on expressing and being receptive to feelings. They feel that for their problem-solving groups to be effective, it is most important that people express ideas clearly and concisely, and they they listen with understanding and try to use the ideas raised by others in the group. It is least important that they express their feelings, help others express their feelings, or keep their feelings hidden and under control.

2. Expressing or controlling feelings and helping others to express feelings are disvalued in the organization and are not often seen in staff and problem-solving meetings. But highly valued actions such as "being open to the ideas of others" (value rank of 1) and "listening and trying to use the ideas raised by others" (value rank of 3.5) rank seventh and eighth respectively in relative frequency of occurrence in these meetings.

In summary, then, the organization disvalues and discourages expression of feelings. The organization highly values openness to ideas, but this behavior is not as effectively encouraged. This pattern is not unexpected, because feeling expression can be effectively suppressed, but actions aimed at suppressing feelings will also decrease openness to, expression of, and experimentation with ideas. Table 1 presents a few examples of situations in which feelings depress openness, expression, and experimentation with ideas.

FEELINGS AND PROBLEM SOLVING

Organizational pressures are so complex that to dismiss feelings as nonexistent or irrelevant is to deny the humanity of man. Personality types are a continually shifting mixture—passive with assertive, warm with aloof, competitive with cooperative, dependent with independent, rational with emotional. How can these complexities fail to yield their residues of irritation, warmth and support, or insecurity? But where is the evidence for this stew of emotionality? Table 2 indicates that managers see little evidence of either expression or suppression of feelings. If feelings are neither expressed nor hidden, are there no feelings at all? The few responses our managers gave to the Frank Maddox case indicate no direct expression of feeling. They also indicate that the managers place little value on either expressing or suppressing feelings. What can this mean except that they consider feelings to be irrelevant for the effective functioning of meetings? Yet experience proves that claims of a nonfeeling world are a myth. Consider the following interaction:

B is a drawling Texan who had the habit of accentuating points in the group by telling rather long and very funny stories ranging in dialect from Texan to Irish to Cajun to Jewish. Each story was followed by widely shared group laughter, although some group members, A in particular, appeared to be getting annoyed at the amount of group time being taken up by B. The group had discussed some of their reactions to B's story-telling behavior for about twenty minutes when the following conversation took place.

A (to B): It just seems to me that you might be more effective if sometimes you came right to the point. Some people might not enjoy your stories and might not understand what you were getting at.

B: Didn't you enjoy them?

A: Oh yes! I think they're great. I wasn't talking about me; I was thinking of other people who might not appreciate . . .

C: Well how did you feel when B was telling his story?

A: I felt he might be more effective if he came to the point more directly.

C: That's what you thought, but how did you feel? Were you angry?

A: Oh no!

C: That's funny, you looked angry. Maybe irritated then?

A: No.

C: Even a little irritated?

A: No.

D: (In exasperation.) For crying out loud! Then if it didn't bother you, why have you been kicking it to death for the last half hour?

A: I just felt that B would be more effective if. . . .

Postscript: Two sessions later, A admitted how much B's behavior had bothered him, and then added, "But now that I've come to know you, it doesn't bother me any more."

In T-Group training such as that sponsored by National Training Laboratories, managers usually become more comfortable in recognizing and expressing their own feelings. They may talk of their reactions of irritation, warmth (usually with great reluctance), frustration, or hostility. But even here the notion generally develops that owning up to feelings is a property unique to the training group and not transferable to organizational life. At the conclusion of a T-group for managers, all of whom were from the same organization, the members began to explore the applications of what they had learned to organizational life. One member asked, "What would happen if you came right out and told someone in your company that his behavior irritated you?" One member reached into his pocket, pulled out a white handkerchief, dangled it effeminately in the air, and muttered, "Tch, tch. Too bad for you!" The rest of the group knowingly nodded their heads in resigned agreement.

TABLE 1
Effects of Feelings on Ideas

Feeling	Effects on Openness, Expression, and Experimentation with Ideas
A *feels competitive* toward B. In any group interaction, he is motivated to increase his own status and decrease B's.	1. A takes premature potshots at B's ideas, thus decreasing the opportunity for others to evaluate or build on B's ideas.
	2. A saves his best ideas for those times when B is not present.
	3. A tends not to express incompletely conceived ideas, which in open discussion might have been productively developed, for fear that critical judgment might lower his status relative to B.
A is *irritated* by a persistent pattern of B's behavior. (For example, he is annoyed by B's constant maligning of others or by B's domination of group discussion.)	4. A tends to tune out B or to distort what B says.
A *feels unsure* of his own ability, which may in fact be equal to or greater than the ability of others in the group.	5. A prefers not to build on others' ideas for fear that his contributions will not be significant.
A *feels dependent* on his superiors' good will.	See 3 and 5 above.
	6. A tends not to critically evaluate or alter in any way his superiors' ideas for fear this will threaten the relationship between them.
A likes B personally and wants him as friend.	See above.

These managers are part of an organizational world in which the expression of ideas is a sign of strength and the admission of feeling a confession of weakness. The avoidance pattern tends to perpetuate this norm in that it allows roadblocks to be temporarily swept aside without any public recognition of the fact that feelings have been aroused. The results are only temporary, however, since the feelings remain. And so the cycle continues with feelings remaining high; these feelings act to suppress the generation, exploration, and experimentation of ideas, all within the myth that no significant feelings are involved anyhow.

We may summarize this section by looking at some typical organizational norms in terms of their effects on problem-solving behavior. In the typical problem-solving setting the following conditions occur:

1. Ideas are considered good. Rewards come from expressing and experimenting with ideas. It is also good to be receptive to ideas, but the primary payoff comes from communicating to others that you produce or are capable of producing good ideas.

2. Feelings are considered bad. Feelings are thought to be either irrelevant or disruptive of smooth organizational functioning. People who characteristically express feelings (whether positive or negative) run the risk of punishment or ostracism.

3. Feelings do exist. Pressures of work, time, quality, and competition, as well as conflicts among different personality styles, do produce feelings of irritation, warmth and support, insecurity, or helplessness.

4. Feelings are either suppressed or expressed indirectly through the avoidance pattern.

5. Because there are so many unresolved emotional issues among managers, the tendency will be to avoid cooperative effort and emphasize individual effort. Cooperative problem solving involves motivation to listen to other ideas and build on them, and freedom to venture vaguely formed ideas with minimal fear of criticism. Unresolved emotional issues will lead to: attacking others' ideas, distorting what others say, uncritical thinking, and withholding of ideas either to maintain a competitive advantage or to avoid fear of retribution.

Our management study indicates that, in fact, the most frequently observed forms of problem-solving behavior are *non-cooperative, idea-oriented* actions. Managers are most frequently described as showing intelligence, demonstrating high technical or professional competence, and thinking quickly (see Table 2). These are clearly important problem-solving skills and abilities, but they do focus on the output of ideas and not on input from others. Individually-oriented problem solving becomes a legitimized way of adapting to interpersonal conflict. It enables one to compete, to attack, and to avoid uncomfortable interpersonal contact. This form of problem-solving behavior—not listening to others, distorting others' ideas, attacking, or withholding one's own ideas—tends to further annoy, irritate, frighten, and alienate others.

If a goal of problem-solving meetings is to create a climate in which ideas are freely expressed, listened to, evaluated, and experimented with, then the avoidance pattern interferes with this goal. Rather than eliminate feelings, which appears to be the intended consequence of

TABLE 2

Twenty Aspects of Problem-Solving Behavior

(ranked by managers)

Problem-Solving Behavior	Frequency of Occurrence (High to Low)	Importance for Effective Problems Solving (Ranks)
Shows intelligence	1	13
Demonstrates high technical or professional competence; knows his stuff	2	7.5
Thinks quickly	3	13
Expresses ideas clearly and concisely	4	2
Listens with understanding to what others say	5	4
Is tolerant and accepting of others in group	6	11
Tries to get things done quickly without beating around the bush	7	7.5
Is open to the ideas of others; looks for new ways to solve problems	8	1
Sticks to the point under discussion	9.5	4
Talks and makes himself heard by others in the group	9.5	17
Pursues points aggressively	11	13
Listens and tries to use ideas raised by others in the group	12	4
Is persuasive, a seller of ideas	13	10
Tries to understand the feelings expressed by others in the group	14	7.5
Keeps feelings hidden and under control	15	18.5
Helps others express their ideas	16	15.5
Helps the group to explore why it is or is not working effectively	17	7.5
Expresses his own feelings (for example, when he is angry, impatient, or ignored)	18	20
Helps other people in the group express their feelings (for example, when they are angry or hurt)	19	18.5
If there are difficulties in his relationships with others, tends to look at himself as one of the causes of the problem	20	15.5

such meetings, they serve only to eliminate discussion of feelings while actually heightening emotionality. This combination of high emotionality and pressures to deny feelings tends to depress the quality of problem solving. People become more closed, more withholding, more attacking, more defensive—and more emotional.

PROBLEM-ORIENTED FEEDBACK

Another way of reacting to hurt feelings, irritation, rejection, anger, or frustration is relatively foreign to organizational life and may appear peculiar in many respects. Whereas in the avoidance pattern we respond to our feelings by sweeping them aside and focusing on the task, in problem-oriented feedback, we recognize and express our feelings *as clearly as we can* and try to specify what it was about our situation which engendered these feelings. Problem-oriented feedback has the following characteristics:

1. Feelings are expressed directly and as clearly as possible. Sometimes our feelings are clear to us. We know that we are angry, hurt, frustrated, bored. At other times, we sense that we are upset but the feeling is so complex that we are unable to specify or label it. Sometimes we are ashamed of our feelings; we think we should be mature enough not to have them. Our choice at these points is often to deny the feeling or expose it at great personal embarrassment. Sometimes we keep the issue alive by reporting a feeling more acceptable to us, which comes close to the actual trouble. In the Frank Maddox case, direct expressions of feeling would be: "I am frustrated," "I am furious," or "I am feeling helpless."

2. Feelings are related as specifically as possible to those elements of the situation that seem to have caused them. If the receiver in an avoidance pattern situation is sensitive enough to pick up the latent feeling message, he will have difficulty determining what is bothering people. It is very easy for him to distort the message, either by attributing their irritation to things beyond his control, or by attributing it to his whole personality and assuming that these others do not like him. In problem-oriented feedback, both the feelings and their causes are stated as explicitly as possible. Unless we are able to focus on the many referents of our feelings, the tendency will be to make an inappropriate scapegoat of one or two more obvious causes. In the early stages of a T-group, for example, it is not unusual for the most outspoken, controlling member of the group to be sharply attacked by other group members. All of the accumulating frustrations, fears, and hostilities,

stemming from many sources—their own ineptness, lack of cooperation from all group members, and lack of direct leadership from the staff—focus on this solitary figure as if he alone were responsible for the group's dilemmas. In describing the referents for such feelings, Frank Maddox might say such things as:

"I'm mad at *myself* for not being able to come up with something brilliant to get us out of this bind. . . ." *"Your stories,* Al, are driving me crazy. Whenever we try to dig into something, you come up with one of your tall tales that takes us off the track. This infuriates me. . . ." "I've got *problems in my own shop* and the longer we stay here, the more anxious I get about being snowed under with work. . . ." "I find myself getting *angry at this whole group* for not being able to function more effectively. We keep shooting down one another's ideas, jockeying for position. . . ."

These statements of feeling and apparent causes of feelings are part of the *facts* of the problem-solving setting. It seems ludicrous to suggest dispensing with feelings and getting down to facts when most of the ineffectiveness of the problem-solving group can be understood only in terms of the group's emotionality. The feelings are there—no matter how hard we wish them away; they depress the problem-solving process; and only as we are able to specify the feelings and the situations creating them are we in a position to improve the process of expressing, building, evaluating, and experimenting with ideas. When we know and are able to discuss the problem, only then are we in a position to at least choose whether we continue things as they are or attempt to change.

3. In the avoidance pattern, we respond to interpersonal dilemmas without time perspective—as if they had no history, and as if our re-actions would not affect the future functioning of the group. In the Maddox case, the responses were aimed at dispensing with this tempo-rary nuisance and getting on with the job. It is clear, however, that the problem, as described, has a long history. Al Green's actions, for example, are characteristic of his past performance in this group, and it is likely that his future responses to this type of feedback will be similar. People can learn more readily from feedback that demonstrates a historical pattern in which certain actions have predictably had certain consequences. This is so for two reasons. First, it may help to explain the magnitude of emotional response in the group. Often, apparently trivial incidents blow the lid off meetings and out we stagger, wondering how such a small event yielded so violent an erup-tion. The sequence becomes more understandable when we are able to link that single emotional outburst with a chain of events, each of which produced lower scale, undiscussed emotional responses.

Secondly, when feedback is placed in some larger time perspective, it helps the recipient understand not only his impact at a particular moment, but, more important, it sheds light on his more general and enduring role in problem-solving groups.

In the avoidance pattern, each incident is treated as an isolated problem. In problem-oriented feedback, the specific incidents are treated as symptoms of more enduring problems, and the commitment is to understand and resolve these more basic problems. In our managers' responses to the Maddox case, it was clear that the goal was to shut up Al Green, as if his talking at that point were the primary problem. The goal of problem-oriented feedback would be to help Al Green learn that this specific incident is characteristic of his performance in groups and that it generally has the same consequences.

Hopefully, this discussion helps dispel the artifical duality between the rationality of ideas and the nonrationality of feelings. Rationality in problem solving implies the willingness and ability to deal with whatever is relevant to the problem situation. Sometimes, expression and clarification of ideas is most relevant; sometimes, understanding of current feelings is most relevant. The competence of a problem-solving group is not measured by the amount of time spent in the discussion of ideas as opposed to feelings, but rather by its capacity to deal effectively with whatever is most relevant to problem solving, whether this be exploration of ideas or feelings.

It makes little sense to argue that feelings are irrelevant, that they get in the way of the job. The one purpose of this discussion has been to demonstrate that it is the suppression, rather than expression, of feelings which interferes with getting the work done. Management development and group problem solving are but two dollars-and-cents organizational activities continually deteriorating in climates that stifle the expression and public exploration of feelings. Test the assumptions you may be making regarding the negative consequences of problem-oriented feedback. Managers frequently refer to problem-oriented feedback as some form of amateur psychoanalysis. It should be clear that I am making a distinction between interpreting people's motives and reacting to people with *your* feelings.

Consider a situation in which you are irritated by another person's continual dominating of group discussion. An interpretive response would be: "You are doing this *because* of your need to influence and control a situation." It is a very safe and uninvolving statement for you to make. The onus lies completely on the dominator while you manage to remain safely aloof from the situation. You are not part of the problem. If you say, "It frustrates me and annoys me when you dominate the discussion," then you are no longer above the interaction, but part of it. You have been willing to admit you are emotionally affected by this behavior. You have communicated something about you, as well as something about him. Both of your actions—past and future—now become more understandable and tolerable. Expressing feelings, as distinct from interpreting motives, is not a therapeutic ploy; it is a very human transaction in which the actions and reactions of both parties are made public and hence more understandable. I am annoyed when people interpret my actions, unless some preconditions have been met. When someone interprets my behavior, he has entered into a learning-emotional relationship with me; he indicates that he is taking some responsibility for my learning about myself. But unless he first responds to me in terms of his own feelings—reactions to my behavior—unless he makes that investment of himself in the relationship—then the relationship is one of teacher to student, or therapist to client, and not person to person. Interpretation, without some relationship based on mutual feeling, is often merely a more sophisticated and more subtle form of keeping feelings out of the discussion.

A second assumption worth testing is that exploring feelings will destroy relationships that are now at least tolerable. In the period that I have been writing this article, I have been doing considerable thinking about many of my relationships. What different feelings do I have in those characterized by the avoidance pattern, as contrasted with those involving problem-oriented feedback? I have many relationships—social and work—not characterized by problem-oriented feedback. These are relationships in which I have strong feelings of irritation, frustration, jealousy, and warmth which have never been explored with those involved. I find myself repeatedly in the same interaction patterns with them—seeing the same actions, experiencing the same feelings. For a number of reasons, I have made no effort to change the nature of our relationships. By some standards, these are probably judged to be tolerable relationships, but for me they are self-denying. In them, I feel uncomfortable and dishonest. I continually am aware of censors over what I should and should not think and feel. If mutual growth and learning and creativity are any criteria of personal relationships, then these relationships are failing. Our mutual inhibitions are so great that we learn nothing about ourselves from each other, and we create nothing together. The boundaries of our interactions seem more determined by the roles we occupy than by our unique capacities and experience. Problem-oriented relationships are, for me, not always happy or comfortable ones, but they are the only ones in which I feel much that is uniquely me is involved. It is an expansive feeling, associated with the idea that I can do, say, and feel spontaneously, and that others feel that they can respond to me in the same way. It is the feeling that either or both of us can be friendly, aggressive, jealous, hurt, elated, brave, or afraid, and the other will accept these feelings as reality and not as weakness. There is a sense of honesty and freedom and being able to be more of myself spontaneously. In such settings, I am more of everything than I am at other times. I am warmer; I am more aggressive; I am funnier; I am more creative; I have greater self-respect, for the me at those times is so much richer than at other times.

The Person as a Manager

This section focuses on managerial behavior, rather than on principles of management or managerial personality types. It attempts to characterize the behavior of managers who are successful in bringing about productivity, constructive change, and effective utilization of people, and provides models against which a manager may gauge his own behavior.

Conditions for
Manager Motivation

M. SCOTT MYERS

- Motivation of the manager is strongest when he is realizing his potential—becoming what he has the capacity and desire to become.

- Motivation is strongly related to the supervisory style of the immediate boss: "developmental" supervisors stimulate motivation; "reductive" supervisors inhibit motivation.

- Motivation is highest among top management.

- Style of supervision is uniformly distributed through all levels of management; however, high level managers tend to know the "right" answers about supervisory practice better than lower level managers.

- All managers prefer a developmental supervisor regardless of their own values or the style of supervision they practice themselves.

- Reductive supervisors are generally insensitive to their propensity for quashing motivation, and in fact rate themselves on a par with developmental supervisors.

These and other interesting conclusions are supported by a recent survey of motivation at Texas Instruments. Based on a study of attitudes of 1,344 managers at all levels and the application of the findings within the company, this article isolates and describes three conditions under which managers and their subordinates are motivated.

1. Interpersonal competence.
2. The opportunity to work toward meaningful goals.
3. The existence of appropriate management systems.

In the balance of this article, I propose to discuss each of these

AUTHOR'S NOTE: I am indebted to Warren J. Bowles, Charles L. Hughes, and Earl D. Weed for their help in interpreting survey data, and to Patrick E. Haggerty and Carl J. Thomsen for concepts of Texas Instruments' goals and systems which provide the framework for the application of research results.

Reprinted from *Harvard Business Review*, Vol. 44, January-February, 1966, pp. 58-71, by permission of author and publisher. © 1966 by the President and Fellows of Harvard College, all rights reserved.

conditions under which managers can motivate and be, in turn, motivated. *Interpersonal competence,* for example, describes a developmental style of supervision which meets one of the requirements for higher motivation, self-realization, and positively expressed creativity. *Meaningful goals* illustrates ways of giving direction to these positive motivations by providing company goals which offer opportunity for achieving personal goals, and keeping the goals clearly in view at all times by slashing away the underbrush of red tape, protocol, and irrelevant objectives. And *management systems* describes the vehicles for speeding positively motivated people on to the achievement of their organization goals, thereby reinforcing and perpetuating this motivation.

A motivation index was computed for each manager on the basis of his responses to the motivation items on the questionnaire. Managers were then sorted into three groups according to level of motivation. The top 30% group of 403 managers was labeled "high motivation"; the middle 40% group of 538, "partial motivation"; and the bottom 30% group of 403, "low motivation." Exhibit I shows the relationship between level of motivation and level of management.

Upper managers—those in key decision-making roles and more closely identified with the overall performance of the organization—understandably derive a higher degree of proprietary enthusiasm from their jobs. From their vantage point, and through the process of getting there, they experience rich satisfaction of their growth, achievement, responsibility, and recognition needs.

Though the incidence of high motivation is much higher at the upper level (57%) than at the lower level (23%), it should be noted that the 91 upper level managers comprise only 7% of the survey group (.91 ÷ 1,344), which means that there are only 52 highly motivated upper

Exhibit I
Relationship of Motivation to Level of Management

LEVEL OF MANAGEMENT	NUMBER	HIGH	PARTIAL	LOW	TOTAL
UPPER	91	57%	31%	12%	100%
MIDDLE	683	32%	39%	29%	100%
LOWER	570	23%	43%	34%	100%
TOTAL	1,344	30%	40%	30%	100%

managers (.57 X 91); whereas the figures for highly motivated lower and middle managers come to 350, thus outnumbering the highly motivated upper managers almost seven to one (350 vs. 52). Stated otherwise, 87% of the company's highly motivated managers are below the upper management level, thereby reflecting the relatively minor role which organizational level per se plays as a motivator.

Style of Supervision

As noted earlier, managers were asked to select items which described the supervisory style of their immediate supervisors. These items describe the boss's style in terms of his ability to stimulate enthusiasm, the level and consistency of his expectations, his recognition of performance, his accessibility and willingness to listen to new ideas, his practices related to dispensing company information, his attitude toward risk taking and mistakes, his manner in dealing with mistakes, and his sensitivity to the feelings of others.

Supervisors described favorably in these terms were labeled "developmental" because of their demonstrated effectiveness in developing subordinates. Supervisors described unfavorably in these terms were labeled "reductive" to denote their propensity for reducing or inhibiting positive expressions of initiative and creativity, and for inducing withdrawal into protective patterns of conformity. Developmental supervision is synonymous with Theory Y supervision, and reductive with Theory X.[1]

Following the same procedure used for grouping managers by levels of motivation, the 1,344 managers were again separated into three groups—this time according to their descriptions of their supervisors' styles. The top 30% was comprised of the 403 managers having the most developmental bosses, and the bottom 30%, the 403 managers having the most reductive bosses. The middle 40% consisted of the 538 managers whose supervisors fit a pattern description between the developmental and reductive styles, labeled here as "traditional," since it probably more nearly characterizes the majority of supervisors who through intuition, experience, and maturation have learned to avoid many of the practices of reductive supervision, yet whose supervisory skills and understanding of human motivation are below requirements for the developmental label.

1. Refers to "The Human Side of Enterprise," by Douglas McGregor. See p. 157.

Exhibit III shows the relationship between levels of motivation and these three supervisory styles. Of the highly motivated managers, one half have developmental bosses and only 8% have reductive bosses. By contrast, almost two thirds of poorly motivated managers have reductive bosses, and only 8% developmental bosses.

Exhibit II
Factors Influencing Management Questionnaire Responses

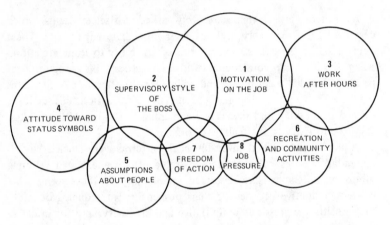

It might seem logical to hypothesize that upper level managers are more developmental, and therefore the relationship of motivation to level of management as shown in Exhibit I is just an expression of the impact of supervisory style. However, Exhibit IV disqualifies that explanation, for it shows that style of supervision is rather uniformly distributed throughout all levels of management.

The study indicated that higher level managers have a good intellectual understanding of developmental assumptions about people. It is not surprising to see greater sophistication at the higher levels where sheer age and experience have provided more opportunity to learn the theoretical answers to questions about human relations. But, from the viewpoint of the subordinate, this intellectual advantage has not been translated into supervisory practice. This phenomenon merely underscores the fact that developmental behavior does not occur automatically as a result of intellectual understanding. Rather, intellectual understanding is but a foundation (and a necessary one) on which habits of interpersonal competence are developed and emotional maturity is acquired.

Exhibit III
Relationship of Motivation to Boss's Style

LEVEL OF MOTIVATION	NUMBER	BOSS'S STYLE			TOTAL
		DEVELOPMENTAL	TRADITIONAL	REDUCTIVE	
HIGH	403	52%	40%	8%	100%
PARTIAL	538	30%	48%	22%	100%
LOW	403	8% 29%	63%		100%
TOTAL	1,344	30%	40%	30%	100%

Exhibit IV
Distribution of Style of Supervision

LEVEL OF MANAGEMENT	NUMBER	BOSS'S STYLE			TOTAL
		DEVELOPMENTAL	TRADITIONAL	REDUCTIVE	
UPPER	91	32%	42%	26%	100%
MIDDLE	683	26%	43%	31%	100%
LOWER	570	34%	37%	29%	100%
TOTAL	1,344	30%	40%	30%	100%

Exhibit V
Ability to Motivate — Self-Ratings Vs. Subordinates' Ratings

	NUMBER	ABILITY TO MOTIVATE			
		EXCELLENT	ABOVE AVERAGE	AVERAGE	POOR
Self-ratings, all managers	1,344	6%	54%	35%	3%
Subordinates' ratings of all managers	1,344	7%	35%	39%	19%
Self-ratings, developmental managers	403	10%	55%	34%	1%
Subordinates' ratings of developmental managers	403	16%	55%	27%	2%
Self-ratings, reductive managers	403	6%	53%	38%	3%
Subordinates' ratings of reductive managers	403	7%	42%	50%	

Managers are generally more objective in describing their boss's style and his effectiveness in motivating subordinates than they are in appraising their own effectiveness. Contrary to expectations, reductive as well as developmental managers are more highly motivated under developmental supervision. Furthermore, though many reductive managers accurately describe their own style of supervision, they often fail to recognize its negative impact on subordinates. Exhibit V illustrates the relationship between self-ratings and subordinates' ratings of their ability to stimulate people to be enthusiastic about their work.

For all managers, the major difference is at the lower end where only 3% of the managers admitted failure, while 19% were rated as failures by their subordinates. The pattern is reversed for developmental managers whose subordinates rated them slightly higher than they rated themselves. But the most spectacular case of introspective myopia is illustrated by reductive managers who rate themselves almost on a par with developmental supervisors. Their subordinates see them differently, however, and rate fully half of them as unsuccessful, and only 8% of them as above average or better.

Exhibit VI presents the collective description of supervisory style by the 403 highly motivated managers (top 30%) as compared to the description of supervisory style by the 403 poorly motivated managers (bottom 30%).

Highly motivated managers rather consistently characterize their supervisors as persons who are approachable and open-minded, maintain high expectations, provide ready access to company information, encourage initiative and risk taking, help them learn from mistakes, and give credit for top performance. This description of supervisors clearly qualifies them for the Theory Y or developmental label.

Poorly motivated managers, though less consistent in describing their supervisors, more often describe them in terms that match Theory X, or reductive supervision. Their supervisors are typically authority-oriented, not usually receptive to conflicting ideas from subordinates, tend to oversupervise and discourage initiative and risk taking, are intolerant of mistakes (particularly those that might embarrass them), are prone to look for someone to blame for mistakes, tend to overlook successes and stress failures.

It is traditional for researchers at this point to conclude that better human relations is the key to organizational effectiveness. Members of the growing cult of sensitivity training offer valid testimonials for its role in improving human relations in work groups, but they provide only spotty evidence of its success in achieving organization goals. It is my belief that sensitivity training can contribute to organization goals, but only if interpersonal competence can find expression through *meaningful goals* and *facilitative systems.* Ideal human relationships in the absence of the other two conditions can, at best, permit cathartic expression for frustrated achievement needs and lead to the trade-off of motivation for satisfaction and complacency.

MEANINGFUL GOALS

The manager's job is to achieve organization goals. He does this through management systems and the proper utilization of human resources.

The foregoing material has dealt primarily with the human factor, and has shown the consequences of developmental and reductive styles of supervision on interpersonal competence. The following discussion attempts to show the synergistic relationship between *interpersonal competence, goals,* and *systems.*

Successful goal setting is a function of:

being able to relate personal goals to organization goals
having helpful systems for setting and achieving goals
being ready to respond favorably to organization goals

Effective management systems are those systems which:

enable individuals to achieve personal goals by achieving organization goals
are managed by the individual (rather than manage the individual) in the achievement of goals
reflect a developmental philosophy of supervision

Motivation for the manager (as well as for the nonmanager) is usually a consequence and symptom of effective job performance, which in turn influences and is influenced by any of the stages in the developmental cycle. Exhibit VII reflects the cyclical relationship of supervisory style, goal setting, and management systems.

The developmental cycle is initiated by conditions of interpersonal competence, opportunity to work toward meaningful goals, and the existence of helpful management systems. These conditions maximize the manager's opportunity to achieve goals and earn approval and reward. The resultant motivation or self-actualization colors his perception of life, his work, and the company, encouraging him to reach out

Exhibit VI
How The Manager Sees His Boss

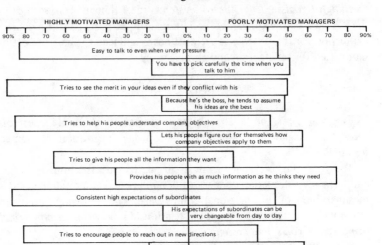

for greater achievements. His positive outlook reinforces the conditions of interpersonal competence, supporting and perpetuating his developmental cycle for as long as these conditions prevail. Job success is both a consequence and cause of the various stages in the developmental cycle.

The reductive cycle, in its extreme, is characterized by interpersonal conflict, unattractive goals, and hopeless red tape. These conditions typically lead to failure, to disapproval and punishment, and to feelings of guilt, frustration, despair, and apathy. The manager's defenses take the form of cynicism, hostility, and efforts to seek gratification from sources unrelated to the goal. This behavior further aggravates interpersonal relationships, reinforcing and perpetuating his cyclical plight.

In actual circumstances individuals seldom find themselves stabilized clearly in one cycle or another. Most persons follow a wavering path in

Exhibit VII
The Motivation Cycle

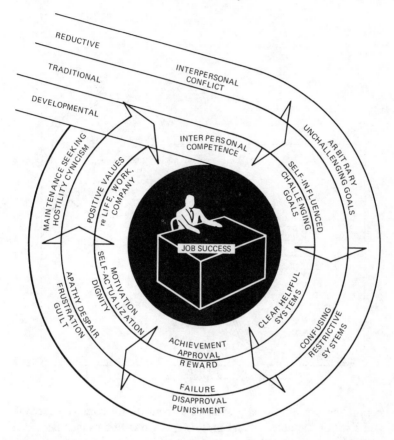

the middle ground of the traditional cycle, from time to time crossing the developmental and reductive borders into the characteristic highs and lows of industrial life. The following case example of goal-setting opportunities, though not immune to reductive mismanagement, is presented as a model for implementing developmental management.

Goal-Setting Model

Having reached the brink of bigness in 1949, with 800 employees and annual sales of $6 million, Texas Instruments managers recognized

Exhibit VIII
Texas Instruments Growth Curves and Goal

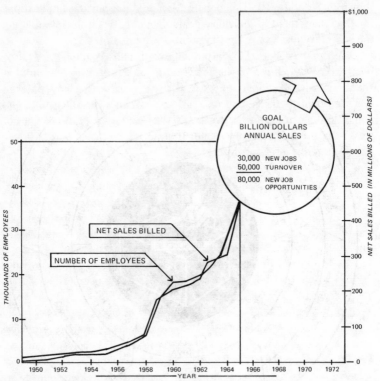

continuing organizational growth as a requisite for company survival, and also for the personal and professional growth of its members. Had growth leveled off at that point, the more competent and highly motivated individuals would have most likely departed for greener pastures, leaving the company to stagnate in the hands of the less competent. Consequently, deliberate growth was planned through strategies related to the following factors:

- Investment in product R & D.
- Product diversification.
- Aggressive and innovative marketing.
- Investment in capital improvements.
- Mergers and acquisitions.
- Expansion to international operations.

These six factors individually, and in a mutually reinforcing manner, resulted in the rapid growth of TI to its 1965 level of 34,000 employees and sales nearing the half-way mark to the 1973 goal of $1 billion as shown in Exhibit VIII. This organization goal has obvious implications for the achievement of individual goals—in a circular fashion stimulating the enthusiasm necessary for their mutual attainment.

Delegation Process. TI's corporate growth and geographical deployment led to the choice of the decentralized product-customer center as the basic organizational unit for pushing goal setting and decision making down to the action areas of engineering, manufacturing, and marketing. Organized around a product or family of products (or services) the product-customer center is a miniature of the parent organization in terms of its organizational role.

Charged with a broad responsibility which, within the bounds of sound management practice, includes the development, manufacture, and marketing of a product or service, and judged in terms of balance sheet criteria, there is little opportunity or incentive for the manager of the product-customer center to dally with irrelevant objectives. Instead of limiting opportunity for autonomy to a few major division heads, the formation of product-customer centers thrust into the eager hands of over 40 young "presidents" of these "small companies" an opportunity for each to build an empire.

This delegation process requires managers of product-customer centers (and their staff counterparts in the supporting and performance-maximizing centers such as industrial engineering, accounting, and personnel) to establish goals and keep score on themselves in the process of achieving them. Motivation abounds under such circumstances, requiring little stimulation from higher company management. Indeed, management influence under these conditions often must include safeguards against overcommitment or overmotivation, and admonishments to be mindful of home and community responsibilities and the developmental needs of the members of their organizational teams.

Administrative Climate. Goal orientation, as opposed to authority orientation, is encouraged at TI. The distinction between these approaches is subtle on the surface, but significant in determining the administrative climate of the organization. The authority-oriented person is typically an "outer-directed" person performing in blind obedience to orders from superiors. His boss calls the shots, giving him little incentive or opportunity to become a thinking person who relates his job to the big picture. Automaton conformity, or obedient "jumping through hoops," is little better than a pattern for "serving time" on the job, even for high-level managers who are generally assumed to be exempt from such domination. The reductive style of supervision described earlier fosters authority orientation.

The goal-oriented person is more likely to see job goals as a meaningful part of the broader organizational objective, and as steppingstones to his long-range personal goals. Unlike the authority-oriented person who becomes overdependent on his boss for direction and affirmation, the more "inner-directed," goal-oriented person receives meaningful feedback and satisfaction directly from work itself and the achievement of goals. His grasp of the job enables him to initiate self-correction and to grow with his accomplishments.

Status, Not Symbols. Deliberate attempts are made at TI to minimize the status symbols which traditionally reinforce authority orientation and undermine goal orientation. Dining and coffee-bar facilities are shared by all employees, identification badges are color-coded on a job-tenure basis, parking privileges and office space are assigned on the basis of factors other than level of responsibility, a hierarchy of office furnishings is nonexistent, and mode of attire is not standardized (and often consists of informal sports apparel at any level). Employees commonly address each other on a first-name basis (vertically as well as horizontally) and communicate with each other (and conduct business) through the informal and fluid grapevine which exists (though is not always recognized) in every organization. The net effect of such a system is to orient employees on a competence basis rather than to sensitize them to, and sandwich them into, an authority hierarchy.

Contrast this, for example, with the class distinctions sometimes created through dining and parking privileges, office size and furnishings, identification badges, mode of attire, and similar status privileges. Symbols associated with these authority-oriented privileges increase social distances and inhibit communication. They create and exaggerate an hourly salaried cleavage of the work force into the "privileged management" group, whose tactics often become manipulative and defensive; and the "exploited worker" group, whose wrath is exploited, and alternately appeased and aggravated, by labor unions.

Not all status symbols are harmful. For example, attractive grounds and buildings and tenure-coded identification badges are not authority oriented, and probably enhance the cohesiveness of the work force. Thus the selective reinforcement and reduction of status symbols serves a key role in improving interpersonal competence and goal setting.

It should be noted that the points enumerated above apply to status *symbols* and not status itself. Status itself differs in terms of amount of accountability, salary, and freedom of action. Increased status is a major incentive for personal and professional growth, and for those who have the talent and desire to achieve it. Earned status is its own reward, and the flaunting of symbols or other reminders of inequality is symptomatic of immaturity which serves only to undermine feelings of dignity and worth of those of lesser status on whom higher status individuals depend for their continued success.

MANAGEMENT SYSTEMS

The foregoing discussion has illustrated the interdependence of interpersonal competence and goal setting. Though the means and philosophy for achieving goals—such as the product-customer center and minimized status symbols—are in a broad sense management systems, they do not define or adequately illustrate the role of formalized systems for catalyzing interpersonal competence and achieving company and employee goals.

A management system is broadly defined at TI as the organization of a manager's effort to accomplish his purpose. Management systems are perceived and serve as extensions of the managers who direct them and, as such, have the same (or greater) motivating, dissatisfying, supporting, or threatening impact that the managers would have without the systems. That is, a system reflects the supervisory style or takes on the "personality characteristics" of the person running it or thought to be running it.

Conversely, the characteristics of a management system impute to its manager a supervisory style. For example, a supervisor's implementation of a company policy to check all expense accounts might tend to brand him as reductive, whereas the existence of company policy encouraging self-audit practices tends to give supervisors a more developmental image. Hence, the design and staffing of a system must take into account the fact that, with few exceptions, people are the media through which systems function. Moreover, the ideal system is both intrinsically well designed and managed in such a manner that people are able to understand and support it.

Five widely used TI management systems are discussed briefly in the following pages to demonstrate their role in satisfying customer-company and employee needs. Before turning our attention to each of these systems, it may be useful to know the reasoning behind their inclusion in this article. Consider:

• The *planning process* is presented as an illustration of a general management system with far-reaching impact on both customer-company and employee needs.

• Both the *performance review* and the *attitude survey* are examples of personnel management systems which, in addition to their unique roles, also serve the common function of measuring managerial effectiveness.

• *Work simplification* is a system for providing expression for employee creativity in the management of the company.

• *Inventory control* is presented as a typical materials management system which attracts little attention unless it fails.

Planning Operation

At TI the planning process includes the ten-year plan, the annual plan, quarterly reviews, sales and billings meetings, technical seminars, and various other regular and ad hoc group meetings. Annual and long-range planning are discussed here to illustrate the many-faceted role of planning in serving customer-company and employee needs.

Managers from worldwide TI operations convene in Dallas each December to participate with company officers in reviewing and finalizing annual goals. Meeting in a large working session of selectively varied memberships, each manager in a 15- to 30-minute period reviews his past year's targets and accomplishments, and outlines his plans for the year ahead. This presentation serves four basic purposes:

1. To communicate goals and achievements to all managers.
2. To appraise managerial effectiveness in planning and achieving organization goals.
3. To establish understandable, acceptable, and challenging charters.
4. To develop managers through their involvement in the planning process.

The annual planning presentations spring from a more profound Objective-Strategy-Tactics (OST) system for managing innovation. Objectives are formal statements of ten-year goals for business areas such as materials, exploration, and electronic components, or for intracompany staff functions such as personnel, facilities, and marketing. Objectives are pursued through one or more supporting "strategies" which, in turn, are implemented through detailed 12- to 18-month "Tactical Action Programs," or TAPs. Strategies and TAPs are the basis for managing innovation in the various create-make-market and staff support groups. Each product-customer center defines its long-range mission through formal strategies, and reports its current effort toward the strategy on the standard TAP form for top management approval and review. Let us look at two typical illustrations:

> Specific ten-year goals have been established for the broad field of functional electronics, and these goals are pursued through several strategies such as one currently implementing the planned evolution of integrated circuits. This strategy is supported by TAPs in the areas of R & D, manufacturing, and marketing.
>
> Similarly, as an example of a staff implementation of the OST system, personnel supports a strategy for locating and developing the company's managerial talent. TAPs supporting this strategy include development of a personnel information retrieval system, identification of criteria and predictors of managerial effectiveness and obsolescence, refinement of a performance measurement and merit compensation procedure, and definition of processes for developing managers.

Reviews of selected strategies and TAPs are presented monthly to the office of the president by strategy and TAP managers who are, in most cases, several organizational levels below the president. This presentation directly to company officers serves several vital purposes not usually satisfied in the large organization. First, it circumvents the traditional multilayer, upward screening process and presents the president and other senior officers with firsthand progress reports on important projects. Second, it also keeps the officers posted on developing technologies. Third, this direct reporting gives the project head immediate feedback, undistorted by the traditional multilayer, downward filtering process, and enables him to align his efforts more directly to the needs of the corporation. Needless to say, the recognition afforded by this process increases the incentive and opportunity for maximum effectiveness.

In short, planning at TI is a dynamic process for involving employees in goal setting, communicating company goals, maximizing professional growth, and earning recognition. More importantly, it is a system for bypassing the traditional impediments to communication, decision making, and involvement which quash innovation and undermine the corporation's capability for competing successfully with smaller and more agile competitors.

Performance Review

This is a dual-purpose management system for setting goals and reviewing accomplishments, and for determining and communicating pay status to employees twice per year. The system, which is implemented through the relationship of the individual to his supervisor, maximizes opportunities for self-direction and self-review. The salaried review form consists of a single sheet on which the ratee fills in three kinds of information—his accomplishments during the past year, his short-term (six months or less) goals, and his long-range (a year or more) goals.

The next step is a discussion with his supervisor which focuses on these accomplishments and goals, their priorities, and the means of achieving them. After talking things over with his supervisor, the subordinate recaps on the reverse side of the form the consensus of their discussion regarding priorities, action plans, and schedules agreed on. Hence, for the salaried person, the systematic review is a performance-planning process in which the subordinate rather than the supervisor is the initiator of corrective action. In this respect, TI's performance review process is similar to General Electric's work performance and review program.[3]

The supervisor of the hourly person typically uses a traditional report card approach based on job-related factors such as quality, quantity, and reliability, but has the option of using a goal-setting approach. If goal setting has little meaning for hourly employees, it is not so much an indictment of the capabilities of the hourly person as it is a consequence of a historical tradition of failing to delegate meaningful chunks of work to him which would provide opportunities and incentives for him to develop initiative, creativity, and company identification.

Attitude Surveys

These are administered annually at TI as a system for helping managers monitor their own effectiveness, and to provide a basis for diagnosing problems and planning remedial actions. Supervisors compare attitude survey results for their department against a current company profile and their own profile for the previous year. Managers appoint and work through committees to review survey results, and formulate recommendations for improvement. These working committees, particularly when they involve non-supervisory salaried and hourly persons who traditionally have little influence on policy and practice, enable employees to understand organizational problems and to make meaningful contributions to their solution.

Attitude surveys often encounter the traditional circular problem: good supervisors have better survey results and freely provide opportunities for employees to participate in the improvement process; inept supervisors receive unfavorable survey results (which they often attempt to rationalize or ignore) and are reluctant to let employees become involved in the improvement process.

Work Simplification

This is perhaps the most potent management system for encouraging creativity at organizational levels where it is traditionally suppressed. It replaces traditional motion-and-time study on the dual assumption that (1) most job incumbents have creative potential for improving their own jobs, and (2) self-initiated change is positively motivational while change imposed by an authority figure (standing behind them with a clipboard and stopwatch) is more likely to evoke fear and hostility.

Skills in work simplification are acquired through a standardized company training program—usually totaling about 24 hours—to learn principles of motion and time economy, process flow charting, cost analysis, and human relations. Endowed with this new ability, an assembler, for example, ceases to be just a pair of hands performing in a routine unthinking capacity. Instead, the individual has a new outlet for personal creativity—involving work planning with supervisor and associates, earning recognition, growing professionally, and in general strengthening self-identification with the company.

Though the major purpose of work simplification is the harnessing of employee creativity, improvements effected through the training program result in considerable savings. Ultimately, these savings are returned to employees through profit sharing, which undoubtedly does much to change the image of profit sharing from that of a handout to an earned reward. Work simplification sensitizes individuals to job processes and develops a proprietary consciousness of proper use of company resources.

Manufacturing processes have, in some instances, narrowed the machine operator's job to the point that opportunities for individual task improvements have been reduced. To adapt to these circumstances, a "work simplification task force" process has been developed to involve all members of a work group in the review and improvement of their total operation.

Guided by a staff conference leader who establishes ground rules against personal accusation, this process usually begins with a meeting of top managers to identify and classify operation bottlenecks. An initial meeting might typically result in the identification of 25 to 50 specific problems which are then classified into perhaps two to five operation areas. The next step takes a deeper dig into the organization through committees to deal with each of these bottlenecks, and may ultimately involve all employees in the department.

Invariably, improvements in operations and attitudes, both of which translate into cost reductions, are the result. Individual and group work improvement processes, if properly goal-oriented, provide opportunities for the growth and recognition of individuals and for the improved achievement of customer-company goals.

Inventory Control

The purpose of an inventory control system is to maintain a proper balance between too lean and too fat an inventory. Too great an inventory increases costs of warehousing, insurance, obsolescence, interest, and price declines; too lean an inventory increases costs of buying, handling, record keeping, and production downtime.

Inventory control is rarely the focus of attention unless something goes wrong. Depletion of a key item can become a serious dissatisfier on the production line. The foreman, for example, faced with the threat of 30 idle assemblers on his hands, scrambles out on a scrounging foray to find the needed part, finding time in the rush to admonish the manufacturing engineer and inventory control people. If he fails to find the part, he tries to avoid idle-time costs by hurriedly farming the assemblers out to other operations. If he succeeds in placing them, he still faces the possibility of tardy delivery, and the cost and personal inconvenience of overtime.

The assemblers' feelings are mixed, depending on factors such as their attitudes toward the work they are doing, frequency of stoppages, nature of the stopgap assignment, pressure to make up schedules, their feelings about overtime, and their attitudes toward their supervisor and the company.

The inventory control manager has problems even when all is well on the production line. He must be ever alert for the surprise opening or closing of a shift or assembly line. He is continuously preoccupied with shortages, obsolescence, and the cost of inventory on hand, particularly when preparing the monthly inventory cost report. If he has done his job well, maintaining a lean and balanced inventory and avoiding work stoppages, his accomplishments may only cause his boss to urge even tighter controls.

Nonetheless, most jobs in inventory control have potential for satisfying motivation needs; and inventory control clerks, when adequately trained and not overloaded, usually enjoy their work. Their responsibility for monitoring the system, organizing their work, and initiating large purchase orders offers opportunities for the satisfaction of achievement needs.

Inventory problems, from shrinkage to imbalance, usually have their origin in the attitudes of those who administer and are influenced by the system. Attitudes, in turn, are traceable in a circular fashion to one or more of the three conditions set forth in this article—interpersonal competence, opportunity to work toward meaningful goals, and the existence of good management systems. Inventory control, as a specimen materials management system, illustrates the potential of such a system for reflecting the positive and negative aspects of the other two conditions.

CONCLUSION

Just as the nonmanager is dependent on his boss for motivational opportunities, so is the manager dependent on his boss for conditions of motivation which have meaning at his level. Since the motivation of an employee at any level is strongly related to the supervisory style of his immediate boss, sound motivation patterns must begin at the top. Being closer to the policy-making level, the manager has more opportunity to understand and relate his work to company goals. However, high position alone does not guarantee motivation or self-actualization.

Motivation for the manager, as well as the nonmanager, is usually both a consequence and a symptom of effective job performance. Job success is dependent on cyclical conditions created by interpersonal competence, meaningful goals, and helpful systems. After sustained conditioning in the developmental cycle, an individual has amazing capacity and incentive to remain in it. Moreover, if forced into the reductive cycle, unless he has pathological needs to remain there, organizational conditions must be remarkably and consistently bad to suppress his return to the developmental cycle.

Sustained confinement of a large percentage of the work force in the reductive cycle is symptomatic of organizational illness. It is usually a culmination of a chain of events beginning with top management, and is reversible only by changes at the top. Consequences of reductive conditions such as militant unionism and other forms of reactive behavior usually provoke management into defensive and manipulative behavior which only reinforces the reductive cycle. The vicarious pleasure sought by the rank and file through seeing the management giant felled by their union is a poor substitute for the self-actualization of being a whole person doing a meaningful job, but, in the absence of motivational opportunities, it is an understandable compromise.

The seeds of concerted reactive behavior are often brought to the job from broadly shared frustrations arising from social injustice, economic deprivation, and moral decadence either to sprout in a reductive climate or become infertile in a developmental climate. Hence, the unionization of a work group is usually precipitated by management failure to provide opportunities for employees to achieve personal goals through the achievement of organization goals. Organizations survive these failures only because most other companies are equally handicapped by the same failures.

Management failures in supervision do not, of course, stem from intentional malice. They may result, in part, from a lingering tradition of "scientific management" which fractionated tasks and "protected" employees from the need to think, and perpetrated management systems based on automaton conformity. But more often such failures stem from the manager's insensitivity to the needs and perceptions of others, particularly from his inability to see himself as others see him.

Insensitivity or the inability to empathize is manifested not only as interpersonal incompetence, but also as the failure to provide meaningful goals, the misuse of management systems, or a combination of both. Style of supervision, then, is largely an expression of the personality characteristics and mental health of the manager, and his potential for inducing developmental or reductive cyclical reactions.

Dynamics of Leadership

JACK R. GIBB

People must be led. People perform best under leaders who are creative, imaginative, and aggressive—under leaders who lead. It is the responsibility of the leader to marshall the forces of the organization, to stimulate effort, to capture the imagination, to inspire people, to coordinate efforts, and to serve as a model of sustained effort.

The leader should keep an appropriate social distance, show no favorites, control his emotions, command respect, and be objective and fair. He must know what he is doing and where he wants to go. He must set clear goals for himself and for the group or institution, and then communicate these goals well to all members of the organization. He must listen for advice and counsel before making decisions. But it is his responsibility to make decisions and to set up mechanisms for seeing that the decisions are implemented. After weighing the facts and seeking expert counsel, he must make policy and rules, set reasonable boundaries, and see that these are administered with justice and wisdom, even compassion.

The leader should reward good performance and learn effective ways of showing appreciation. He must be equally ready to give negative criticism where warranted and to appraise performance frequently, fairly, and unequivocally. He must command strong discipline, not only because people respect a strong leader, but because strength and firmness communicate care and concern. Good leadership requires good followship. People tend to follow good leaders. Leaders are born. Methods of election and selection are thus very important. Finding the right chairman or president is the critical variable in the success of a program or an institution. The quality of an organization is often judged by the perceived quality of the leadership.

The above is an oversimplified statement of one view of leadership theory and practice. A similarly oversimplified statement of an alternative viewpoint follows.

People grow, produce, and learn best when they set their own goals, choose activities that they see as related to these goals, and have a wide

Reprinted by permission of author and the *National Education Association—Current Issues in Higher Education*, 1967.

range of freedom of choice in all parts of their lives. Under most conditions persons are highly motivated, like to take responsibilities, can be trusted to put out a great deal of effort toward organizational goals, are creative and imaginative, and tend to want to cooperate with others.

Leadership is only one of several significant variables in the life of the group or the institution. Leaders can be helpful and often are. The most effective leader is one who acts as a catalyst, a consultant, and a resource to the group. His job is to help the group to grow, to emerge, and to become more free. He serves the group best when he is a whole person, is direct, real, open, spontaneous, permissive, emotional, and highly personal. The leader at his best is an effective member. He acts in such a way as to facilitate group strength, individual responsibility, diversity, nonconformity, and aggressiveness. The leader is thus not necessary to the group and quickly becomes replaceable, dispensable, and independent. The good leader tends not to lead. He permits, feels, acts, relates, fights, talks—acts human as do other members of the group and the institution. The leader is present, available, and with the group as a person, not as a role.

We find many shades and variations of each of these two oversimplified statements of the theory and practice of leadership in our society. Several years of consulting and research in representative organizations make it very clear to me that attitudes toward leadership tend to cluster around these two poles. This bifurcation has analogues in current educational theory, politics, religion, philosophy, and administration.

The first view, described variously as authoritarian, paternalistic, or conservative, I classify as defensive because dynamically the view defends the administrator against his own fears and distrusts and against perceived or anticipated attack from the outside.

This authoritarian or defensive view is particularly appropriate to some viable aspects of the culture we live in: to organizational forms inherited from the medieval church and military; to a life of vertical hierarchy, prescribed role responsibilities, and delegated authority; to a highly competitive economic and educational system; to the current dominant values of efficiency, excellence, productivity, task performance, and perfectionism; to the impersonality, alienation, loneliness, impotence, and indifference in our people; to a world of automation, programming, data processing, and engineering; to a forensic, persuasive, public relations, and marketing mode of interpersonal commerce; to a world continually at war, threatened by war, or preparing for war; in short, to a world of machines. It is not accidental that all around the country when administrators administer the ultimate forensic weapon in arguing against participative forms of leadership they say, "But it would never work in the military or on the production line." Actually, research indicates that this point is probably not true, but in any event the image of the leaders of our educational and governmental institutions using as a reference point for administrative theory the demands of the military organization and the production line is at least disconcerting.

It seems to me equally clear that defensive leadership is highly inappropriate and perhaps even fundamentally dissonant with another viable side of the world we live in: with education for growth, intimacy, authenticity, humanness, and creativity; with the Judeo-Christian ethics of love, honesty, intimacy, faith, cheek-turning, and brotherhood; with a climate for research, inquiry, scholarship, contemplation, and learning; with cooperation, group planning, team building, and various successful forms of group effort; with the new emerging models of industrial organization and manufacturing productivity; with what might be thought of as the behavioral science approach to organizational productivity and organizational change; with the world of ambiguity, feeling, conflict, sorrow, creativity, and diversity; with many new and exciting developments in education, architecture, the creative arts, economics, management, and all phases of modern life; in short, with the world of human beings, with people.

I have deliberately drawn sharp and oversimplified distinctions in a problem area which is very complex and legitimately polemic. It is essential today that those who are administratively responsible for the colleges and universities of America see clearly this conflict and its implications for all facets of American Life. It is my observation that much of the dysfunctional disturbance that the papers report daily from the college campuses is created as unintended but inevitable effects of defensive leadership practices among administrators of American colleges.

Let us look at the dynamics of defensive leadership. The major dynamic of the defensive model is fear and distrust. Observations indicate that people who have mild or more serious fears tend to do several things: distrust the people being led; filter the data that are given to the followers and develop strategies for such filtering and programming of data dissemination; attempt to control and manipulate the motivations of the followers; and attempt to control their behavior. The incidence and degree of low trust, strategic, persuasional, and controlling behavior varies directly with the amount of fear. Most of us who are leaders or are placed in leadership roles have varying degrees of fear about our own adequacy, how we are seen by others, the effectiveness of our leadership strategies, the effects of rebellion, the anxieties about insubordination and other unfollowerlike behavior. I guess that our major fear has to do with anxiety about being followed!

The behavior of leaders tends to camouflage, perhaps even to themselves, the underlying fears which support the strategic, manipulative, and controlling behavior. For images of fear on assuming leadership roles one has but to think of the new teacher in the schoolroom, the new mother bringing back her first baby from the hospital, the new lieutenant guiding a patrol into action, or the newly appointed administrative official handling a student riot. The fears that we all have are quelled and softened by various adaptive, self-deceptive, and facade-building mechanisms for presenting ourselves to ourselves and to others.

Some educational leaders are today more fearful than ever. In reaction to student strikes, riots, demonstrations, and protests, as well as to the more normal vicissitudes of campus life, college and university leaders utilize defensive practices that generate unintended byproducts of fear, distrust, hostility, and counter-defensive behavior. The classical models of leadership are time and again proved to be ineffective. Why does defensive leadership arise and persist among educational leaders?

A reciprocal or circular process seems to be operating. Normal fears of life are exacerbated by the ambiguity, high control, and threat of the group or organization. However necessary this ambiguity and control is thought to be, it serves to create fears and hostilities which in turn call forth still more restrictive ambiguity and controlling behavior. This reciprocal fear-distrust cycle sustains the defensive behavior of leadership. The fears accompany and reinforce feelings of inadequacy and self-rejection in leaders and other members of the group or organization.

But the fears, hostilities, and distrusts are so successfully camouflaged in the social defenses that the casual observer might well think the above description of educational life to be strangely out of touch with reality as he sees it. Certainly it is not the conscious intent of educational leaders to create such a state of affairs.

Why is it then that we get in the university so many unintended effects? These unintended effects seem to result from a kind of self-fulfilling prophecy: low-trust, high-fear theories, when put into practice, actually generate distrust and fears that not only confirm the assumptions underlying the theories, but also provide emotional support and strong motivation to continue the low-trust, high-fear behavior. An interactive and self-preserving cycle is thus set in motion, supported in depth by latent fear-distrust and by rationalized theories which appear to be confirmed. Leadership behavior, thus supported, is exceedingly difficult to change.

Behind the facade of paternalism, politeness, one-big-happy-family-living, heartiness, and the accompanying soft-sell influence and velvet-glove control lie defensive relationships that pervade the colleges. Defensive leadership is characterized by low trust, data distortion, persuasion, and high control. These four aspects of defensive leadership are parallel to four basic dimensions of all group or social behavior: the feeling climate, the flow of data within the system, the formation of goals, and the emergence of control.

The key to defensive leadership is a state of low trust. The defensive leader assumes that the average person cannot be trusted, he is essentially lazy and irresponsible, action must be taken to inspire and motivate him, and he requires supervision and control. The defensive leader can counteract his feelings of inferiority by assuming that his subordinates are less than they actually are; and he can service his hostile feelings by keeping the subordinate in demeaning, dependent, and inferior roles in relation to himself and to leadership as a class.

The defensive leader or administrator rationalizes the service of his needs by developing formal or informal leader theories which both justify and camouflage his fears and hostilities. An essential step in theory and in practice is to manipulate the flow of information and communication within the organization. Information sent down from the top is often deliberately "corrected" to increase morale, to allay fears, to put the best administrative foot forward, and to justify administrative action. "Correction" is achieved by consciously or unconsciously filtering and distorting information to present a good image, to encourage positive thinking, or to build loyalty.

Strategies are devised to improve the administrative image: a worker's name is remembered to make him feel good; a birthday file is kept to demonstrate that the administrator feels the subordinate is important enough to warrant a birthday card. The "good" administrator is especially careful to smile acceptingly at those members of the "family" team towards whom he has temporary or sustained feelings of animosity. Interpersonal cues are thus manipulated and distorted to present a facade of warmth, friendliness, or cohesiveness.

The defensive leader is continually challenged to create new prods, rewards, and gimmicks as the old ones become ineffective. Thus the responsibility for sustaining motivations is thrust upon the administrator or teacher rather than upon the student. The inherent impetus to derive self-satisfaction and self-respect through accomplishment for its own sake becomes atrophied and lost. Self-satisfaction becomes dysfunctional as an incentive system.

The person who is being motivated by others through extrinsic rewards tends either to resist being influenced or to come under the control of the rewarder. He is motivated, not to achieve something, but to gain the approval of the teacher or administrator, to hunt for his satisfactions in status, grade, and social approval rather than to look for his satisfactions within, in terms of self-respect, self-approval, and the achievement of personal goals.

Thus the roots of dependence and apathy lie in the reward system, for the person who learns to find his values from without is always at the mercy of other persuaders—teachers, companions, demagogues, groups, or other sources of approval and authority. He becomes dependent, passive, and susceptible to all sorts of external controls.

The reward system may in others foster resistance and rebellion, resentment, cynicism, and a variety of negative and competitive feelings. People who work under competition learn to be competitive, and the extrinsic rewards do not satisfy the deep needs for self-satisfaction and self-respect which are gained by achieving our personal goals as unique individuals.

Both dependency and resistance require controls, and the defensive leader expends a considerable amount of energy devising a variety of controls both for the people and for the processes of the enterprise. The more fearful and anxious he is, the more he feels caught in recurring emergencies and the greater is his need to control. Regulations are put on car-parking, coffee break duration, channels of reporting, library schedules, methods of work, habits of dress, use of safety devices, more and more complex filing systems, rigid report systems—until all aspects of living in the organization are controlled.

The conscious and official reasons given for the controls usually relate to organization and productive efficiency, but the underlying impulses often spring from, or are reinforced by, the leader's personal needs for rigid order or needs to demonstrate his superiority and strength, express hostility, exercise power, justify his position ("What else would I do if I didn't plan these controls?"), reinforce hierarchy, force people to be orderly or conforming, and keep them in line.

Control systems become functionally autonomous—traditional and conventional elements of the organizational system—and often outlive any practical utility. Indeed, people seem to sense that many regulations actually serve personal needs for punishment or power and bear little relation to the actual needs of the organization itself. In looking at organizations we have often found that many controls are universally violated in the system by common consent. In fact, there is clear indication—and often conscious awareness—that some controls are so dysfunctional that if everyone obeyed them the system would come to a grinding halt.

These defensive techniques of leadership produce certain predictable results. Fear and distrust beget fear and distrust. People who are distrustful tend to see untrustworthy behavior in others. If the relationship between an administrator and his subordinate is basically one of distrust, almost any action on either's part is perceived by the other as untrustworthy. Thus a cycle is created which nurtures self-corroborating leadership hypotheses.

This cycle is well illustrated in connection with communications. Any restriction of the flow of information and any closed strategy arouses energy devoted to circumventing the strategy and fosters counter-strategies that are at least as imaginative and often more effective than the original inducing strategy. A familiar example is the strategy of countering the top brass by distorting the upward-flowing data: feelings of hostility are camouflaged by deferential politeness; reports are "fixed up," records are doctored or "cooked" to fit administrative goals and directives. Such attempts are augmented by emergency and threat; the greater the fear and distrust, the greater the circumvention, counter-strategy, and counter-distortion.

Defensive leaders use various forms of persuasion to motivate subordinates toward the organization's goals, but often the results are either apathy and passivity or frenetic conformity. Persuasion is a form of control and begets resistance, which may take many subtle forms. Open and aggressive cold war between teachers and administrators, for instance, is an obvious form. More common—and less easy to deal with—is passive, often unconscious resistance such as apathy, apparent obtuseness, dependent demands for further and more minute instructions, bumbling, wheel-spinning, and a whole variety of inefficiencies that reduce creative work.

As we have seen, tight control leads to some form of dependency and its accompanying hostility; it may vary from the yes-man's deference and conformity to the no-man's rebellion against even the most reasonable and normal requests and rules. Deference and rebellion are cut from the same cloth. When unnecessary and arbitrary controls are imposed, or when normal controls are seen as unnecessary or arbitrary, as is the case when there is fear and distrust, then almost all members of the hierarchy become concerned with their feelings about authority. Most of us are ambivalent toward authority figures, and these mixed feelings are augmented in periods of stress and fear. In tightly controlled, disciplining, and disciplined organizations members demand clarity in rules and in boundary demarcations. But rules can never be made completely clear in practical work situations; boundaries are always permeable and inadequately defined. Thus the demands for further clarification are endless, and controls lead to further controls.

We see how the cycle is set up: hostility and its inevitable counterpart, fear, are increased by the distrust, distortion, persuasion-reward, and control systems of defensive leadership; and the continuing cycle is reinforced at all stages, for as fear breeds distrust, distrust is rationalized and structured into theories which sanction distrustful leadership practices. The practices reinforce distrust; now the theorist is justified, and latent motivation to continue the cycle is itself reinforced.

Defensive leadership theories and practices permeate our society. We find them in the home, in school, and in the church, as well as in business organizations. Let us see, for instance, how the child-rearing patterns of our culture fit the picture described above. There are so many frightening things in the world that can harm helpless children. The fearful person can, with little effort, find a variety of frightening aspects in the environment of the child—anything from matches and electric outlets to busy roads and unacceptable playmates. Anxiety makes it easy to exaggerate the number of people ready to kidnap and even rape one's child; the fears of the parent embellish natural dangers and provide nourishment and comforting rationalization for defensive practices.

Communications must be managed for the good of the child. Because he might be worried or upset, emotional and financial discord must be camouflaged and a facade of security and serenity maintained. Children are inexperienced and immature, therefore they cannot be trusted to do things on their own. Moreover, since the natural interests of the child are likely to be frivolous, demeaning, or harmful, he should be carefully guided and persuaded to do what is right—to select appropriate playmates, read good books, and generally adopt goals set by the parental culture or aspirations. To protect the child from ubiquitous dangers and to set his feet on the proper path, parents readily learn to use bribes, praise, and deprivation as tools of coercion. And because children are initially dependent and helpless, it is easy for the fearful parent to prolong the period of dependency.

Schools reinforce these patterns. They receive children whose dependency has been created by defensive parental techniques, and they
maintain the dependency by continuing these practices. Having been
distrusted, children continue to be untrustworthy. The insecure teacher
finds it necessary to maintain a protective facade; she rationalizes her
behavior by making a number of low-trust, right-control assumptions
about the children under her tutelage. She builds a changing repertoire
of tricks to keep them busy, orderly, neat, attentive, and—she hopes—
motivated. Impressed by the awesome culture heritage she is charged to
transmit, she feels it imperative that she instill in her pupils the goals,
ideals, and rules of the culture. As bodies of knowledge become increasingly standardized, pressures towards indoctrination increase. By codi-
fying rules, regulations, and standards, the teachers build internal
control systems—in the classroom, and hopefully, in the children
themselves. As part of the informal curriculum, children are taught
facade-building; they are encouraged to put the best foot forward, to be
polite, to be decorous, and to adopt the essentially hypocritical social
graces of the dominant middle class.

What is the alternative to defensive leadership? This is not as easy to
specify. The key to emergent leadership centers in a high degree of trust
and confidence in people. Leaders who trust their colleagues and subordinates and have confidence in them tend to be open and frank, to be
permissive in goal setting, and to be noncontrolling in personal style
and leadership policy. People with a great deal of self-acceptance and
personal security do trust others, do make trust assumptions about
their motives and behavior. The self-adequate person tends to assume
that others are also adequate and, other things being equal, that they
will be responsible, loyal, appropriately work-oriented when work is to
be performed, and adequate to carry out jobs that are commensurate
with their levels of experience and growth.

Just as we saw that distrust arises from fear and hostility, so we can
see that people with little fear and minimal needs to be hostile are
ready to trust others. Of course, there is some risk in trusting others, in
being open and freedom-giving.

People naturally tend to share their feelings and concerns with those
whom they trust, and this is true at the simplest and most direct level
of inter-personal relationships as well as at more complex levels of
organizational communication. Thus a high-trust system may institute
open planning meetings and evaluation meetings; public criteria for
promotion; easily available information on salaries, cost figures, and
budgets; and easy access to material in the files. There is comparatively

little concern with public relations, with the corporate or family image, or with communications programs. Communication in such a system is a process rather than a program.

The participative leader is permissive in his relations with subordinates, for he assumes that as people grow they learn to assess their own aptitudes, discover their deep-lying interests, and develop their basic potentials. Therefore he gives his subordinates every opportunity to maximize self-determination and self-assessment, to verbalize their goals, to try new jobs or enlarge the scope of the work they are doing, and he trusts them to make mature judgments about job assignments. Where he is dealing with a work-team or a group, he lets the group make decisions about job allotments and work assignments.

This process of allowing people to be responsible for their own destinies, for setting their own targets, assessing their own development needs, searching out resources to aid in job accomplishment, and participating in setting organizational objectives is basic to high-trust leadership. Instead of using conventional defensive-leadership techniques of skilled persuasion to induce acceptance of leadership goals, the high-trust administration participates in cooperative determination of goals and in cooperative definition of production and staff problems. He knows that goal-information is a significant skill that must be learned, and that to develop such skill students and adults must exercise a variety of opportunities to make decisions, explore goals, and experiment with many kinds of activities.

The participative administrator joins in creating a climate in which he has no need to impose controls. He knows that in a healthy group controls emerge from group processes as the need is perceived. Then controls are mediated by group or organization objectives and by such relevant data as deadlines and target dates. People or groups who have set their own objectives and have clearly stated their own goals build internal tension-systems which maintain goal orientation and create appropriate boundaries.

Formal and written rules about such things as work space, library use, and stockroom neatness are less and less necessary when people are engaged in a common task with others whose feelings and perceptions they freely share; when there is trust and mutuality, people are inclined to respect the rights and concerns of fellow members. This principle applies to large and small systems alike—in either, the participative administrator reduces as far as practicable all formal controls evidenced by rules, regulations, written memoranda, signs, formal job specification sheets, rigid lines of responsibility and authority, and the like.

The effects of participative leading are diametrically contrary to those of defensive leading. Love begets love. Respect begets respect. Trust produces trust. People who are trusted tend to trust themselves and to trust those in positions of responsibility. Moreover, the feeling that one is trusted encourages exploration, diversity, and innovation, for the person spends little time and energy trying to prove himself. His time and energy are freed to define and solve problems, accomplish work, and create new dimensions of his job. A fearful person uses a great deal of energy in defending himself against present or anticipated threat or attack; a confident and self-assured person can direct his energy towards goals that are significant to him as a person.

Again, openness begets openness. In the long run, at least, one who freely shares data, whether of feelings or of figures, reduces fear and distrust in himself and in others. Defensive administrators build massive communication programs, not to disseminate objective information but to mold attitudes, create favorable and appropriate images, and influence people. Such persuasional and distortive communication produces resistance. Direct and open flow of information, on the other hand, serves to create an atmosphere which encourages people to share information with those above as well as with those below.

In general, openness and information giving improves the decision-making process, for experience in giving information and expressing feelings enhances consensus; and the more nearly a group can reach consensus on operational issues, the higher the quality of the decision and the greater the group's commitment to the program.

Moreover, participative goal-information optimizes self-determination and self-assessment. Intrinsic motivations become increasingly relevant and powerful. People explore their own capacities and interests, and try to find or create work for themselves that is satisfying and fulfilling. They enlarge their own jobs, asking for more responsibility and more creative and interesting work. Such work is fulfilling to the person, and extrinsic rewards are secondary to satisfaction in accomplishing the task. Administrators find that people like to work; they "own" their jobs and feel great loyalty and responsibility toward the common goals of the group. People feel little need to escape from the work situation, and the "thank goodness it's Friday" clubs become less enticing. Concerns over salary and merit increases are symptomatic of defensive-leading pressures.

Participative administration creates interdependence and diminishes the problem of authority. For instance, work is allocated by consensus—people assess their abilities and select or create appropriate tasks.

Where there is interdependence, conflict and disagreement are openly expressed and can thus be resolved and integrated into productive work. Where people feel they are working together for a common goal, the organization of work can be flexible, diverse, and informal, with a minimum of written job boundaries and rigid role requirements. Channels of communication are free, open and spontaneous.

The attainment of emergent leadership on the college campus is a developmental task of awesome proportion. If the above analysis of the leadership problem has some validity, then it is clear where some responsibilities lie.

These concepts are a challenge to the university. The Ohio State studies, particularly, showed how far behind even the military and industry the university administration is in achieving some kind of more participative and less authoritarian administrative relationships. The headlines today are filled with conflicts. The university is in many ways more susceptible to the pressures which produce fear than is industry, government, or business. The university is at one and the same time vulnerable to attacks from public opinion and also historically inviolate. The products of the university are highly intangible, and it is difficult to apply vigorous controls to the product and to tell if the university is successful in the same way that a business or even the military is with its hard criteria for productivity, profit, or victory. Thus highly vulnerable, the university has preserved a historical isolation from social pressures; and administrative behavior is often medieval and out of touch with the vigorous demands of democratic growth. The university, strangely, is sometimes a citadel for autocratic administrative behavior.

I should say a word about the implications of this model for ethical behavior. In abstract, this model of leadership specifies a theory of ethics: That behavior is more ethical which is most trusting, most open, most self-determining, and most interdependent. Thus one would look in the university setting for unethical behavior in the areas of distrust, strategic filtering of feelings and ideas (honesty), manipulative abridgement of self-determination, and dependency-producing or rebellion-producing high control behavior.

It seems to me that joint, interdependent, and shared planning is the central concept of the kind of participative, consultative leadership that we are considering. Planning, to be moral, in this framework, to be efficient, and to be growth-producing must be organic to the institution, involve to an optimal degree all of the participants, and must be done interdependently. It is easy to find illustrations on the university campus of buildings in architectural styles that are unrelated to experimental learning theory, fund-raising methods that are planned by a special group of people who are usually collecting funds in ways that would be anathema to other members of the college community, athletic programs that arise from financial need rather than from educational policy, personnel practices that are inherited unabashedly from business institutions, planning as a fragmentary, emergency process engaged in by small groups of people who are often out of touch with the university as a community.

Our assumption is that the blocks to innovation and creativity are fear, poor communication, imposition of motivations, and the dependency-rebellion syndrome of forces. People are innovative and creative. The administration of innovation involves freeing the creativity that is always present. The administrative problem of innovation is to remove fear and increase trust, to remove strategic and distortional blocks to open communication, to remove coercive, persuasional, and manipulative efforts to pump motivation, and to remove the tight controls on behavior that tend to channel creative efforts into circumvention, counter-strategy, and organizational survival rather than into innovative and creative problem-solving.

Valid, direct, authentic, and open communication among all segments of the organic institution is a central process of effective leadership in the model we are examining. Effective leadership grows with communication in depth. Effective leadership is hampered by all forces which inhibit or restrain communication in depth. If emergent or participative leadership were prevalent on the campus, communication programs would become less and less necessary. Defensive administration breeds the conditions that require an increasing escalation of massive communication programs to hopefully alleviate the conditions produced by the defensive leadership.

We are attempting to become as a people and as a culture. We are in the process of discovering and creating models of interdependent, high-trust, self-determining, and open behavior. We are trying to create an interdependent, achieving, free, becoming culture. This has never been done in the world, and the strains of transition are awesome and somewhat frightening. But for those of us who are dedicated to the university as a way of life, the challenge to the college and university administrator and leader is clear. The challenge is there. The road is unclear. The goal is at one and at the same time preservation of certain concepts we hold dear and the achievement of a more free, a more open, a more self-determining, and a more human environment for learning and growth.

The Problem of Leadership: A Look at Some Recent Findings of Behavioral Science Research

JAMES V. SPOTTS

The problem of leadership has been one of man's major concerns since the days of antiquity. Leadership was a matter of concern in the days when Alexander set out with a small band of Greeks to conquer the world, when Caesar led his troops across the Rubicon, and when Columbus set out with a mutinous crew in leaky boats to discover a "New World."

Early writers frequently wrote lengthy treatises on problems of leadership. Plato in his *Republic* devoted considerable attention to the characteristics of the "philosopher-king," the ideal and just ruler of men. Machiavelli's *The Prince* presented detailed strategies on how a leader could gain and maintain power over others. Some investigators assert that history itself is a poignant record of the successes and failures of man's leadership efforts. While interest in leadership has been a phenomenon of long historical concern, the problem of leadership has become one of crucial importance in our modern era of rapid social change, escalating crises, revolution, and nuclear stalemate. In view of this fact, it seems worthwhile to examine what behavioral scientists have discovered about this aspect of interpersonal behavior.

Although literally hundreds of leadership studies have been conducted during the last two decades, there is, at present, no universally accepted theory of leadership. In fact, many divergent and contradictory theories have been proposed. However, during the last few years, research has reached a point where some consistent findings have begun to emerge. This paper will examine some of the past discoveries that are relevant for understanding leadership phenomena and will provide one assessment of the current status of research in this field.

What do people mean when they talk about leadership? What is a leader? If one were to ask any collection of people what they think about leaders and leadership, he would receive ready answers. Everyone

Reprinted by permission of author and the *Kansas Business Review,* School of Business, University of Kansas, Vol. 17, No. 6, June 1964, pp. 3-13.

has ideas and opinions about leadership, even children. If a hypothetical investigator were to jot down what people say about leadership,
he would probably get a collection of statements something like the
following:

> A leader's job is to make decisions and exercise authority.
> A leader's job is to develop responsibility and initiative among his
> subordinates.
> Most leaders are too bossy, or most leaders are not bossy enough.
> A group is only as strong as its leader.
> The trouble in most groups and organizations is that a few people run
> everything.
> Once a leader shows weakness he's dead.
> To be a leader you must be aggressive and ambitious and tell people what to
> do.
> If you want to be a leader you have to be sensitive to the needs of others and
> tell them what they want to hear anyway.[1]

Thus, it would appear that people have all kinds of ideas about leadership. The general conclusion that one might draw is that there is very
little consensus about what leadership *is* or what it *should be*.

The mixed and conflicting assumptions about leadership noted
above are, frankly, remarkably similar to ideas held, at one time or
another, by investigators who have attempted to study and understand
leadership from a scientific point of view. Cartwright and Zander
(1953) assert that two major problems seemed to have caused behavioral scientists the most trouble. The first is that it has been extremely
difficult for investigators to separate and disentangle their assumptions
about what leadership *should be* from the straightforward research on
the question of *what consequences follow specific leadership practices.*
That is, the scientific investigation of problems like leadership is a
difficult task; particularly, because it involves value judgments or statements implying that something is "good" or "bad." Scientists are
notoriously poor at dealing with questions of value, and it has been
difficult for them to separate their own armchair assumptions about
what constitutes "good" or "poor" leadership from the variables they
are attempting to study. It is only in recent years that investigators have
begun to deal with the value question in empirical terms. Thus, leadership is increasingly being defined in operational terms such as behavior
that increases production and employee morale or decreases turnover,
absenteeism, and so on.

The second, and perhaps more complex, problem has been that of

---

1. Cartwright, D. and A.F. Zander (eds.) *Group Dynamics: Research and
Theory.* Row, Peterson, Evanston, Ill., 1953. pp. 535-36.

trying to find acceptable scientific definitions for terms like leader and leadership. For some investigators, leadership is viewed as a *characteristic of the individual;* for others, it is seen as a *property of the group.* Some workers define leadership as anyone who performs leadership *acts;* while others define it in terms of *prestige, status,* or *ability to influence others.* The complexity of the definitional problem is reflected by the fact that in a recent review one investigator compiled a list of 130 different definitions of leadership in a sampling of research literature prior to 1949.[2]

THE STUDY OF LEADERSHIP

Many of the scientist's conceptions about man have their historical roots in philosophical assumptions and ideas that have been a part of the cultural heritage for some time. These philosophical notions are sometimes very valuable in that they sharpen the scientist's conceptions of the phenomena under investigation and help him take into account factors that might otherwise be ignored. However, such ideas can just as easily blind him to other scientific data.

During the eighteenth and nineteenth centuries, philosophers were engaged in heated arguments as to the relative importance of *great men* versus the *situation* these men found themselves in. One group of philosophers believed that the personal characteristics of the great men— men of destiny, such as Napoleon, Caesar, Churchill, and the like— determined the course of history. Some exponents of this view were Thomas Carlyle, Friedrich Nietzsche, Francis Galton, and William James. For example, Carlyle argued vehemently that a true genius would contribute no matter where he was found, and James asserted that the great men were the major forces behind the creative mutations and innovations in society.

Opposed to this group were the environmentalists, a group of thinkers who boldly asserted that it was the *Zeitgeist* or situation rather than the great man that determined the course of history. These philosophers declared that the great man was nothing more than an expression of the needs of his time; if one man did not fill this need, another would step forward to do so. This group contended that no man could change society and that any changes wrought by a great man were illusory in that they were only another expression of the needs of the period.

2. Bentz, V.J., "Leadership: A Study of Social Interaction." An unpublished manuscript.

There are concrete parallels to these two kinds of thinking and speculation in current leadership research. That is, much of the early work aimed at discovering the *traits* of the leader is a logical outgrowth and development from the philosopher's *great man* theme. Similarly, the modern exponents of the environmentalist position may be reflected in the work of the investigators who have attempted to study the effects of *situational* factors upon leadership behavior.

The Trait-Oriented Approach

One major vein of early research focused upon isolating the physical, intellectual, or personality traits that distinguished a leader from his followers. Such studies have found that leaders tend to be somewhat bigger than their followers (but not much) and somewhat brighter than the rest of the group (but not much). Well-accepted leaders also evidence somewhat better adjustment than do followers (but, again, not much).

In one early study, Tead (1935) reported that the traits of the effective leader were nervous and physical energy, a sense of purpose and direction, enthusiasm, friendliness, integrity, technical mastery, decisiveness, intelligence, teaching skills, and faith! In another study, Barnard (1948) stated that the significant traits that distinguished leaders from their followers were physique, technical skill, perception, knowledge, memory, imagination, determination, persistence, endurance, and courage! Other investigators have asserted that the "successful" leader has an above average education, is active in social organizations, and has high moral and ethical standards. (Wald and Doty, 1954) Characteristics such as adjustment, good appearance, need for achievement, assertiveness, and fear of failure have also been reported as necessary leadership traits. (Henry, 1948) While these qualities would be desirable in a leader, none of them seem essential. In this context, Solomon aptly stated:

> The world has seen numerous great leaders who could hardly lay claim to any kind of formal education. History is replete with non-trained, non-academic Fords, Edisons and Carnegies who could not even claim a grammar school education yet managed to become leaders whose influence was felt around the globe.
>
> As for appearance or robust health, need we mention more than the delicate Ghandi, or George Washington Carver, the frail, shriveled, insignificant little Negro who was one of America's greatest scientists, and so many more like them. As for high ideals, fine character, etc., where would Hitler, Capone or Attila the Hun rate here? [3]

---

3. Solomon, B., *Leadership of Youth.* Youth Services, New York, 1954. p. 15.

While Solomon characterized some of the exceptions to trait-oriented leadership research, a casual examination of the studies cited above quickly reveals one of the major shortcomings of this kind of approach; namely, that rarely, if ever, do two lists agree on the *essential* characteristics of the effective leader. Bird (1940) and Stogdill (1948) have surveyed well over one hundred studies in this area. The discouraging finding was that less than five per cent of the traits reported as characteristic of the effective leader were common in four or more of the studies surveyed. Secondly, there was some evidence to suggest that the leaders, in fact, cannot be markedly different from their followers. Thus, while the leader must be intelligent he cannot be—or appear to be—too much more intelligent that the other group members. Extremes in personality are not usually associated with leadership, if for no other reason than they make the person too different from the other members of his group.

Investigators appear to be generally coming to the conclusion that certain minimal abilities may be required of all leaders. However, these same traits will probably be widely distributed among the non-leaders as well. Moreover, there seems to be an increasing recognition of wide variations in the characteristics of individuals who become leaders in similar situations and of even greater divergence in the traits of leaders working in different situations. (Jenkins, 1947)

The Situational Approach

General dissatisfaction with the failure to isolate leadership traits led some investigators to focus their research efforts more upon the problem of the situation in which leadership occurs. These workers share the assumption that the traits and skills that characterize a "good" leader will vary from group to group and from situation to situation. Associated with this assumption is the notion of *emergent* leadership, which postulates that temporary or situational leaders will arise in groups when necessary to meet the demands of new situations.

The notion that "new" leaders will emerge when groups are in periods of stress or crisis is well documented. Crockett (1955) found that, when a designated leader failed to provide the leadership functions he was supposed to perform, other members provided them, so there would be a minimal loss in group effectiveness. Similar results were reported by Kahn and Katz (1956) in the work situation. These investigators found that, when foremen failed to provide adequate leadership, informal leaders arose in the work groups and provided the needed functions.

Situation-oriented research has assumed that it is unreasonable to expect one leader to always be able to do everything better than anyone else. In our terms, the question might be posed as follows: Is it reasonable to expect a successful businessman to be equally as "effective" in other types of leadership, such as the president of General Motors, a commander of a B-52, the president of a local P.T.A., or a leader of a Special Forces platoon in the jungles of Viet Nam? Obviously, the situation has much to do with determining what leadership skills will be required. Stogdill cogently stated the problem [pp. 64-65].

It is not especially difficult to find persons who are leaders. It is quite another thing to place these people in different situations where they will be able to function as leaders. Thus, any adequate analysis of leadership involves not only a study of the leaders but also of the situation in which leadership acts occur.

There are many studies in the literature that support the notion of situational leadership. For example, Thrasher (1927) in a study of street gangs reported that the particular activity of the group was a major factor in determining who would be the gang leader. In a similar study, Whyte (1943) found that the leaders of these informal gangs actively manipulated their group's activities so as to maintain their leadership. The leader tended to involve his group in activities where he knew he would excel and avoided those situations and activities where his leadership might be threatened.

In a study of the leadership patterns of navy enlisted men on ships during wartime discussed by Burke (1943), it was found that three different patterns of leadership emerged depending upon the situation. In combat, the officers were the effective leaders of the enlisted group. However, during the periods of rest and boredom between battles, it was the "jokesters" and entertainers who seemed to occupy major leadership roles. Finally, when the ships were returning to port the men with previous shore "contacts" emerged as leaders. Similarly, Dunkerly's study (1940) of leadership patterns among college women points to the significance of situational factors. Those girls chosen as *intellectual leaders,* such as house president and the like, were found to be superior to their peers in judgment, initiative, and intellectual ability. Those girls selected as *social leaders* were generally superior to others in dress and appearance. Finally, girls selected as *religious leaders* were reported as being less "neurotic" than the others. Surprisingly enough, or perhaps not so surprisingly, the social leaders were found to be most "neurotic."

Bass (1960) reports that cross-cultural studies by anthropologists also support the importance of situational leadership factors. He notes that among the Samoans, where there was a highly developed sensitivity to position and social rank, quite different patterns of leadership were evidenced than were found in the individualistic Eskimo society where no man's importance was considered relative to another. Again, leadership among the Iroquois Indians was attained through acts of generosity, hospitality, and cooperation, but, among the Kwakiutls of the Northwest, leadership was established through one's ability to compete financially with others.

Clearly then, there is a wealth of scientific evidence pointing to the significance of situational factors as determinants of leadership behavior. However, this has been found to be only one facet of the leadership problem.

The Functional Approach

A third approach to the study of leadership developed from a functional orientation to the problem. This approach developed under the influence of Kurt Lewin, founder of field-theory in social science, from subsequent theorizing and research in group dynamics and, to some extent, from the human relations movement.

With the Functional Approach, emphasis in research shifted from the study of the leader as a person to the study of the group. One major aim here has been to discover the kinds of behavior that are necessary for a group to survive and attain its goals. In this context, leadership is defined as all those member acts that aid in the development of the group and accomplishment of the group's task. Thus, leadership may be performed by one or many members of the group. It is viewed as a quality that a person may display in varying degrees rather than as something he possesses entirely or not at all. Consequently, leadership may be "possessed" to some degree by any member of a group, regardless of his formally designated office or position.

The Functional Approach considers both the individual and the situation in which leadership occurs. This approach assumes that groups (and leaders) are continually faced with two interrelated tasks. The first is that groups must find ways to deal with problems associated with attainment of agreed-upon goals, i.e., resolve task problems. Secondly, group members must find ways to improve and strengthen the group itself, i.e., resolve internal maintenance problems, to achieve its goals.

Benne & Sheats (1948), Bales (1950), and others have attempted to isolate some of the major task and maintenance behaviors that appear in well-functioning groups. Those member (or leader) functions that seem to be effective in moving groups toward resolution of task problems include such acts as asking for clarification of issues at hand, summarizing the contributions of others, proposing new ideas and courses of action, giving and receiving information, coordinating the ideas and suggestions made by others, and so on. Members or leader functions that seem to aid in the resolution of internal problems and maintenance of the group include giving minority views a chance to be heard, mediating and harmonizing conflict within the group, maintaining open channels of communication, ventilating feelings for the group and so on.

There are a number of studies to suggest that the behavior of the leader varies considerably depending upon the task at hand. For example, Carter and his associates (1950) studied the activities of leaders on three different tasks; reasoning, mechanical assembly, and group discussion. In the reasoning tasks, the leaders more frequently asked for information or facts. When confronted with the mechanical assembly task, the leader most frequently expressed the need for action and worked actively with his men. Finally, in the group discussion situation, he was most likely to give information and ask for expression of opinions.

The results of the Carter study were based upon data obtained with artificially created laboratory groups. However, similar results have been reported from studies of real-life work groups. Stogdill (1951), in a study of leadership patterns of officers in 46 naval organizations, found that the relative emphasis placed upon particular leadership functions was highly influenced by the task situation. While all officers did some coordinating, this function was most frequently stressed in the work of the executive officer. The function of exercising administrative control was most prominent in the activities of the district medical officer; technical supervision was most frequently observed with the electrical officer; and consultation was practiced most often by the legal officer.

Two other classic studies are worthy of mention in this area. The first, by White and Lippitt (1956), investigated the effects of three different styles of leadership, which these workers designated as Democratic, Autocratic, and Laissez-Faire, on productivity and member morale.

Democratic leaders generally tended to encourage their members to participate in the decision making, did not give rigid rules as to how things were to be done, and gave suggestions, information, and praise to the groups as a whole rather than to individuals. Autocratic leaders, on the other hand, made all final decisions for the groups, told them how to do things, supervised members closely, and praised and punished individual members. The Laissez-Faire leaders gave no suggestions unless specifically requested to do so. They performed a minimum of leader functions and neither praised nor punished group members.

The results of this investigation show clearly that the behavior of the group members differed markedly under the different patterns of leadership. The following was found in this study [p. 595].

Democratic leadership resulted in greater productivity (measured by the amount of work done) than did Laissez-Faire leadership. On the other hand, Autocratic leadership led to greater productivity than did Democratic leadership. However, the quality of work was consistently better in the Democratic than Autocratic groups.

There was more direct and indirect discontent expressed in the Autocratic groups than in Democratic ones. When the Autocratic leaders were absent, their groups collapsed. In Democratic groups, there was only a slight drop in work involvement during "leader-out" periods.

Members of the Democratic groups expressed greater cohesiveness and satisfaction with their group experience than did either the Autocratic or Laissez-Faire group members. In this respect, the Autocratic groups were characterized by two patterns of member behavior: either the greatest amount of hostility, aggressiveness, and scapegoating among members or the greatest apathy.

Democratic groups showed the least absenteeism and dropouts while Autocratic groups evidenced the most absenteeism and terminations.

Group members evidenced more submissive and dependent behavior in the Autocratic groups than in the other two and showed unsurprisingly less "talking back" to leaders.

While the findings reported in this study were based upon data gathered from youth groups, subsequent investigations (Baumgartel, 1957; Bovard, 1951; Hare, 1953; Preston & Heintz, 1949) with a variety of adult work groups yielded highly similar results. Taken together, these studies suggest that the "style" of the leader can have marked effects upon group member performance.

The second classic leadership study is by Coch and French, (1948). In the factory studied, changes in products and methods of doing jobs were a necessary result of existing competitive conditions in the field. In addition, a marked increase in absenteeism and turnover in recent years had resulted in unbalanced production lines and had made frequent shifting of individuals from job to job necessary. Job changes were, therefore, frequent and were nearly always accompanied by sharp drops in employee productivity. One serious problem that had developed out of this situation was an intense resistance by the production workers to the necessary changes in methods and jobs. This resistance was expressed in frequent grievances to the union about the piece rates that accompanied the new methods and in high turnover, low efficiency, restriction of output, and marked hostility and aggression towards management.

After an initial survey, the experimenters felt that the reactions described above resulted not from the objective difficulties of changing to a new job but from the difficulty of getting people to accept the need for change and to aid actively in creating change. The investigators, therefore, set up a study based upon the idea that participation in the planning and carrying out of change would be helpful. A total of four different work groups were set up; three, the experimental groups, were allowed to participate in the change in different ways, and the fourth, the control group, was treated the same as the groups had been treated in the past.

The control group went through the usual factory routine when jobs were changed. They were told that a change was necessary and that a new piece rate had been set. In this group, there was *no participation* by employees in planning the change though an explanation was given them. The first experimental group involved *participation through*

EXHIBIT I
THE EFFECT OF PARTICIPATION ON PRODUCTIVITY

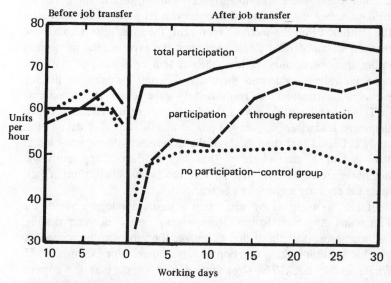

Reproduced by permission from John R. P. French, Jr., C. H. Lawshe, and Floyd C. Mann, "Training for Effective Leadership," *Planning and Training for Effective Leadership* (Ann Arbor, Mich.: The Foundation for Research on Human Behavior, 1956), p. 11.

representation in designing the changes to be made; that is, the group elected representatives who met with management to work out the new methods and piece rates. The third variation, used in the other two experimental groups, involved *total participation* by all of the workers in the designing of the new jobs and establishment of the new rates. Exhibit I shows rather clearly what happened. The control group showed the usual drop in productivity and did not return to its previous level during the period shown. This group continued to carry grievances to the union about the new rates and showed increased absenteeism, job terminations, deliberate restriction of work output, and hostility towards the foremen and management. The first experimental group, with participation through representation, evidenced an initial drop with fairly rapid recovery. The last two experimental groups (combined in the exhibit), in which total participation was allowed, showed practically no drop and then went to a higher level of productivity than before the change.

Two months after the original study, the control group was involved in a new job transfer using the total participation method. With the total participation procedure, this group quickly recovered its previous efficiency rating and, like the other groups, continued on to new production levels. There was no aggression and turnover in the group for 19 days, a fact that contrasted sharply with its previous behavior after the transfer. From the second experiment, the investigators concluded that the obtained results depended upon the experimental procedures rather than personality factors, such as skill or aggression, since the same individuals evidenced markedly different behavior in the no-participation treatment as contrasted with the total-participation one.

This particular study gives a striking picture of the effects that participatory leadership may have upon productivity. Other data in this study indicated that the morale of the experimental groups was better than that of the control group. Thus, high production apparently was not obtained at the cost of employee morale or satisfaction; in fact, quite the contrary appeared to be true.

It has been argued by some that research developing out of the Functional Approach fosters "group-think," group decision making, and management methods that encourage the supervisor or manager to give his decision-making function to subordinates. For example, W. H. Whyte in his book *The Organization Man* asserts that the current focus upon groups only encourages in leaders a loss of individuality, conformity, and mediocrity. However, it should be noted that this approach makes no value judgments as to whether a leader should or should not practice a particular leadership pattern. It only asks the question of what consequences are associated with different leadership behavior, and it then leaves the problem of deciding what particular leadership practices will be most effective in a given situation to the practitioner.

Actually, results from studies that have attempted to answer the question of whether leadership should be widely distributed in a group or concentrated in the hands of a few have generally been mixed. For example, Bavelas (1942) found that concentrated leadership resulted in both more efficient performance and lower morale. Similarly, Kahn and Katz (1956), in a study of a variety of high- and low-producing groups in business and industry, found that the supervisors of high-producing group units tended to take clear control of several leadership functions such as planning, coordinating, and so on. However, these supervisors were also more inclined to delegate responsibilities to others, encourage subordinates to make decisions, and take initiative in many activities.

The Interactionistic Approach

Finally, consideration should be given to what may be defined, for lack of a better term, as an Interactionistic Approach to the study of leadership. In many respects, this approach is a logical outgrowth and extension of the Functional Approach. However, there is value in distinguishing the two approaches, if for no other reason than to examine the interactionist's methodology. This approach also has a certain uniqueness in that it stresses the quality of the leader-subordinate relationship as an important determinant of productivity, morale, and other goals seen as "good" or desirable by organizations.

One basic assumption of this approach is that leadership cannot be studied in isolation, because it represents an *interaction* between members of a group. One argument leveled at some of the functional studies was that the results were based upon experimentally constituted laboratory groups that were transitory and divorced from the "real-life" conditions in which leadership occurs. Such complaints can hardly be leveled at interactionistic research, since these investigations characteristically have been field studies in all kinds of work groups and organizations.

A favorite methodology in this kind of research is to select "high productive" and "low-productive" or "effective" and "ineffective" work groups doing the same tasks in an organization and then study the leader-follower interactions. In these studies "productive," "effective,"

The answer to the question—Are there significant differences in the superior-subordinate relationships of "productive" and "nonproductive" work groups?—seems to be basically "Yes." Evidence from field studies with B-52 bomber crews, factory assembly lines, public utility companies, infantry combat squads, insurance companies, government agencies, petroleum companies, and so on would suggest that the leader-follower interaction may differ quite markedly in "productive" and "nonproductive" groups (Likert, 1961).

Contrary to what one might suspect, the leaders or supervisors of highly productive units—crews, departments, or divisions—do not appear to devote their greatest time and efforts to technical or job-oriented functions with subordinates. Rather, supervisors or leaders with the best records of performance focus their primary attention upon the human aspects of their subordinate relationships and attempt to build effective work groups with high-performance goals.

High-productive leaders—supervisors and managers—tend to spend more time than low-productive supervisors in motivating their subordinates, providing structure, and keeping them informed as to what is going on, getting their ideas and suggestions on important matters before going ahead, training their subordinates for more responsibilities, trying out new ideas with them, and, in general, showing consideration for the follower and his needs.

At the other extreme, the ineffective or low-production leader frequently demands more from his subordinate than can be done, criticizes them in front of others, treats subordinates without respect for their feelings, rides them for making mistakes, initiates actions without consulting them, and refuses to accept their ideas and suggestions or even explain the actions he has taken.

High- and low-production leaders differ not only in their relationships with their subordinates but also in their relationships with their supervisors. Pelz (1951) found that high-production leaders tended to have much greater influence upon their own superiors on matters relating to subordinates' pay, working conditions, promotions, and so on, than did low-production leaders. In this study, it was also found that, when leaders who had above average influence with their own bosses followed "good" supervisory practices, the subordinates tended to react favorably. However, when supervisors who were below average in the amount of influence they had with their supervisors practiced these same desirable supervisory procedures, they usually failed to obtain a favorable reaction and not infrequently obtained adverse reactions from their subordinates. Apparently, if the leader is to influence his followers effectively, he must also be able to influence his own supervisor as well. Interactionistic research findings constitute perhaps the closest thing to what might be regarded as leadership "principles" in the whole literature. Although the maxims are fairly well documented by research and experience, they do not form any kind of compact "cookbook" or guide to effective leadership. None of the findings is universally applicable; in fact, one may sometimes obtain similar results with almost opposite leadership practices. Some representative leadership "principles" that are frequently reported in the research literature are as follows.

1. Supervisors of high-productive units spend a greater amount of time developing their work groups into "close," highly cohesive teams than do supervisors or managers of low-productive units.

One assumption here is that a supervisor or leader cannot treat his subordinates with full effectiveness unless he recognizes the work group as a source of morale and motivation. Seashore's study (1954) of high- and low-"cohesive" work groups in a large manufacturing company indicates clearly the powerful influences a small group can exert upon a member's behavior and adjustment. This investigator found that members of high-cohesive groups exhibited much less anxiety than low-cohesive groups when feeling "jumpy" and nervous, feeling under pressure to achieve higher productivity, and feeling a lack of support from the company were used as measures of anxiety. Seashore concluded that membership in a cohesive group provides the worker with effective support in his encounters with work-associated anxiety and provides direct satisfactions that are anxiety reducing.

Similarly, research by Trist and Bamforth (1951) with English coal miners supports the importance of the group as a determinant of worker effectiveness and morale. As a part of a program of increasing the mechanization and "efficiency" of mining operations, management broke up the miner's small, face-to-face work groups and assigned the workers to more isolated tasks. The reorganization of the small work groups led to serious problems of absenteeism, turnover, and sickness (including psychosomatic disorders). This problem became so acute that it was necessary to alter attempts at increased mechanization and restore the small work groups, even though, from an outsider's point of view, this seemed "inefficient."

While the principle of utilization of group factors such as loyalty and group cohesiveness appears to be one of the most firmly established findings in the literature, highly cohesive groups are *not always* the most productive. In Seashore's study, high productivity among cohesive groups was found *only* if the group members saw the company as a supportive and secure situation. Among crews who saw the company as threatening, high cohesiveness was associated with low productivity.

2. *General rather than close supervision is more often associated with a high rather than a low level of productivity.*

A number of investigators have found that high-production supervisors and managers supervise their employees less closely than low-production supervisors. High-production supervisors make clear to their subordinates what needs to be done then let these subordinates use their own ideas and experience to do the job in the way they find best. Low-production supervisors frequently spend more time with their subordinates than do high-production ones, but the time is broken up into short periods because the supervisors give specific instructions such as "Do this," "Don't do that."

An interesting parallel to this proposition is that leaders tend to supervise their subordinates as they themselves are supervised. (Pfiffner, 1955) Thus, if a department head utilizes general or close supervision, his foremen tend to follow similar practices. It would appear reasonable to assume that low-production subordinates might require more close supervision; however, on the other hand, there is some evidence to suggest that close supervision may actually *cause* poor performance in that it emphasizes precise rules and procedures, at the expense of long-range goals, subordinate morale, and job satisfaction (Likert, 1961).

While general rather than close supervision practices are often more characteristic of high-producing managers than of low ones, research findings *do not* show that all high-producing managers adhere to this pattern. Some technically competent, job-centered, intensive, and tough managers have achieved impressive levels of productivity. However, the members of these work groups showed unfavorable attitudes towards their work and supervisors, hostility and resentment towards management, a high number of grievances that went to arbitration, frequent slowdowns, work stoppages, waste, and high job turnover.

Likert and Kahn (1956) reported a study that attempted to evaluate the effects of (1) tighter controls and direction and (2) greater employee autonomy and participation as alternative ways to achieve high productivity and employee satisfaction in the same organization! In some sections of the company, results were sought through closer supervision, more detailed work procedures, and other forms of tighter control and direction. In other sections, a program of encouraging more autonomy and participation in decision making was followed. Responsibility for decisions was pushed down to lower levels of the organization and greater freedom was given employees. *In both situations, productivity was increased about 15-20 percent.* Thus, contradictory leadership practices were effective in increasing productivity; however, employee morale changed for the worse in units where tighter controls were imposed and changed for the better in those units where greater autonomy was instituted.

3. The greater the amount of unreasonable pressure toward production that men feel from their supervisors, the lower the productivity and the less confidence and trust they have in their supervisors.

Even this finding must be tempered by situational factors; that is, increasing management pressures toward productivity may have different results depending upon the initial level of pressure. At initially low levels of pressure, an increase in emphasis upon productivity by supervisors not only results in higher productivity but also increases the satisfaction of the men with their supervisor. However, at higher levels of pressure, further increases in emphasis upon productivity by supervisors frequently tend to result in lower productivity and adverse reactions toward the supervisor.

SUMMARY

The studies surveyed represent a fair sampling of more than two decades of leadership research, and, on the basis of these findings, some general conclusions can be drawn.

The available evidence seems to indicate that there are probably no personality traits or characteristics that consistently distinguish the leader from his followers. There is some evidence, however, to suggest that the leader probably cannot be markedly different from his subordinates if he is to be followed.

The results of a number of studies indicate that leadership does not occur in a vacuum but at a particular time and place and under a particular set of circumstances. Therefore, the situation determines to some degree the kinds of leadership skills and behavior that may be required. One reassuring finding that has emerged from these studies has been the "discovery" that, when formal or designated leadership fails to provide its required functions, there is a tendency for other members of the group to step in and perform the "needed" functions so that there will be a minimal loss in group effectiveness.

Some workers have investigated the effects of differing kinds of leadership styles and have begun the process of explicating what kinds of leadership acts or behavior helps groups "move forward" and function effectively. Some of these studies suggest that there is a tendency for democratic or participatory leadership behavior to be associated with productivity, increased worker morale, and a number of other factors. Directive leadership has been found to lead to equally high productivity but often results in low morale and commitment to work. However, the relationship between leadership styles and job performance is much too complex to be explained simply by "democratic" or "authoritarian" leadership practices. Different leadership practices seem appropriate for different situations. Thus, under certain conditions, participative leadership may be most effective. Under other conditions, a more directive leadership may be required. Again, the personality characteristics and expectations of subordinates will influence the kinds of leadership practices that are most effective. An increase in the degree of follower participation will often have favorable effects if the subordinates have relatively high needs for independence, a readiness to assume responsibility, the necessary knowledge and experience to deal with problems, and an identification with the goals of the organization. (Tannenbaum & Schmidt, 1958) However, the use of participatory practices with workers who lack these attributes might have highly adverse and undesirable effects.

There is a growing body of research indicating rather clear differences between the behavior of high- and low-production workers in real-life work situations. These studies suggest that high-production supervisors tend to supervise their subordinates less closely, spend more time consulting with their workers, and give them more opportunities to participate in decisions that affect them than do low-production leaders. The quality of the leader-subordinate relationship—the degree of genuine respect and consideration that the leader shows for the follower's needs—appears to be a crucial factor here. This is perhaps another way of saying that employee-centered leadership tends to be more closely associated with subordinate productivity, morale, and job satisfaction than does production-centered leadership.

On the basis of the research surveyed in this presentation, it would seem clear that leaders accomplish their work through other people and their success as leaders depends upon their ability to enlist and maintain follower commitment and collaboration for the attainment of group or organizational goals. In this respect, some of the research considered here may provide ideas that may be worth considering in the concrete work situation. However, at the present time, there is no straight-forward set of supervisory practices that will always yield the best results. Research reported in this presentation suggests that a leader's objectives may be reached through multiple and sometimes even contra-dictory means. At this point, it would appear that the choice of alterna-tive leadership practices for a given individual will depend upon a num-ber of factors, such as the following:

The leader's personal preference or "style."

The leader's skill in applying various leadership practices.

The leader's confidence in his subordinates.

The leader's value system or the importance that he attaches to organizational efficiency, personal growth of subordinates, company profits, et cetera.

The leader's assessment of the "situation" of his subordinates.

The leader's evaluation of possible undesirable side effects of a particular practice.

Viewed from a historical point of view, the studies considered indi-cate that behavioral scientists are making progress in understanding the phenomena of leadership. Research has come a long way from the early study of leadership traits, and investigators can now state with some certainty what they know and do not know. Moreover, they are in a position to begin to specify some of the conditions under which given leadership practices may be effective. However, while behavioral scien-tists may be able to provide managers and supervisors with some tenta-tive "guidelines," leadership research can never specify the "proper" practices for all situations. *In the concrete leadership situation, the final choice and responsibility for specific action must always fall back upon the judgment and good common sense of frail human beings, and, in all due respects to the "leader," this is as it should be.*

REFERENCES

Bales, R. F., *Interaction Process Analysis: A Method for the Study of Small Groups* (Cambridge, Mass.: Addison-Wesley Press, 1950).

Barnard, C. J., *The Function of the Executive* (Cambridge, Mass.: Harvard University Press, 1948).

Bass, B., *Leadership, Psychology and Organizational Behavior* (New York: Harper, 1960).

Baumgartel, Howard, "Leadership Style as a Variable in Research Administra-tion," *Administrative Science Quarterly*, Vol. II (1957).

Bavelas, A., "Morale and Training of Leaders," *Civilian Morale*, G. Watson, ed. (Boston, Mass.: Houghton-Mifflin, 1942).

Benne, K. D. and P. Sheats, "Functional Roles of Group Members," *Journal of Social Issues*, Vol. IV (1948).

Bird, C., *Social Psychology* (New York: Appleton-Century, 1940).

Bovard, E. W., Jr., "Group Structure and Perception," *Journal of Abnormal & Social Psychology*, Vol. XLVI (1951).

Burke, R., "Approaches to Understanding Leadership" (an unpublished manuscript).

Carter, L., Beatrice Haythorn & J. Lanzatta, "The Behavior of Leaders and Other Members," *Journal of Abnormal & Social Psychology*, Vol. XLV (1950).

Cartwright, D. and A. F. Zander (eds.), *Group Dynamics: Research and Theory* (Evanston, Ill.: Row, Peterson, 1953).

Coch, L. and J. French, Jr., "Overcoming Resistances to Change," *Human Relations*, Vol. I (1948).

Crockett, W., "Emergent Leadership in Small, Decision-Making Groups," *Journal of Abnormal & Social Psychology*, Vol. LI (1955).

Dunkerly, M. D., "A Statistical Study of Leadership Among College Women," *Studies in Psychology and Psychiatry*, Vol. IV (Washington, D. C.: Catholic University of America, 1940).

Hare, A. P., "Small Discussions with Participatory and Supervisory Leadership," *Journal of Abnormal & Social Psychology*, Vol. LVIII (1953).

Henry, W. E., "Executive Personality and Job Success," *American Management Association*, Personnel Series, No. 120 (1948).

Jenkins, W. O., "A Review of Leadership Studies with Particular Reference to Military Problems," *Psychological Bulletin*, Vol. XLIV (1947).

Kahn, R. and D. Katz, "Leadership Practices in Relation to Productivity and Morale," *Group Dynamics: Research and Theory*, Cartwright and Zander, eds. (Evanston, Ill.: Row, Peterson, 1953).

Likert, R., *New Patterns of Management* (New York: McGraw-Hill, 1961).

Likert, R. and R. L. Kahn, "Planning for Effective Leadership," *Planning and Training for Effective Leadership*, S. Seashore, ed. (Ann Arbor, Mich.: Foundation for Research on Human Behavior, 1956).

Pelz, D. C., "Leadership Within a Heirarchical Organization," *Journal of Social Issues*, Vol. VII (1951).

Pfiffner, J. M., "The Effective Supervisor: An Organization Research Study," *Personnel*, Vol. XXXI (1955).

Preston, M. G. and R. K. Heintz, "Effects of Participatory Versus Supervisory Leadership on Group Judgment," *Journal of Abnormal & Social Psychology*, Vol. XLIV (1949).

Seashore, Stanley, *Group Cohesiveness in the Industrial Work Group* (Ann Arbor, Mich.: Institute for Social Research, 1954).

Stanton, E. S., "Company Policies and Supervisors' Attitudes Toward Supervision," *Journal of Applied Psychology*, Vol. XLIV (1960).

Stogdill, R. M., "Personal Factors Associated with Leadership: A Survey of the Literature," *Journal of Psychology*, Vol. XXV (1948).

Stogdill, R. M., "Studies in Naval Leadership, Part II," *Groups, Leadership and Men*, H. Buetzkow, ed. (Pittsburgh, Pa.: Carnegie Press, 1951).

Tannenbaum, R. and W. H. Schmidt, "How to Choose a Leadership Pattern" *Harvard Business Review*, Vol. XXXVI (1958).

Tead, O., *The Art of Leadership* (New York: McGraw-Hill, 1935).

Thrasher, F. M., *The Gang* (Chicago: University of Chicago Press, 1927).

Trist, E. L. and K. W. Bamforth, "Some Social and Psychological Consequences of the Long-wall Method of Coal Getting," *Human Relations*, Vol. IV (1951).

Wald, R. M. and R. A. Doty, "The Top Executive: A Firsthand Profile," *Harvard Business Review*, Vol. XXXII (1954).

White, R. and R. L. Lippitt, "Leadership Behavior and Member Reaction in Three Social Climates" *Group Dynamics*, D. Cartwright and A. Zander, eds. (New York: Row, Peterson, 1956).

Whyte, W. H., *The Organization Man* (New York: Simon & Schuster, 1956).

Whyte, W. F., *Street Corner Society* (Chicago: University of Chicago Press, 1943).

The Manager in the Organization

In this section, Douglas McGregor's classic discussion is used as a reference point for reviewing concepts of organization. Emphasis is placed on new ways of viewing organizations which go beyond the traditional bureaucratic or administrative management approaches. Newer models are provided which take into account the people who are members of the organization.

The Human Side
of Enterprise

DOUGLAS M. McGREGOR

It has become trite to say that industry has the fundamental know-how to utilize physical science and technology for the material benefit of mankind, and that we must now learn how to utilize the social sciences to make our human organizations truly effective.

To a degree, the social sciences today are in a position like that of the physical sciences with respect to atomic energy in the thirties. We know that past conceptions of the nature of man are inadequate and, in many ways, incorrect. We are becoming quite certain that, under proper conditions, unimagined resources of creative human energy could become available within the organizational setting.

We cannot tell industrial management how to apply this new knowledge in simple, economic ways. We know it will require years of exploration, much costly development research, and a substantial amount of creative imagination on the part of management to discover how to apply this growing knowledge to the organization of human effort in industry.

MANAGEMENT'S TASK: THE CONVENTIONAL VIEW

The conventional conception of management's task in harnessing human energy to organizational requirements can be stated broadly in terms of three propositions. In order to avoid the complications introduced by a label, let us call this set of propositions "Theory X":

1. Management is responsible for organizing the elements of productive enterprise—money, materials, equipment, people—in the interest of economic ends.

2. With respect to people, this is a process of directing their efforts, motivating them, controlling their actions, modifying their behavior to fit the needs of the organization.

Reprinted by permission of the publisher from "The Human Side of Enterprise," by Douglas M. McGregor, *Management Review*, November 1957, © 1957 by the American Management Association, Inc.

3. Without this active intervention by management, people would be passive—even resistant—to organizational needs. They must therefore be persuaded, rewarded, punished, controlled—their activities must be directed. This is management's task. We often sum it up by saying that management consists of getting things done through other people.

Behind this conventional theory there are several additional beliefs— less explicit, but widespread:

4. The average man is by nature indolent—he works as little as possible.

5. He lacks ambition, dislikes responsibility, prefers to be led.

6. He is inherently self-centered, indifferent to organizational needs.

7. He is by nature resistant to change.

8. He is gullible, not very bright, the ready dupe of the charlatan and the demagogue.

The human side of economic enterprise today is fashioned from propositions and beliefs such as these. Conventional organization structures and managerial policies, practices, and programs reflect these assumptions.

In accomplishing its task—with these assumptions as guides—management has conceived of a range of possibilities.

At one extreme, management can be "hard" or "strong." The methods for directing behavior involve coercion and threat (usually disguised), close supervision, tight controls over behavior. At the other extreme, management can be "soft" or "weak." The methods for directing behavior involve being permissive, satisfying people's demands, achieving harmony. Then they will be tractable, accept direction.

This range has been fairly completely explored during the past half century, and management has learned some things from the exploration. There are difficulties in the "hard" approach. Force breeds counter-forces: restriction of output, antagonism, militant unionism, subtle but effective sabotage of management objectives. This "hard" approach is especially difficult during times of full employment.

There are also difficulties in the "soft" approach. It leads frequently to the abdication of management—to harmony, perhaps, but to indifferent performance. People take advantage of the soft approach. They continually expect more, but they give less and less.

Currently, the popular theme is "firm but fair." This is an attempt to gain the advantages of both the hard and the soft approaches. It is reminiscent of Teddy Roosevelt's "speak softly and carry a big stick."

IS THE CONVENTIONAL VIEW CORRECT?

The findings which are beginning to emerge from the social sciences challenge this whole set of beliefs about man and human nature and about the task of management. The evidence is far from conclusive, certainly, but it is suggestive. It comes from the laboratory, the clinic, the schoolroom, the home, and even to a limited extent from industry itself.

The social scientist does not deny that human behavior in industrial organization today is approximately what management perceives it to be. He has, in fact, observed it and studied it fairly extensively. But he is pretty sure that this behavior is *not* a consequence of man's inherent nature. It is a consequence rather of the nature of industrial organizations, of management philosophy, policy, and practice. The conventional approach of Theory X is based on mistaken notions of what is cause and what is effect.

Perhaps the best way to indicate why the conventional approach of management is inadequate is to consider the subject of motivation.

PHYSIOLOGICAL NEEDS

Man is a wanting animal—as soon as one of his needs is satisfied, another appears in its place. This process is unending. It continues from birth to death.

Man's needs are organized in a series of levels—a hierarchy of importance. At the lowest level, but pre-eminent in importance when they are thwarted, are his *physiological needs*. Man lives for bread alone, when there is no bread. Unless the circumstances are unusual, his needs for love, for status, for recognition are inoperative when his stomach has been empty for a while. But when he eats regularly and adequately, hunger ceases to be an important motivation. The same is true of the other physiological needs of man—for rest, exercise, shelter, protection from the elements.

A satisfied need is not a motivator of behavior! This is a fact of profound significance that is regularly ignored in the conventional approach to the management of people. Consider your own need for air: Except as you are deprived of it, it has no appreciable motivating effect upon your behavior.

SAFETY NEEDS

When the physiological needs are reasonably satisfied, needs at the next higher level begin to dominate man's behavior—to motivate him. These are called *safety needs.* They are needs for protection against danger, threat, deprivation. Some people mistakenly refer to these as needs for security. However, unless man is in a dependent relationship where he fears arbitrary deprivation, he does not demand security. The need is for the "fairest possible break." When he is confident of this, he is more than willing to take risks. But when he feels threatened or dependent, his greatest need is for guarantees, for protection, for security.

The fact needs little emphasis that, since every industrial employee is in a dependent relationship, safety needs may assume considerable importance. Arbitrary management actions, behavior which arouses uncertainty with respect to continued employment or which reflects favoritism or discrimination, unpredictable administration of policy—these can be powerful motivators of the safety needs in the employment relationship *at every level,* from worker to vice president.

SOCIAL NEEDS

When man's physiological needs are satisfied and he is no longer fearful about his physical welfare, his *social needs* become important motivators of his behavior—needs for belonging, for association, for acceptance by his fellows, for giving and receiving friendship and love.

Management knows today of the existence of these needs, but it often assumes quite wrongly that they represent a threat to the organization. Many studies have demonstrated that the tightly knit, cohesive work group may, under proper conditions, be far more effective than an equal number of separate individuals in achieving organizational goals.

Yet management, fearing group hostility to its own objectives, often goes to considerable lengths to control and direct human efforts in ways that are inimical to the natural "groupiness" of human beings. When man's social needs—and perhaps his safety needs, too—are thus thwarted, he behaves in ways which tend to defeat organizational objectives. He becomes resistant, antagonistic, uncooperative. But this behavior is a consequence, not a cause.

EGO NEEDS

Above the social needs—in the sense that they do not become motivators until lower needs are reasonably satisfied—are the needs of greatest significance to management and to man himself. They are the *egoistic needs,* and they are of two kinds:

1. Those needs that relate to one's self-esteem—needs for self-confidence, for independence, for achievement, for competence, for knowledge.

2. Those needs that relate to one's reputation—needs for status, for recognition, for appreciation, for the deserved respect of one's fellows.

Unlike the lower needs, these are rarely satisfied; man seeks indefinitely for more satisfaction of these needs once they have become important to him. But they do not appear in any significant way until physiological, safety, and social needs are all reasonably satisfied.

The typical industrial organization offers few opportunities for the satisfaction of these egoistic needs to people at lower levels in the hierarchy. The conventional methods of organizing work, particularly in mass-production industries, give little heed to these aspects of human motivation. If the practices of scientific management were deliberately calculated to thwart these needs, they could hardly accomplish this purpose better than they do.

SELF-FULFILLMENT NEEDS

Finally—a capstone, as it were, on the hierarchy of man's needs—there are what we may call the *needs for self-fulfillment.* These are the needs for realizing one's own potentialities, for continued self-development, for being creative in the broadest sense of that term.

It is clear that the conditions of modern life give only limited opportunity for these relatively weak needs to obtain expression. The deprivation most people experience with respect to other lower-level needs diverts their energies into the struggle to satisfy *those* needs, and the needs for self-fulfillment remain dormant.

MANAGEMENT AND MOTIVATION

We recognize readily enough that a man suffering from a severe dietary deficiency is sick. The deprivation of physiological needs has behavioral consequences. The same is true—although less well recognized—of deprivation of higher-level needs. The man whose needs for safety, association, independence, or status are thwarted is sick just as surely as the man who has rickets. And his sickness will have behavioral consequences. We will be mistaken if we attribute his resultant passivity, his hostility, his refusal to accept responsibility to his inherent "human nature." These forms of behavior are *symptoms* of illness—of deprivation of his social and egoistic needs.

The man whose lower-level needs are satisfied is not motivated to satisfy those needs any longer. For practical purposes they exist no longer. Management often asks, "Why aren't people more productive? We pay good wages, provide good working conditions, have excellent fringe benefits and steady employment. Yet people do not seem to be willing to put forth more than minimum effort."

The fact that management has provided for these physiological and safety needs has shifted the motivational emphasis to the social and perhaps to the egoistic needs. Unless there are opportunities *at work* to satisfy these higher-level needs, people will be deprived, and their behavior will reflect this deprivation. Under such conditions, if management continues to focus its attention on physiological needs, its efforts are bound to be ineffective.

People *will* make insistent demands for more money under these conditions. It becomes more important than ever to buy the material goods and services which can provide limited satisfaction of the thwarted needs. Although money has only limited value in satisfying many higher-level needs, it can become the focus of interest if it is the *only* means available.

THE CARROT-AND-STICK APPROACH

The carrot-and-stick theory of motivation (like Newtonian physical theory) works reasonably well under certain circumstances. The *means* for satisfying man's physiological and (within limits) his safety needs can be provided or withheld by management. Employment itself is such a means, and so are wages, working conditions, and benefits. By these means the individual can be controlled so long as he is struggling for subsistence.

But the carrot-and-stick theory does not work at all once man has reached an adequate subsistence level and is motivated primarily by higher needs. Management cannot provide a man with self-respect, or with the respect of his fellows, or with the satisfaction of needs for self-fulfillment. It can create such conditions that he is encouraged and enabled to seek such satisfactions for *himself,* or it can thwart him by failing to create those conditions.

But this creation of conditions is not "control." It is not a good device for directing behavior. And so management finds itself in an odd position. The high standard of living created by our modern technological know-how provides quite adequately for the satisfaction of physiological and safety needs. The only significant exception is where management practices have not created confidence in a "fair break"—and thus where safety needs are thwarted. But by making possible the satisfaction of low-level needs, management has deprived itself of the ability to use as motivators the devices on which conventional theory has taught it to rely—rewards, promises, incentives, or threats and other coercive devices.

The philosophy of management by direction and control—*regardless of whether it is hard or soft*—is inadequate to motivate because the human needs on which this approach relies are today unimportant motivators of behavior. Direction and control are essentially useless in motivating people whose important needs are social and egoistic. Both the hard and the soft approach fail today because they are simply irrelevant to the situation.

People, deprived of opportunities to satisfy at work the needs which are now important to them, behave exactly as we might predict—with indolence, passivity, resistance to change, lack of responsibility, willingness to follow the demagogue, unreasonable demands for economic benefits. It would seem that we are caught in a web of our own weaving.

A NEW THEORY OF MANAGEMENT

For these and many other reasons, we require a different theory of the task of managing people based on more adequate assumptions about human nature and human motivation. I am going to be so bold as to suggest the broad dimensions of such a theory. Call it "Theory Y," if you will.

1. Management is responsible for organizing the elements of productive enterprise—money, materials, equipment, people—in the interest of economic ends.

2. People are *not* by nature passive or resistant to organizational needs. They have become so as a result of experience in organizations.

3. The motivation, the potential for development, the capacity for assuming responsibility, the readiness to direct behavior toward organizational goals are all present in people. Management does not put them there. It is a responsibility of management to make it possible for people to recognize and develop these human characteristics for themselves.

4. The essential task of management is to arrange organizational conditions and methods of operation so that people can achieve their

own goals *best* by directing *their own* efforts toward organizational objectives.

This is a process primarily of creating opportunities, releasing potential, removing obstacles, encouraging growth, providing guidance. It is what Peter Drucker has called "management by objectives" in contrast to "management by control." It does *not* involve the abdication of management, the absence of leadership, the lowering of standards, or the other characteristics usually associated with the "soft" approach under Theory X.

SOME DIFFICULTIES

It is no more possible to create an organization today which will be a full, effective application of this theory than it was to build an atomic power plant in 1945. There are many formidable obstacles to overcome.

The conditions imposed by conventional organization theory and by the approach of scientific management for the past half century have tied men to limited jobs which do not utilize their capabilities, have discouraged the acceptance of responsibility, have encouraged passivity, have eliminated meaning from work. Man's habits, attitudes, expectations—his whole conception of membership in an industrial organization—have been conditioned by his experience under these circumstances.

People today are accustomed to being directed, manipulated, controlled in industrial organizations and to finding satisfaction for their social, egoistic, and self-fulfillment needs away from the job. This is true of much of management as well as of workers. Genuine "industrial citizenship"—to borrow again a term from Drucker—is a remote and unrealistic idea, the meaning of which has not even been considered by most members of industrial organizations.

Another way of saying this is that Theory X places exclusive reliance upon external control of human behavior, while Theory Y relies heavily on self-control and self-direction. It is worth noting that this difference is the difference between treating people as children and treating them as mature adults. After generations of the former, we cannot expect to shift to the latter overnight.

STEPS IN THE RIGHT DIRECTION

Before we are overwhelmed by the obstacles, let us remember that the application of theory is always slow. Progress is usually achieved in small steps. Some innovative ideas which are entirely consistent with Theory Y are today being applied with some success.

Decentralization and Delegation

These are ways of freeing people from the too-close control of conventional organization, giving them a degree of freedom to direct their own activities, to assume responsibility, and, importantly, to satisfy their egoistic needs. In this connection, the flat organization of Sears, Roebuck and Company provides an interesting example. It forces "management by objectives," since it enlarges the number of people reporting to a manager until he cannot direct and control them in the conventional manner.

Job Enlargement

This concept, pioneered by I.B.M. and Detroit Edison, is quite consistent with Theory Y. It encourages the acceptance of responsibility at the bottom of the organization; it provides opportunities for satisfying social and egoistic needs. In fact, the reorganization of work at the factory level offers one of the more challenging opportunities for innovation consistent with Theory Y.

Participation and Consultative Management

Under proper conditions, participation and consultative management provide encouragement to people to direct their creative energies toward organizational objectives, give them some voice in decisions that affect them, provide significant opportunities for the satisfaction of social and egoistic needs. The Scanlon Plan is the outstanding embodiment of these ideas in practice.

Performance Appraisal

Even a cursory examination of conventional programs of performance appraisal within the ranks of management will reveal how completely consistent they are with Theory X. In fact, most such programs tend to treat the individual as though he were a product under inspection on the assembly line.

A few companies—among them General Mills, Ansul Chemical, and General Electric—have been experimenting with approaches which involve the individual in setting "targets" or objectives *for himself* and in a *self*-evaluation of performance semiannually or annually. Of course, the superior plays an important leadership role in this process—one, in fact, which demands substantially more competence than the conventional approach. The role is, however, considerably more congenial to many managers than the role of "judge" or "inspector" which is usually forced upon them. Above all, the individual is encouraged to take a greater responsibility for planning and appraising his own contribution to organizational objectives; and the accompanying effects on egoistic and self-fulfillment needs are substantial.

APPLYING THE IDEAS

The not infrequent failure of such ideas as these to work as well as expected is often attributable to the fact that a management has "bought the idea" but applied it within the framework of Theory X and its assumptions.

Delegation is not an effective way of exercising management by control. Participation becomes a farce when it is applied as a sales gimmick or a device for kidding people into thinking they are important. Only the management that has confidence in human capacities and is itself directed toward organizational objectives rather than toward the preservation of personal power can grasp the implications of this emerging theory. Such management will find and apply successfully other innovative ideas as we move slowly toward the full implementation of a theory like Y.

THE HUMAN SIDE OF ENTERPRISE

It is quite possible for us to realize substantial improvements in the effectiveness of industrial organizations during the next decade or two. The social sciences can contribute much to such developments; we are only beginning to grasp the implications of the growing body of knowledge in these fields. But if this conviction is to become a reality instead of a pious hope, we will need to view the process much as we view the process of releasing the energy of the atom for constructive human ends—as a slow, costly, sometimes discouraging approach toward a goal which would seem to many to be quite unrealistic.

The ingenuity and the perseverance of industrial management in the pursuit of economic ends have changed many scientific and technological dreams into commonplace realities. It is now becoming clear that the application of these same talents to the human side of enterprise will not only enhance substantially these materialistic achievements, but will bring us one step closer to "the good society."

Managerial Grid

ROBERT R. BLAKE, JANE SRYGLEY MOUTON
and ALVIN C. BIDWELL

The purpose of this article is to compare seven managerial theories in terms of how each deals with (1) organizational needs for production and profit and (2) human needs for mature and healthy relationships.

Five of these seven are shown in the chart, "The Managerial Grid."[1] They are referred to as *country club management, impoverished management, dampened pendulum, team management,* and *task management.* The remaining two are combined forms.

The term *concern for,* as used in the Grid, is a theoretical variable which reflects basic attitudes or styles of control. The term does not necessarily reflect how much production or profit is obtained or the degree to which human needs are met. The horizontal axis of the Grid represents concern for production and profit. The vertical axis represents concern for mature and healthy relations among those engaged in production. Each axis is on a 1 to 9 point scale, with the 1 representing minimum interest or concern and the 9, maximum concern.

In the discussion that follows, the emphasis is on analysis of the corners and mid-point of the Grid, although these extreme positions are rarely found in pure form in the working situation.

In several of the theories, the concerns for production and those for people will be seen in conflict. In three of the theories, the assumption is that attention to needs of individuals does not contribute automatically to production requirements.

Turning again to the chart, note that the lower right-hand corner represents the task management approach (9, 1). Here, primary concern is for output of the enterprise. People are viewed solely in terms of their contribution to production.

This theory is based on the notion that a manager's central responsibilities are to achieve production objectives. Those who are engaged in planning and controlling, in other words, are not those who carry out

---

1. The line of thinking that leads to the generalized version of the Managerial Grid is consistent with work by Rensis Likert, Edwin A. Fleishman, Edwin F. Harris, and Harold E. Burtt, Chris Argyris, and Douglas McGregor.

Reprinted by permission of the Administrative Management Society from the September 1962 *Advanced Management-Office Executive.*

the actions directly. Under the task management theory, a job is a job and someone has to do it. Like machines, people are seen as production tools, obligated to comply when told what they are to do.

At lower levels, concern for production may be thought of as actual output. Concern for production at the managerial levels is just as critical as units of output are among operators. The following kind of advice which was given to managers in the middle levels is characteristic of a task management orientation.

> For an executive to challenge orders, directions and instructions, policy and procedures, rules and regulations, etc., smacks of insubordination or lack of co-operation. It shows his failure to understand the need for decisions at higher levels and for direction and control.

Thoughts, attitudes, and feelings are given little or no attention. When interpersonal conflict arises, the way to handle it (as well as all types of feelings) is to suppress it through disciplinary types of actions. Under the task management theory, if people don't comply after a certain amount of control has been applied, they should be replaced.

THE MANAGERIAL GRID

Concern for People

9 Country Club Management–(1,9)						Team Management–(9,9)		
8 Production is incidental to lack of conflict and						Production is from integration of task		
7 "good fellowship."						and human requirements.		
6					Dampened Pendulum–(5,5) (Middle of the Road) Push			
5 Impoverished Management–(1,1) Effective production					for production but don't go "all out." Give some, but			
4 is unobtainable because people are lazy, apathetic					not all. "Be fair but firm."			
3 and indifferent. Sound and mature relationships						Task Management–(9,1) Men are a commodity just		
2 are difficult to achieve because human						as machines. A manager's responsibility is to plan,		
1 nature's being what it is, conflict is inevitable.						direct and control the work of those subordinate to him.		
1	2	3	4	5	6	7	8	9

Concern for Production

Thus, this theory has been referred to as an impersonal approach to managing.

The task management theory tends to produce unsound relationships among those who should be operating in an interdependent way within the organizational structure. Since Chris Argyris has hammered home the negative consequences of this theory, little more needs to be said here.

Production Incidental to Satisfaction

The country club management theory (see 1,9, upper left-hand corner of the chart) is the reverse of the task management theory in a number of respects. In the former, production is incidental to satisfaction through social relations, good fellowship, and fraternity. Goal of this theory of management is to achieve harmony even though needs for output may suffer as a result. Assumption is that contented people will produce as well as contented cows, if given the chance.

This theory is not well suited to organizations which strive for increased effectiveness. When, because of outside forces, the organization has to increase efficiency, it is frequently unable to respond to the demands. The country club theory does tend to flourish in organizations that approach monopolies and in bureaucratic structures.

Aware of the Need to Be Nice

Under the country club theory, too, executives are aware of the need to be nice. Moreover, the people in the system sense the phony quality in *good* human relations which are *not* related to conditions of work and production.

The be-nice approach leads to few overt production or personnel problems, because conflict is smothered and denied. The manager is seen as a likable fellow, a good Joe, or a big brother. He is prepared to make his subordinates happy, carefree, and satisfied at almost any economic price.

Also, the country club approach is unlikely to achieve any meaningful human relations gains, since conflict and frustration are smoothed over, not dealt with. This is the style which is sometimes called *soft* management, in contrast with *hard* management. Frequently the only alternative seen by hard managers is the country club theory.

The impoverished management theory (1,1) is shown in the lower left corner of the chart. The manager at this position de-emphasizes concerns for production, with just enough being done to get by. He also disregards or diminishes the importance of human relationships. He takes the ostrich approach to feelings—instead of suppressing or denying them, he ignores them.

Within the executive level an impoverished management orientation can be found in circumstances in which a person has been passed by repeatedly. Rather than looking elsewhere, he adjusts to the work setting by giving minimal performance, seeking satisfaction elsewhere.

This managerial style is not so prevalent throughout an entire company. In a competitive economy, a company operated under this style is unlikely to stay in business long. On the other hand, many individuals who manage in the impoverished management style are able to survive in bureaucratic organizations, and in country club managerial structures where the rule is that "no one gets fired."

Three approaches to management consider the task (9,1), the country club (1,9) or the impoverished (1,1) types simultaneously. All stem from the notion that needs of mature individuals and organizational requirements of production oppose each other.

The wide-arc pendulum theory, for example, describes a relationship between the task (9,1) and the country club (1,9) positions as: When management tightens up to get increased output, as often happens under recession pressures, it does so consistently with the task (9,1) attitude. Later, relationships become so disturbed that production suffers. Then management feels forced to ease off and to start being concerned with the thoughts, feelings, and attitudes of people.

Output Pressures Are Lessened

Because of the negative results of the task approach, a swing in the direction of the country club position takes place. Output pressures are lessened to make people feel that management's intentions are good. Thus, the pendulum tends to swing from the one position to the other.

When a degree of confidence in management has been restored among the people, the tightening up occurs again to regain the losses in production suffered during the previous pendulum swing. Cracking down to get efficiency and easing up to restore confidence is the pendulum swing from hard to soft.

Another kind of pendulum swing within an organization is one associated with task management (9,1) pressures for production. In this cycle, as described by Robert L. Katz (1960), top management's plans and commands lead to lower management's reacting in an impoverished manner (1,1), with indifference, apathy, and minimal output.

Tries to Tighten Up on Lower Levels

The failure of middle- and lower-levels of management to respond with concrete contributions to production is followed by top management's redoubling of its efforts to tighten up. Once successful influence from top to middle has been achieved, the middle tries to tighten up on lower levels. Thus the cycle goes from the task, to the impoverished, and back to the task management theory.

In the center of The Managerial Grid is shown the dampened pendulum (5,5) or the middle-of-the-road theory. This theory says, push enough to get acceptable production, but yield to the degree necessary to develop morale. When the happy medium is achieved, don't expect too much production. Recognize that one must be flexible and must give. Under the dampened pendulum theory, it is believed that by clever string-pulling, management can prevent either of the two concerns from blocking the complete attainment of the other.

In a number of respects it would appear that managements which have abandoned the task theory tended over time to slide toward the dampened pendulum position. However, the shift is not a healthy one because the dampened pendulum position retains the theory of work direction contained in the task management position. The shift adds to the theory of human relations of country club management. The dampened pendulum approach does not solve the problem. Rather, a live-and-let-live situation is created under which the real problem is muted.

Paternalistic management pushes for output in a task management way, but in time it recognizes feelings of alienation that separate the workers from the management. Therefore, an additional step is taken to satisfy lower-management levels and workers. Concern for people is expressed through *taking care of them* in a country club management fashion. Organizational members are *given* many fine things—good pay, excellent benefit programs, recreational facilities, retirement programs, and even low-cost housing.

However, these are not given to acknowledge contribution to output. They are given to *buy* subservience. A paternalistic executive retains tight control in work matters, but is benevolent in a personal way. In other words, he treats his junior executives as part of his managerial family. Paternalism is a more or less stable mix of two anchor positions. Although it has failed repeatedly to solve the basic problems of getting production through people, it is still current in managerial thinking.

Accept Conflict as Inevitable

All the managerial styles just described accept conflict between concerns for production and concerns for people as inevitable. Each attempts to deal with the assumed basic incompatibility in a different way. The task management and impoverished management and pendulum theories are one or another in that the emphasis is either on production or on people.

The middle-of-the-road, or dampened pendulum, and the paternalistic modes try to achieve some sort of balance. Under the impoverished management approach, the manager does the minimum. Only under the team approach, description of which follows, is an integration achieved where the goal is production through people.

In the team management position (9,9), the building block in the organization is the team. It is not the individuals on a one-to-one basis, as though isolated from one another.   To a country club style manager, the style of a task manager and that of a team manager seem similar, since both express a high concern for production. However, the way in which production is achieved is vastly different.

A team manager describes his philosophy on work planning in this way:

> When a change is required, I meet with the work group, present the picture, discuss and get reactions and ideas, *build* in their ideas, commitment, and ownership. Together we set up procedures and ground rules and assign individual responsibilities. The work group sets goals and flexible schedules.

Planning, as but one example, is a product of team effort rather than of individual skill. In a well-integrated team operation, all voices carry weight in final positions.

Gaining effective integration among members of multi-level teams is seen as another important task of leadership. Here, joint effort is centered on production, and members share responsibilities for planning, directing, and controlling.

A third key objective of team management is that of linking teams into effective communication and problem-solving systems which have a peer relationship with one another. Union and management or correlated divisions in different departments would be examples.

Knowledge of human relations needed under the team management theory is far greater than most managers possess today. When problems of feelings and emotions arise in the working relationships, the manager who uses the team approach recognizes the problems and confronts them directly. He deals with and works through conflict as it appears.

Morale Achieved Is Task Related

The manager who uses the task management approach finds it difficult to distinguish team management from country club management because both reflect high concern for people. Yet the concern expressed by the country club manager is more in terms of satisfaction based on non-work aspects of the situation, such as good social relations. The team manager seeks to integrate people around production. The morale achieved under team management conditions is task-related.

Also, the manager who uses the team approach must have greater appreciation of and skill in unleashing individual motivation than managers using any other approach. Behavioral science theory and research findings have identified many of the conditions of team management. In addition, the theory and ways of teaching are available for the manager who wants to shift from any of the other approaches to the team situation.

Production Improvement

Many organizational efforts of the past fifteen years have intuitively aimed toward improving the achievement of production through people in a team management approach. Without explicit managerial theory available to guide them, many efforts have been built on trying to shore up bad human relations brought about by the task management approach.

One result has been what is called phony human relations. All too frequently, managers have adopted a managerial strategy in the country club area of The Managerial Grid as a soft approach. They have been led down this path by the assumption that there must be a conflict between the organizational requirements and needs of individuals. Other managers have confused the emphasis on using the team as the building block with that of destroying individual self-expression and freedom.

By now, in a number of instances, managerial effort has successfully employed behavioral science concepts and methods as the basis for moving toward a team managerial orientation. Some have used team training with specific development of The Managerial Grid for setting meaningful organization objectives to which all team members are committed.

Sheds Light on Controversies

Understanding of The Managerial Grid is basic for appreciating present organizational structures and the relationships between organizational and human needs. In addition, the Grid sheds light on many of the day-by-day controversies present in managerial thinking.

Heaviest emphasis here is placed on the team management (9,9) position. Generally, the best long-term production is achieved and sustained when concerns for production and needs of people are integrated in the team direction, regardless of economic conditions.

When managements have tried to move away from the task management anchor position, without behavioral science training, the movement has tended to drift, unwittingly, in the country club direction. The movement frequently stabilizes somewhere around the dampened pendulum (5,5) position, where some push for production is balanced against some concern for people. The major difference between the task management and the dampened pendulum theories is in the increased recognition placed on people. The task management theory of work control is retained, however.

The skills involved in moving toward the team management position are difficult to attain. The theory for integrating effective production through sound human relationships is complex in concept and application. Just as the physical sciences have become the indispensable underpinning of product development and technological innovation, a new era can be seen on the managerial horizon where the behavioral sciences are beginning to undergird the design of production structures.

REFERENCES

Katz, Robert L., "Toward a More Effective Enterprise," *Harvard Business Review* (September-October 1960).

Organizational Climate and Individual Growth

GORDON L. LIPPITT

Mankind's continual search for compatability between his organized relationships and individual growth is being constantly explored by social scientists and practitioners. That kind of organizational system which manifested itself early in history frequently exhibited a high degree of control by managerial coercion that is no longer meeting the needs of today's organized society or the needs of the individuals in it. The rapid changes in society have brought with them changes in organizational system, and need for even greater change. One of the most apparent changes has been that of control through benevolence and persuasion. Whether viewed from the paternalism of large organizations in the thirties in the United States, or the "sell-the-other-fellow" approach used by sales and pseudo-human relations advocates, such an approach has been very much in evidence in the leadership of industrial, governmental, social, and welfare organizations. In fact, some writers give a great deal of credence to this approach to leadership.

There is, however, a third way by which influence can be manifested in organizational life. This has been referred to as the "helping" approach in work relations, and finds itself in existence where one finds the consultative organizational system at work. This kind of influence on others, as expressed by McGregor [p. 19] as "typified by the exceptionally sophisticated and sensitive individual in any professional field, does not consist in playing God with the client, but in placing the professional's knowledge and skill at the client's disposal. It is a particularly important form of social influence which is not at all well understood." The effects of the coercive, benevolent or consultative ways of influencing others are measured by the degree to which they help change the ability of persons to achieve goals and meet evident needs. In an organization, the ability of others to help me meet my needs is a very important dimension in the acceptance of the method of influence.

Reprinted by permission from the Sept.-Oct., 1960, issue of *Personnel Administration*, copyright 1960, Society for Personnel Administration, 485-87 National Press Building, 14th and F Streets, N.W., Washington, D.C. 20004.

Man's needs differ, collectively or individually, at any particular time. Nevertheless, certain levels of needs have been determined as common to man's life experience. Maslow organizes man's needs into a "hierarchy of needs." At the fundamental level of man's existence one finds the *physical needs*. Food, water, and air form the basic elements of life itself. One does not search for much else in life when these elements are not provided. Historically, even the earliest coercive examples of industrialized civilization helped man to meet these basic life needs.

At the next level of need, however, we have the basic *social needs* of man. Needs for affection, belonging, achievement, and recognition a⋅ ⋅ part of the motivational system of each individual. The historical sh ⋅ft in organizational influence patterns from autocratic (coercive) systems to benevolent (paternalistic) systems was brought to the fore by the increasing standard of living in which man's physical needs were being met, and he was now wanting and expecting more from his work relations. The provision, for workers, employees, clients, of swimming-pools, retirement benefits, annual picnics, and similar activities has been a "reaching-out" by the organization to meet the "needs" of the workers. Such endeavors were motivated by multiple causes—desire by management for higher production, to combat increased unionization, to help the workers enjoy life more adequately, to meet the requirements of government regulations, and to help the increasing size of organizations to be able to function effectively.

These endeavors to meet some of the social needs of individuals through benevolent patterns of activity and leadership have been partially successful. Certain improved working conditions, closer relationships with the workers, more effective controls, and less frustration have resulted from the benevolent system. On the other hand, the paternalism implicit in this approach to relations with others creates dependence, does not account for man's change and growth, and creates a tension between the highest level of man's needs and the organization at work.

Argyris points out some significant incompatabilities between individual personality growth and the organizational system. As he states it: "If the principles of formal organization are used as ideally defined, then the employees will tend to work in an environment where (1) they are provided minimal control over their work-a-day world, (2) they are expected to be passive, dependent, subordinate, (3) they are expected to have a short-time perspective, (4) they are induced to perfect and value the frequent use of a few superficial abilities, and (5) they are expected to produce under conditions leading to psychological failure." Argyris, in describing his maturation of personality, refers to the fact that as an individual grows from childhood to adulthood he moves from passivity to a more active social role, from dependence on his environment to independence, from specialized functioning to flexibility, and from a subordinate to a supraordinate position in life.

The concept and practices in many organizations are such as to delimit the opportunity for individual growth. Even organizations with lofty ideals and purposes—such as church, health, welfare, and educational systems—while giving "lip service" to the practice of something they refer to as "democratic administration," actually execute only the rather obvious, good-intentioned kind of concern for others that may develop dependency and warmth but limits the individual's growth to achieve his highest needs.

Let us examine these needs at the top of man's "hierarchy of needs."

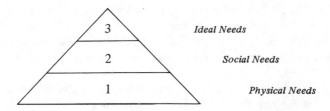

A number of social scientists have listed the concept of self-actualization as one of man's highest needs. In the writings of Jung, Rogers, Maslow, and Allport we find this concept discussed. Maslow (1950), in his interviews of selected subjects, found self-actualizing persons to be characterized by the following:

1. Efficient perception of reality and comfortable with reality
2. Acceptance of self, others, and nature
3. Spontaneity
4. Problem-centered
5. Quality of detachment
6. Autonomy, independence from culture and environment
7. Continual freshness of appreciation
8. Effective in interpersonal relations
9. "Gemeinschaftsgefuhl" (empathy for mankind)

Such persons are idiosyncratic in the expression of themselves, "for self-actualization is actualization of a self, and no two selves are altogether alike." Other writers have referred to the concept of self-fulfillment as one of the highest goals of man. These two concepts would seem to be closely linked.

An additional concept to which much attention has been given is the *creative ability* of man. In today's organization we need persons who will create new methods, new products, new ideas, and new solutions. Studies of originality have been undertaken in the past few years. One (1958) shows that "originality results from divergent thinking; it means getting out of a mental rut and looking at things in a new and different way. This kind of thinking occurs at the discovery phase, the insight phase, the inventive phase." Such creativity is essential for social growth and problem solving. Most organizations have more creative talent than they are using effectively. In many organizations the need and ability for creativity are stifled by the size of the organization, control factors in organization programs, and the pattern of leadership being manifested in the leadership of others.

The third of man's highest needs is his *sense of values.* The need for man to find meaning out of existence, to develop a philosophy of life, to see the world as something of and beyond himself, and to give an expression of faith in something meaningful, is one of the great potentials of man.

If an individual is primarily concerned with his physical needs, it is difficult for him to reach for this "higher" man. It would seem, however, that in most organizations, to meet the challenge of a changing society will require the organization's functioning in such a way as to encourage the individual to achieve his highest goals and in so doing contribute to the goals of the organization.

This does not mean that individuals shall function in a completely "free" way, unfrustrated, and non-conforming. All of life requires the mutual adjustment amongst law, order, and freedom. The concept of an organizational climate to provide growth opportunities for the individual does not imply that *all* of man's needs shall or can be met in the life of work. It does imply, however, that organizational leaders and members need to search and work diligently for those kinds of human relationships that will provide the best possible opportunities for an individual to reach his full potential.

Consultative System Defined

What is meant by this concept of the consultative relationship in the organization? A number of scholars have contributed to the concept. Bennis (1959) has dealt with some of the characteristics, and in a recent program of the NTL Institute the staff further conceptualized some of the differences between the consultative versus the authoritarian systems.

1. *In the consultative system the organization is viewed as an organism—not as a machine.*

Implicit in this characteristic is the reality that an organism, whether singular or multiple, must adapt to exist. It must change its functioning to meet new needs. In this context, the organization is seen not just as a formal structure, but as a living, flexible, changing, and complex network of relationships among people to achieve both individual and organizational goals.

2. *Provision is made in the organization for relevant decision making by the members of the organization as over against centralized decision-making.*

The process of involving persons in the decisions which they will implement is an important aspect of a consultative process. Obviously, all persons will not be involved in every decision, even though effective communication is one level of involvement. The degree of participation will depend on forces in the situation, forces in the leader, and forces in the subordinate, or member, groups. Those forces will provide guidelines for the degree to which an organization leader involves members in decision making that is relevant to their competency, experience, and meets the leader pattern of response to a particular situation (Schmidt & Tannenbaum, 1958).

3. *Mutual confidence is the basis for cooperation rather than authority-obedience basis.*

A consultative relationship is built upon the confidence persons have in one another's integrity, goal orientation, and commitment to a problem-solving process. Such confidence does not need to depend upon authority or status in the organization for its success.

4. *Face-to-face groups are the units of organization rather than persons seen as individuals in assigned "places" in the organization.*

Recent research has given a great deal of recognition to the importance of the group as a functional unit in the organization. This has been made particularly evident from the productivity and morale studies research. Likert (1956), comments thus on the importance of organizational work units [p. 7]:

Each of us seeks to satisfy our desire for a sense of personal worth and importance primarily by the response we get from people we are close to, in whom we are interested, and whose approval and support we are eager to have. The face-to-face groups with whom we spend the bulk of our time are, consequently, the most important to us. Our work group is one of the most important of our face-to-face groups and one from which we are particularly eager to derive a sense of personal worth.

Studies in the field of psychology, sociology, and psychiatry reinforce this statement. It clearly indicates that if an organization is to make the maximum use of the human resources and meet the highest level of man's needs it will best come to function in situations where the individual relates effectively in those organizational groups in which he is a member and those in which he is a leader. Such well-knit and effective face-to-face work units will develop out of conditions which provide the consultative relationship between leader and members.

Such emphasis on the group is an aid to individual growth and development (Bradford & Lippitt, 1954).

Social science, by discovering what happens in group situations and what causes different individual behavior, and by contributing to the recent growing movement of leadership and membership training, has aided materially in freeing and developing the individual, rather than submerging him in the group [p. 487].

To develop such group relations is one of the goals in the consultative organizational process.

5. *Leadership is person-centered as over against task-centered.*

Many factors in the traditional organizational pattern cause the persons in an organization to be seen as the "doers of work." The task is the important concern of the supervisor. In the consultative approach, the supervisor sees his major responsibility as the development of others to adult patterns of self-control, developing effective work-group functioning, and to focus on the "person-centered" needs so as to "release" the potential of others. Fortunately, this kind of supervision fits the job to the person, rather than fitting a person to a job description.

In the area of performance improvement, the supervisor will make possible opportunities for the person to set his own "targets" for good achievement, work standards, and personal growth. Through the "target-setting" type of experience the individual meets his task goals in terms of his own drives, standards, and needs.

6. *There is a two-way flow of communication with appropriate feedback opportunities as over against a one-way pattern of communication.*

In the assumptions underlying the consultative system is the importance of the two-way process of communication which is found in both the formal and informal aspect of organization life. Opportunities to see oneself and the effect of one's supervision are a prime necessity of effective organizational accomplishment. The need for a "feedback" communication system is essential.

Engineers have built into guided missiles a mechanism that enables the missile to guide or steer itself. This mechanism, called a feedback mechanism, collects information showing how far the missile is off the target. This information then enables the feedback mechanism automatically to change or correct the flight of the missile so that it gets back on the target . . .

Each individual and group needs a feedback process. Each individual needs to get accurate information about the difference between what he is trying to do and how well he is doing it. He needs to be able to use this information to correct or change his action. Then, basically, he is steering himself.(Bradford, 1952).

An organization, through the policies, philosophy, and practice of its management, can develop the climate of acceptance of the appropriate skills to permit this level of interpersonal communication.

Implications for the Organization

1. *To develop clearly the objectives of the organization so that standards of work relations can be relevant to these objectives.*

A number of organizational theorists have written recently in the literature about "management by objective." Such clear goals for the organization make it possible for supervisor-subordinate relationships to develop in such a way that the goals of the individual may be seen in terms of the organizational goals. The degree of incompatability between these two sets of goals will be mainly affected by the kinds of relationships between supervisor and subordinate.

2. *Supervisory training at all levels of management that focuses on the ability of supervisors to develop a collaborative relationship with their supervisors, peers, and subordinates.*

In the multiple roles in which the supervisor finds himself, he will recognize the necessity not only to take into account factors of interdependence, but the reality of the task considerations. The supervisor is a "helper, trainer, consultant, and coordinator; and . . . the arm of reality, a person with power over a subordinate."[1] To make meaningful the power-and-growth role, the supervisor must exercise his many

1. Bennis, W. G. "Leadership Theory and Administrative Behavior; The Problem of Authority," *Administrative Science Quarterly,* Vol. 4, No. 3, Dec., 1959, p. 6.

roles in a sensitive, insightful, and diagnostic manner. Such skills should be in the focus of an enlightened supervisory-training program.

3. *To develop a performance-improvement process along with appraisal and manpower inventory procedures that are consistent with the organization's philosophy and training program.*

In many instances, performance appraisal is combined or confused with performance improvement. The concept of continued growth by the individual on the job is the responsibility of each individual and of the supervisor. If a consultative organizational system is to work, there must be present opportunities for individuals in the organization to set their performance standards and, in relationship with others, to try to achieve, revise, and secure "feedback" on the objectives so set. This two-person continued growth is separate from the process of appraisal by superiors and the need for organizational management to have an inventory of persons to fill positions from within the organization.

The goals of an organization, the personnel (rewards system) policy, and training programs of the organization must have common understanding and commitment to the consultative organizational process if it is to work effectively and be the direction in which an organization is developing.

Implications for the Individual

The concept of the consultative organizational system has the following implications for the individual in the organization:

1. *To further an increased awareness of one's own behavior and one's effect on others.*

In whatever way the individual finds possible, he should, through training, through additional educational opportunities, and through opportunities to assess himself, increase his own self-insight. In this way, the individual is more capable of relating himself effectively with others.

2. *To examine one's attitudes and assumptions as they affect one's job performance and relationships.*

Part of one's personal growth is the need to test the assumptions we make about other individuals. Our behavior is determined by these assumptions. If we assume that a person is lazy and "cutting corners," we will behave accordingly in our relationship with that person. If, on the other hand, our assumption about another person is conditioned by our perception of him as "eager, makes mistakes but learns from them, and is willing to listen," then our relationship will be so conditioned. These assumptions about others are closely related to one's own value system.

3. *To increase one's knowledge of persons, work groups, and industrial organizations.*

The "knowledge lag" between what is known about human behavior and the practitioner's application is considerable. New research has confirmed some old truths of human behavior, as well as indicated new approaches to effective resolution of conflict and decision making. The new research in the behavioral sciences related to the individual, groups, organizational life, and community dynamics, as now reported and written in readily available resources, indicates that today's individual can improve his understanding of this knowledge through a variety of learning opportunities.

4. *To increase one's skill in diagnosing human situations.*

The ability of an individual to diagnose the causes of situations rather than to deal only at the symptomatic level, is an area of growth for an individual to perform in a helping role with others. The ability to look "beneath the surface" and probe for underlying causes in the work situation is essential to effective relationships with others. One of the skills explicit in this regard is the skill to *listen* to other persons. The biggest block to personal communication is man's inability to listen intelligently, understandingly, and skillfully to another person. This deficiency in the modern world is widespread and appalling. This skill of listening is but one of several ways by which the individual becomes more diagnostic in his relationship with others.

5. *To envision one's understanding and skill relative to continuing social change and the process of change.*

While it is necessary for all leaders to understand the phenomena of change which are inevitable and universal, it is also important that leaders who are to function in a "helping" fashion with others understand the phenomena of *planned change*, that is, change which derives from a purposeful decision to effect improvement in a personality system or social system and which is achieved with the help of professional guidance.

Such change, if it is not to be manipulative, results in A moving toward A's goals, and, in so doing, helping B to move toward B's goals. Such a cooperative relationship situation is one in which effective understanding of resistance to change is taken into account through proper goal-setting, involvement, alternative-testing, participative decision making, and attention to reassessment of the change by the persons initiating the change and receiving it. Such skills are a part of the helping relationship.

Summary

The author does not intend to indicate that the authoritative system and consultative system are in reality "alternatives." The consultative system works only so long as a combination of self-control, member responsibility, and scientific method are ingredients of decision-making. When and if these break down, the authority structure is brought into action. As implied earlier in this article, man's physical and social needs must be met before we can reach those levels of functioning that will release the fullest of man's potential. In a society where we have reached the highest standard of living in history, it seems appropriate that this higher level of organizational functioning is realistic and possible. If we affirm that the strength of democracy is directly proportioned to the practice of it by its citizen leaders, then we must search for those kinds of leadership behavior and organizational climate that can provide for this optimum of individual growth while attaining the objectives of organized man.

REFERENCES

Argyris, C., "The Individual and Organization: Some Problems of Mutual Adjustment," *Administrative Science Quarterly*, Vol. II, No. I, 1957.

Bennis, W. G., "Leadership Theory and Administrative Behavior: The Problem of Authority," *Administrative Science Quarterly*, Vol. 4, No. 3, Dec., 1959.

Bradford, L. P., "A Fundamental of Education," *Adult Education*, Vol. 11, No. 4, April 1952.

Bradford, L. P., and Lippitt, G., "The Individual Counts in Effective Group Relations," *NEA Journal*, Nov. 1954.

"Creativity and Conformity: A Problem for Organizations," *The Foundation for Research on Human Behavior*, 1958.

Likert, R., "Developing Patterns of Management," *American Management Association*, No. 182, 1956.

Maslow, A. H., *Motivation and Personality*, (New York: Harper, 1954).

McGregor, D. *The Human Side of Enterprise*, McGraw-Hill Book Company, 1960.

Schmidt, W., and Tannenbaum, R., "Choosing a Leadership Pattern," *Harvard Business Review*, 1958.

Organizational Revitalization

WARREN G. BENNIS

Many years ago, in downtown Boston, a foreign visitor walked up to an American sailor and asked why the ships of his country were built to last only a short time. In the words of the foreign tourist,

The sailor answered without hesitation that the art of navigation is making such rapid progress that the finest ship would become obsolete if it lasted beyond a few years. In these words, which fell accidentally from an uneducated man, I began to recognize the general and systematic idea upon which your great people direct all their concerns.

This shrewd observer of American morals and manners was Alexis de Tocqueville, and the year was 1835. In that brief exchange, he caught the central theme of our country, its preoccupation, its *obsession with change*. This central theme has persisted, but one thing is new since de Tocqueville's time—the *prevalence of newness*, the changing scale and scope of change itself, so that, as Oppenheimer said, ". . . the world alters as we walk in it, so that the years of man's life measure not some small growth, or rearrangement, or moderation of what was learned in childhood, but a great upheaval." [1]

Numbers have a magic all their own. Take population. In 1789, when George Washington was inaugurated, American society comprised fewer than 4,000,000 people, of whom 750,000 were Negroes. Few people lived in cities; New York, then the capitol, had a population of 33,000. In all, 200,000 people lived in what were then defined as "urban areas"—places with more than 2,500 inhabitants. By way of comparison, in the past ten years, the population of Los Angeles increased by 2,375,000, almost equal the population of present-day Boston.

In July 1964, the population of the United States was about 192 million, and the United States Census Bureau estimates that population in 1975 will be between 226 and 235 million; by 1980 population will be between 246 and 260 million. World population was over 3 billion in 1964. If fertility remains at present levels until 1975 and then begins to

1. Oppenheimer, J. R., "Prospects in the Arts and Sciences," *Perspectives U.S.A.*, Spring 1955, pp. 10, 11.

decline, the population of the world will reach 4 billion in 1977, 5 billion by about 1990.

In 1960, when President Kennedy was elected, more than half of all Americans alive were over thirty-three years old, and most had received their formative experiences during the Great Depression. By 1970, only ten years later, more than half of all Americans alive will be under twenty-five and will have been born after World War II. In one short decade, the mid-age of the United States will have dropped by a full eight years—the sharpest such age drop recorded in history.

Observe the changes taking place in education. Thirty years ago, only one out of every eight Americans at work had been to high school. Today four out of five attend high school. Thirty years ago, only 4 per cent or less of the population attended college and today the figure is around 35 per cent, in cities about 50 per cent.

We are all aware of the momentous social change of the Scientific Revolution—moving like a juggernaut, transforming or ossifying everything in its path. But its magnitude, its scale, and its accelerating rate (to say nothing of its consequences) are truly staggering. By 1980 it will cut an even wider path and require an even wider berth: In that year, the federal government will spend close to 35 billion for research and development, 10 billion for arms and arms control, 7 billion for basic research, and 18 billion on vast civilian welfare programs and new technology.

"Everything nailed down is coming loose," an historian said recently, and it does seem that no exaggeration, no hyperbole, no outrage can realistically convey the extent and pace which modernization involves. It takes only a year or two for the exaggerations to come true. Nothing will remain in the next ten years—or there will be twice as much of it.

It is to our credit that the pseudo-horror stories and futuristic fantasies about accelerations of the rate of change of obsolescence, technology, and science have failed to deter our complusive desire to invent, to overthrow, and to upset inherited patterns and comfort in the security of the future.

We can all feel the impact of overwhelming numbers and social changes on the job, in the school, in the neighborhood, in our professions, in our everyday lives. President Lyndon Johnson said recently, "We want change. We want progress. We want it both at home and abroad—and we aim to get it!" I think he has it.

How will these changes taking place in our society influence human organizations? First, it might be useful to describe the dominant form of human organization employed throughout the industrial world. We spend all of our working day in it and a great deal of our nonworking day. It is a unique and extremely durable social arrangement called "bureaucracy." I use this term "bureaucracy" not as a swear word about those "guys in Washington" or as a metaphor *a la* Kafka which conjures up an image of red tape or faceless and despairing masses standing in endless queues.

Bureaucracy, as I use the term, is a social invention, perfected during the industrial revolution to organize and direct the activities of the business firm. But it is also today the prevailing and supreme type of organization wherever people direct concerted effort toward the achievement of some goal. This holds for university systems, for hospitals, for large voluntary organizations, for governmental organizations, and so on.

Corsica, according to Gibbon, is much easier to deplore then to describe. The same holds true for bureaucracy. Basically, bureaucracy is a social invention which relies exclusively on the power to influence through rules, reason, and the law. Max Weber, the German sociologist who developed the theory of bureaucracy around the turn of the century, once described bureaucracy as a social machine:

. . . . (bureaucracy is like) a modern judge who is a vending machine into which the pleadings are inserted together with the fee and which then disgorges the judgment together with its reasons mechanically derived from the code. [2]

The bureaucratic "machine model" Weber outlined was developed as a reaction against the personal subjugation, nepotism, cruelty, and capricious and subjective judgments which passed for managerial practices in the early days of the industrial revolution. The true hope for man, it was thought, lay in his ability to rationalize, to calculate, and to use his head as well as his hands and heart. Bureaucracy emerged out of the need for more predictability, order, and precision. It was an organization ideally suited to the values of the Victorian Empire.

Most students of organizations would say that the anatomy of bureaucracy consists of the following "organs":

- A division of labor based on functional specialization.
- A well-defined hierarchy of authority.
- A system of procedures and rules for dealing with all contingencies relating to work activities.
- Impersonality of interpersonal relations.
- Promotion and selection based on technical competence—the pyramidal arrangement we see on most organizational charts.

2. Bendix, R., *Max Weber: An Intellectual Portrait*. Doubleday & Co., Inc., Garden City, N.Y., 1960.

It is my premise that the bureaucratic form of organization is out of joint with contemporary realities, that new shapes, patterns, and models are emerging which promise drastic changes in the conduct of the corporation and of managerial practices in general. In the next twenty-five to fifty years, we should witness, and participate in, the end of bureaucracy as we know it and the rise of new social systems better suited to twentieth-century industrialization.

I think every age develops an organizational form appropriate to its genius. This is my personal vision of these coming events and of the potentialities of new forms of organization, beyond bureaucracy.

Social Changes

I see two main reasons for the changes in organizational life. One has been implied earlier in terms of the changes taking place in society, commonly referred to as the population and knowledge explosions.

The other is more subtle and muted, perhaps less significant, but for me, profoundly exciting. I have no easy name for it nor is it easy to designate. It has to do with man's historical quest for self-awareness, for using reason to achieve and stretch his potentialities—his possibilities. This deliberate self-analysis has spread to large and more complex social systems—to organizations. There has been a dramatic upsurge of this spirit of inquiry over the past two decades. At new depths and over a wider range of affairs, organizations are opening their operations to self-inquiry and analysis. This really involves two parallel shifts in values and outlooks, between the men who make history and the men who make knowledge. One change is the scientist's realization of his affinity with men of affairs and the other is the latter's receptivity and new-found respect for men of knowledge.

I am calling this new development *organizational revitalization*, a complex social process which involves a deliberate and self-conscious examination of organizational behavior and a collaborative relationship between managers and scientists to improve performance.

For many this new form of collaboration may be taken for granted. I have simply regarded reciprocity between the academician and the manager as inevitable and natural. But I can assure you that this development is unprecedented, that never before in history, in any society, has man in his organizational context so willingly searched, scrutinized, examined, inspected, or contemplated—for meaning, for purpose, for improvement.

This shift in outlook has taken a good deal of courage from both partners in this encounter. For the manager, he has had to shake off old prejudices about "eggheads" and "long-hair" intellectuals. More important, the manager has had to make himself and his organization vulnerable and receptive to external sources and to new, unexpected, even unwanted, information. The academician has had to shed some of his natural hesitancies. Scholarly conservatism is admirable except to hide behind, and for a long time caution was a defense against reality.

It might be useful to dwell a bit longer on the role of academic man and his growing involvement with social action, using the field of management education as a case in point. Until recently, the field of business was unknown to, or snubbed by, the academic establishment. There, management education and research were at best regarded with dark suspicion as if contact with the world of reality—particularly monetary reality—was equivalent to a dreadful form of pollution.

In fact, historically, academic man has taken one of two stances toward "The Establishment," **any** establishment: that of a rebellious critic or of a withdrawn snob. The stance of the rebel is currently popular. Witness the proliferation of such paperback titles as: *The Power Elite, The Lonely Crowd, The Organization Man, Hidden Persuaders, Tyranny of Testing, Mass Leisure, Exurbanites, Life and Death of Great American Cities, American Way of Death, Compulsory Miseducation, Status Seekers, Growing Up Absurd, Paper Economy, Silent Spring, Child Worshippers, Affluent Society,* and *Depleted Society.*

The withdrawn stance can still be observed in some of our American universities, but less so these days. However, it continues to be the prevailing attitude in many European universities. There, the universities seem intent on preserving the monastic ethos of their medieval origins, offering a false but lulling security to their inmates, and sapping the curriculum of virility and relevance. Max Beerbohm's whimsical and idyllic fantasy of Oxford, *Zuleika Dobson*, dramatizes this:

> It is the mild, miasmal air, not less than the grey beauty and the gravity of the buildings that has helped Oxford to produce, and foster, eternally, her peculiar race of artist-scholars, scholar-artists. . . . The buildings and their traditions keep astir in his mind whatsoever is gracious; the climate enfolding and enfeebling him, lulling him, keeps him careless of the sharp, harsh exigent realities of the outer world. These realities may be seen by him. . . . But they cannot fire him. Oxford is too damp for that.

"Adorable dreamer," said Matthew Arnold in his valedictory to Oxford:

> Adorable dreamer, whose heart has been so romantic! who has given thyself so prodigally, given thyself to sides and to heroes not mine, only never to the

Philistine! . . . what teacher could ever so save us from that bondage to which we are all prone . . . the bondage of what binds us all, the narrow, the mundane, the merely practical.

The intellectual and the manager have only recently come out of hiding and recognized the enormous possibilities of joint ventures. Remember that the idea of the professional school is new, even in the case of the venerable threesome—law, medicine, and engineering—to say nothing of the recent upstarts like business and public administration. It is as new as the institutionalization of science itself, say, around fifty years. And even today, this change is not greeted with unmixed joy. Colin Clark, the economist, writing in a recent issue of the magazine *Encounter,* referred to the "dreadful suggestion that Oxford ought to have a business school."

It is probably true that in the United States we have had a more pragmatic attitude toward knowledge than anywhere else. Many observers have been impressed with the disdain European intellectuals seem to show for practical matters. Even in Russia, where one would least expect it, there is little interest in the "merely useful." Harrison Salisbury, the New York *Times* Soviet expert, was struck during his recent travels by the almost total absence of liaison between research and practical application. He saw only one agricultural experimental station on the American model. There, professors were working in the fields and told him, "People call us Americans."

There may not be many American professors working in the fields, but they can be found, when not waiting in airports, almost everywhere else: in factories, in government, in less advanced countries, and more recently, in backward areas of our own country, in mental hospitals, in the State Department, in practically all the institutional crevices Ph.D. candidates can worm their way into. They are advising, counselling, researching, recruiting, interpreting, developing, consulting, training, and working for the widest variety of clients imaginable. This is not to say that the deep ambivalence which some Americans hold toward the intellectual has disappeared, but it does indicate that academic man has become more committed to action, in greater numbers, with more diligence, and with higher aspirations than at any other time in history.

Indeed, Fritz Machlup, the economist, has coined a new economic category called the "knowledge industry," which, he claims, accounts for 29 per cent of the Gross National Product. And Clark Kerr, the President of the University of California, said not too long ago:

What the railroads did for the seccød half of the last century and the automobile did for the first half of this century may be done for the second half of this century by the knowledge industry: that is, to serve as the focal point of national growth. And the university is at the center of the knowledge process.[3]

Change in Philosophy

I will now turn to my main theme and put the foregoing remarks about the reciprocity between action and knowledge into the perspective of changing organizations. Consider some of the relatively recent research and theory concerning the human side of enterprise which have made such a solid impact on management thinking and particularly upon the moral imperatives which guide managerial action. I will be deliberately sweeping in summarizing these changes as much to hide my surprise as to cover a lot of ground quickly. (I can be personal about this. I remember sitting in Douglas McGregor's class some seven years ago when he first presented his new theories, and the sharp antagonism his Theory X and Theory Y analysis provoked. Today most take these ideas as self-evident.)

It seems to me that we have seen, over the past decase, a fundamental change in the basic philosophy which underlies managerial behavior, reflected most of all in the following three areas:

• A new concept of *man*, based on increased knowledge of his complex and shifting needs, which replaces the oversimplified, innocent push-botton idea of man.

• A new concept of *power*, based on collaboration and reason, which replaces a model of power based on coercion and fear.

• A new concept of *organizational values*, based on humanistic-democratic ideals, which replaces the depersonalized mechanistic value system of bureaucracy.

I do not want to overstate the case. I do not mean that these transformations of man, power, and organizational values are fully accepted or even understood, to say nothing of implemented, in day-to-day affairs. These changes may be light years away from actual adoption. I do mean that they have gained wide intellectual acceptance in enlightened management quarters, that they have caused a terrific amount of rethinking and searching behavior on the part of many organizations, and that they have been used as a basis for policy formulation by many large-scale organizations.

All the changes affecting organizations, both from the behavioral sciences and trends in our society, are summarized in the box. These problems (or predicaments) emerge basically from twentieth-century changes, primarily the growth of science and education, the separation

3. Kerr, Clark, *The Uses of the University*. Harvard University Press, Cambridge, Mass., 1963.

of power from property, the correlated emergence of the professional manager, and other kinds of changes. The bureaucratic mechanism, so capable of coordinating men and power in a stable society of routine tasks, cannot cope with contemporary realities. The table shows five major categories, which I visualize as the core tasks confronting the manager in coordinating the human side of enterprise.

1. The problem of *integration* grows out of our "consensual society," where personal attachments play a great part, where the individual is appreciated, and where there is concern for his well-being, not just in a veterinary-hygiene sense, but as a moral, integrated personality.

2. The problem of *social influence* is essentially the problem of power, and leadership studies and practices reveal not only an ethical component but an effectiveness component: People tend to work more efficiently and with more commitment when they have a part in determining their own fate and a stake in problem solving.

3. The problem of *collaboration* grows out of the same social processes of conflict, stereotyping, and centrifugal forces, which inhere in and divide nations and communities. They also employ the same furtive, often fruitless, always crippling mechanisms of conflict resolution: avoidance or suppression, annihilation of the weaker party by the stronger, sterile compromises, and unstable collusions and coalitions. Particularly as organizations become more complex, they fragment and divide, building tribal patterns and symbolic codes which often work to exclude others (secrets and noxious jargon, for example) and on occasion to exploit difference for inward, and always fragile, harmony. Some large organizations, in fact, can be understood only through an analysis of their cabals, cliques, and satellites, their tactics resembling a sophisticated form of guerrilla warfare, and a venture into adjacent spheres of interest is taken under cover of darkness and fear of ambush.

The university, for example, is a wondrous place for these highly advanced battle techniques, far over-shadowing the business field in the use of subterfuge and sabotage. Quite often a university becomes a loose collection of competing departments, schools, and institutes, largely noncommunicating because of the multiplicity of specialist jargons and interests and held together chiefly, as Robert Hutchins once said, by a central heating system or, as Clark Kerr amended, by questions of what to do about the parking problem.

4. The real *coup de grace* to bureaucracy has come as much from our turbulent environment as from its incorrect assumptions about human behavior. The *pyramidal structure of bureaucracy*, where power was concentrated at the top—perhaps by one person or a group who

had the knowledge and resources to control the entire enterprise—seemed perfect to "run a railroad." And undoubtedly, for tasks like building railroads—the routinized tasks of the nineteenth and early twentieth centuries—bureaucracy was and is an eminently suitable social arrangement.

Nowadays, primarily because of the growth of science, technology, and research and development activities, the organizational environment of the firm is rapidly changing. Instead of a placid and predictable environment, today it is turbulent. There is a deepening interdependence among the economic and other facets of society. This means that economic organizations are increasingly enmeshed in legislation and public policy. Put more simply, it means that government will be in almost everything more of the time. It might also mean (and this is radical) that maximizing cooperation rather than competition between firms—particularly if their fates are correlated—may become a reality.

5. Finally, the problem of *revitalization*: Alfred North Whitehead sets the problem neatly before us: "The art of free society consists first in the maintenance of the symbolic code, and secondly, in the fearlessness of revision. . . . Those societies which cannot combine reverence to their symbols with freedom of revision must ultimately decay."

Organizations, as well as societies, must be concerned with those social conditions that engender buoyancy, resilience, and a fearlessness of revision. Growth and decay emerge as the penultimate problem in contemporary society where the environment is turbulent and uncertain.

Forecast of the future

A forecast falls somewhere between a prediction and a prophecy. It lacks the divine guidance of the latter and the empirical foundation of the former. On thin empirical ice, I want to set forth some of the conditions that I believe will dictate organizational life in the next twenty-five to fifty years.

Those factors already mentioned in the environment will continue in force and increase. Rapid technological change and diversification will lead to interpenetration of the government—its legal and economic policies—with business. Partnerships between business and government will be typical. Because of the immensity and expense of the projects, there will be fewer identical units competing for the same buyers and sellers. The three main features of the environment will be *interdependence* rather than competition, *turbulence* rather than steadiness, and *large-scale* rather than small-scale enterprises.

The Knowledge Industry

The most distinctive characteristic of our society is, and will become even more so, its *education*. Peter Drucker calls us the "educated society," and for good reason: Within fifteen years, two-thirds of our population living in metropolitan areas will have attended college. Adult education is growing even faster. It is now almost routine for the experienced physician, engineer, and executive to go back to school for advanced training every two or three years. Some fifty universities, in addition to a dozen large corporations, offer advanced management courses to successful men in the middle and upper ranks of business. Before World War II, only two such programs existed, both new, and struggling to get students.

All of this education is not just "nice," but necessary. For, as Secretary of Labor Wirtz recently pointed out, computers can do the work of most high school graduates—cheaper and more effectively. Fifty years ago, education used to be regarded as "nonwork" and intellectuals on the payroll (and many staff workers) were considered "overhead." Today the survival of the firm depends more than ever before on the proper exploitation of brain power.

The Working Atmosphere

One other characteristic of the population which will aid our understanding of organizations of the future is increasing *job mobility*. The lowered expense and ease of transportation, coupled with the real needs of a dynamic environment, will change drastically the idea of "owning" a job—or "having roots," for that matter. Participants will be shifted from job to job and even employer to employer with little concern for roots and homestead.

The increased level of education and mobility will change our *work values*. People will be more intellectually committed to their jobs and will probably require more involvement, participation, and autonomy in their work.

Also people will be more "other directed"; taking cues for their norms and values from their immediate environment more than from tradition. We will tend to rely more heavily on temporary social arrangements, on our immediate and constantly changing colleagues. We will tend to be more concerned and involved with relationships rather than with relatives.

The *tasks of the firm* will be more technical, complicated, and un-programmed. They will rely more on the intellect than muscle. And they will be too complicated for one person to comprehend, to say nothing of control. Essentially, they will call for the collaboration of specialists in a project or team form of organization.

A Structure of Goals

There will be a *complication of goals*. Business will increasingly con-cern itself with its adaptive or innovative-creative capacity. In addition, meta-goals will have to be articulated and developed, that is, *supra-goals* which shape and provide the foundation for the goal structure. For example, one meta-goal might be a system for detecting new and chang-ing goals; another could be a system for deciding priorities among goals.

Organizational Structure

Finally, there will be *more conflict and contradiction among diverse standards of organizational effectiveness*, just as in hospitals and univer-sities today there is conflict between teaching and research. The reason for this is the increased number of professionals involved, who tend to identify more with the goals of their profession than with those of their immediate employer. University professors can be used as a case in point. More and more of their income comes from outside sources, such as foundations and consultant work. They tend not to be good "com-pany men" because they divide their loyalty between their professional values and organizational goals.

The social structure of organizations of the future will have some unique characteristics. The key word will be "temporary"; there will be adaptive, rapidly changing temporary systems. These will be "task forces" organized around problems-to-be-solved by groups of relative strangers who represent a diverse set of professional skills. The groups will be arranged on an organic rather than mechanical mode; they will evolve in response to a problem rather than to programmed role expec-tations. The "executive" thus becomes a coordinator or "linking pin" between various task forces. He must be a man who can speak the diverse languages of research, with skills to relay information and to mediate between groups. People will be differentiated not vertically according to rank and status but flexibly and functionally according to skill and professional training.

Creative Systems

Adaptive, problem-solving, temporary systems of diverse specialists, linked together by coordinating and task-evaluating specialists in an organic flux—this is the organizational form that will gradually replace bureaucracy as we know it. I call this an *organic-adaptive structure*.

The organic-adaptive structure should increase *motivation* and thereby effectiveness because it enhances satisfactions intrinsic to the task. There is a harmony between the educated individual's need for meaningful, satisfactory, and creative tasks and a flexible organizational structure.

There will, however, also be reduced commitment to work groups, for these groups, as I already mentioned, will be transient and changing. While skills in human interaction will become more important, due to the growing needs for collaboration in complex tasks, there will be a concomitant reduction in group cohesiveness. It is possible to predict that, in the organic-adaptive system, people will have to learn to develop quick, intense relationships on the job and learn to bear the loss of more enduring work relationships. Because of the added ambiguity of roles, more time will have to be spent on the continual rediscovery of the appropriate organizational mix.

In general, I do not agree with those who emphasize a New Utopianism, in which leisure, not work, becomes the emotional-creative sphere of life. Jobs should become more rather than less involving; man is a problem-solving animal and the tasks of the future guarantee a full agenda of problems. In addition, the adaptive process itself may become captivating to many.

At the same time, the future described is not necessarily a "happy" one. Coping with rapid change, living in temporary work systems, quickly developing meaningful relations—and then breaking them—all augur social strains and psychological tensions. Learning how to live with ambiguity, to identify with the adaptive process, to make a virtue out of contingency, and to be self-directing will be the task of education, the goal of maturity, and the achievement of the successful manager. To be a wife in this era will become a profession of providing stability and continuity.

In these new organizations, participants will be called on to use their minds more than at any other time in history. Fantasy, imagination, and creativity will be legitimate in ways that today seem strange. Social structures will no longer be instruments of psychic repression but will increasingly promote play and freedom on behalf of curiosity and thought.

Bureaucracy was a monumental discovery for harnessing the muscle power of the Industrial Revolution. In today's world, it is a lifeless crutch that is no longer useful. For we now require structures of freedom to permit the expression of play and imagination and to exploit the new pleasure of work.

One final word: While I forecast the structure and value coordinates for organizations of the future and contend that they are inevitable, it should not bar any of us from giving a little push here and there to the inevitable. And while the French moralist may be right in saying that there are no delightful marriages, just good ones, it is possible that, if managers and scientists continue to get their heads together in organizational revitalization, they might develop delightful organizations—just possibly.

I started with a quote from de Tocqueville and I think it would be fitting to end with one:

I am tempted to believe that what we call necessary institutions are often no more than institutions to which we have grown accustomed. In matters of social constitution the field of possibilities is much more extensive than men living in their various societies are ready to imagine.

Participative Management: Time for a Second Look

ROBERT C. ALBROOK

The management of change has become a central preoccupation of U.S. business. When the directors have approved the record capital budget and congratulated themselves on "progress," when the banquet speaker has used his last superlative to describe the "world of tomorrow," the talk turns, inevitably, to the question: "Who will make it all work?" Some people resist change. Some hold the keys to it. Some admit the need for new ways but don't know how to begin. The question becomes what kind of management can ease the inevitable pains, unlock the talent, energy, and knowledge where they're needed, help valuable men to contribute to and shape change rather than be flattened by it.

The recipe is elusive, and increasingly business has turned to the academic world for help, particularly to the behavioral scientists—the psychologists, sociologists, and anthropologists whose studies have now become the showpieces of the better business schools. A number of major corporations, such as General Electric, Texas Instruments, and Standard Oil (N.J.), have brought social scientists onto their staffs. Some companies collaborate closely with university-based scholars and are contributing importantly to advanced theoretical work, just as industry's physicists, chemists, and engineers have become significant contributors of new knowledge in their respective realms. Hundreds of companies, large and small, have tried one or another formulation of basic behavioral theory, such as the many schemes for sharing cost savings with employees and actively soliciting their ideas for improved efficiency.

For forty years the quantity and quality of academic expertise in this field have been steadily improving, and there has lately been a new burst of ideas which suggest that the researchers in the business schools and other centers of learning are really getting down to cases. The newest concepts already represent a considerable spin-off from the

appealingly simple notions on which the behavioral pioneers first concentrated. The essential message these outriders had for business was
this: recognize the social needs of employees in their work, as well as
their need for money; they will respond with a deeper commitment and
better performance, help to shape the organization's changing goals and
make them their own. For blue-collar workers this meant such steps as
organizing work around tasks large enough to have meaning and inviting
workers' ideas; for middle and upper management it meant more participation in decision making, wider sharing of authority and responsibility, more open and more candid communication, up, down, and
sideways.

The new work suggests that neither the basic philosophy nor all of
the early prescriptions of this management style were scientifically
sound or universally workable. The word from the behavioral scientists
is becoming more specific and "scientific," less simple and moralistic.
At Harvard, M.I.T., the University of Michigan, Chicago, U.C.L.A.,
Stanford, and elsewhere, they are mounting bigger, longer, and more
rigorous studies of the human factors in management than ever before
undertaken.

One conclusion is that the "participative" or "group" approach
doesn't seem to work with all people and in all situations. Research has
shown that satisfied, happy workers are sometimes more productive—
and sometimes merely happy. Some managers and workers are able to
take only limited responsibility, however much the company tries to
give them. Some people will recognize the need to delegate but "can't
let go." In a profit squeeze the only way to get costs under control fast
enough often seems to be with centralized, "get tough" management.

Few, if any, behaviorists espouse a general return to authoritarian
management. Instead, they are seeking a more thorough, systematic
way to apply participative principles on a sustained schedule that will
give the theory a better chance to work. Others are insisting that management must be tailor-made, suited to the work or the people, rather
than packaged in a standard mixture. Some people aren't and never will
be suited for "democracy" on the job, according to one viewpoint,
while others insist that new kinds of psychological training can fit most
executives for the rugged give-and-take of successful group
management.

As more variables are brought into their concepts, and as they look
increasingly at the specifics of a management situation, the behaviorists
are also being drawn toward collaboration with the systems designers
and the theorists of data processing. Born in reaction to the cold

scientism of the earlier "scientific management" experts with their stopwatches and measuring tapes, the "human relations" or behavioral school of today may be getting ready at last to bury that hatchet in a joint search for a broadly useful "general theory" of management.

Why Executives Don't Practice What They Preach

Before any general theory can be evolved, a great deal more has to be known about the difficulty of putting theory into practice—i.e., of transforming a simple managerial attitude into an effective managerial style. "There are plenty of executives," observes Stanley Seashore, a social psychologist at the University of Michigan's Institute for Social Research, "who'll decide one morning they're going to be more participative and by the afternoon have concluded it doesn't work."

What's often lacking is an understanding of how deeply and specifically management style affects corporate operations. The executive who seeks a more effective approach needs a map of the whole terrain of management activity. Rensis Likert, director of the Michigan institute, has developed a chart to assist managers in gaining a deeper understanding of the way they operate. A simplified version is on pp. 302-303. By answering the questions in the left-hand column of the chart (e.g., "Are subordinates' ideas sought and used?"), an executive sketches a profile of the way his company is run and whether it leans to the "authoritative" or the "participative." Hundreds of businessmen have used the chart, under Likert's direction, and many have discovered a good deal they didn't realize about the way they were handling people.

Likert leads his subjects in deliberate steps to a conclusion that most of them do not practice what they say they believe. First, the executive is asked to think of the most successful company (or division of a company) he knows intimately. He then checks off on the chart his answers as they apply to that company. When the executive has finished this exercise, he has nearly always traced the profile of a strongly "participative" management system, well to the right on Likert's chart. He is next asked to repeat the procedure for the least successful company (or division) he knows well. Again, the profiles are nearly always the same, but this time they portray a strongly "authoritative" system, far to the left on the chart.

Then comes the point of the exercise. The executive is asked to describe his own company or division. Almost always, the resulting profile is that of a company somewhere in the middle, a blend of the "benevolent authoritative" and the "consultative"—well to the left of what the executive had previously identified as the most successful style. To check out the reliability of this self-analysis, Likert sometimes asks employees in the same company or division to draw its profile, too. They tend to rate it as slightly more "authoritative" than the boss does.

Likert believes that the predominant management style in U.S. industry today falls about in the middle of his chart, even though most managers seem to know from personal observation of other organizations that a more participative approach works better. What accounts for their consistent failure to emulate what they consider successful? Reaching for a general explanation, Likert asks his subjects one final question: "In your experience, what happens when the senior officer becomes concerned about earnings and takes steps to cut costs, increase productivity, and improve profits?" Most reply that the company's management profile shifts left, toward the authoritarian style. General orders to economize—and promptly—often result in quick, across-the-board budget cuts. Some programs with high potential are sacrificed along with obvious losers. Carefully laid, logical plans go down the drain. Some people are laid off—usually the least essential ones. But the best people in the organization sooner or later rebel at arbitrary decisions, and many of them leave.

At the outset, the arbitrary cost cutting produces a fairly prompt improvement in earnings, of course. But there is an unrecognized trade-off in the subsequent loss of human capital, which shows up still later in loss of business. In due course, management has to "swing right" again, rebuilding its human assets at great expense in order to restore good performance. Yet the manager who puts his firm through this dreary cycle, Likert observes, is often rewarded with a bonus at the outset, when things still look good. Indeed, he may be sent off to work his magic in another division!

Likert acknowledges that there are emergencies when sharp and sudden belt-tightening is inescapable. The trouble, he says, is that it is frequently at the expense of human assets and relationships that have taken years to build. Often it would make more sense to sell off inventory or dispose of a plant. But such possibilities are overlooked because human assets do not show up in the traditional balance sheet the way physical assets do. A company can, of course, lose $100,000 worth of talent and look better on its statement than if it sells off $10,000 worth of inventory at half price.

A dollars-and-cents way of listing the value of a good engineering staff, an experienced shop crew, or an executive group with effective, established working relations might indeed steady the hand of a hard-pressed president whose banker is on the phone. Likert believes he is now on the trail of a way to assign such values—values that should be at least as realistic as the often arbitrary and outdated figures given for real estate and plant. It will take some doing to get the notion accepted by bankers and accountants, however sophisticated his method turns out to be. But today's executives are hardly unaware that their long payrolls of expensive scientific and managerial talent represent an asset as well as an expense. Indeed, it is an asset that is often bankable. A merely more regular, explicit recognition of human assets in cost-cutting decisions would help to ensure that human assets get at least an even break with plant and inventory in time of trouble.

Likert and his institute colleagues are negotiating with several corporations to enlist them in a systematic five-year study, in effect a controlled experiment, that should put a firmer footing under tentative conclusions and hypotheses. This study will test Likert's belief that across-the-board participative management, carefully developed, sustained through thick and thin, and supported by a balance sheet that somehow reckons the human factor, will show better long-run results than the cyclical swing between authoritarian and participative styles reflected in the typical middle-ground profile on his chart.

Conversion In A Pajama Factory

Already there's enough evidence in industry experience to suggest that participative management gets in trouble when it is adopted too fast. In some cases, an authoritarian management has abruptly ordered junior executives or employees to start taking on more responsibility, not recognizing that the directive itself reasserted the fact of continuing centralized control. Sometimes, of course, a hard shove may be necessary, as in the recent experience of Harwood Manufacturing Corp. of Marion, Virginia, which has employed participative practices widely for many years. When it acquired a rival pajama maker, Weldon Manufacturing Co., the latter's long-held authoritarian traditions were hard to crack. With patient but firm prodding by outside consultants, who acknowledge an initial element of "coercion," the switch in style was finally accomplished.

Ideally, in the view of Likert and others, a move of this kind should begin with the patient education of top executives, followed by the development of the needed skills in internal communication, group leadership, and the other requisites of the new system. Given time, this will produce better employee attitudes and begin to harness personal motivation to corporate goals. Still later, there will be improved productivity, less waste, lower turnover and absence rates, fewer grievances and slowdowns, improved product quality, and, finally, better customer relations.

The transformation may take several years. A checkup too early in the game might prove that participative management, even when thoroughly understood and embraced at the top, doesn't produce better results. By the same token, a management that is retreating from the new style in a typical cost squeeze may still be nominally participative, yet may already have thrown away the fruits of the system. Some research findings do indicate that participation isn't producing the hoped-for results. In Likert's view, these were spot checks, made without regard to which way the company was tending and where it was in the cycle of change.

A growing number of behaviorists, however, have begun to question whether the participative style is an idea toward which all management should strive. If they once believed it was, more as a matter of faith in their long struggle against the "scientific" manager's machine-like view of man than as a finding from any new science of their own, they now are ready to take a second look at the proposition.

It seems plain enough that a research scientist generally benefits from a good deal of freedom and autonomy, and that top executives, confronted every day by new problems that no routine can anticipate, operate better with maximum consultation and uninhibited contributions from every member of the team. If the vice president for finance can't talk candidly with the vice president for production about financing the new plant, a lot of time can be wasted. In sales, group effort—instead of the usual competition—can be highly productive. But in the accounting department, things must go by the book. "Creative accounting" sounds more like a formula for jail than for the old behaviorists' dream of personal self-fulfillment on the job. And so with quality control in the chemical plant. An inspired adjustment here and there isn't welcome, thank you; just follow the specifications.

In the production department, automation has washed out a lot of the old problem of man as a prisoner of the assembly line, the kind of problem that first brought the "human relations" experts into the factories in the 1920's and 1930's. If a shop is full of computer-controlled machine tools busily reproducing themselves, the boy with the broom who sweeps away the shavings may be the only one who can put a personal flourish into his work. The creativity is all upstairs in the engineering and programing departments. But then, so are most of the people.

"Look what's happened in the last twenty years," says Harold J. Leavitt, a social psychologist who recently moved to Stanford after some years at Carnegie Tech. "Originally the concern of the human-relations people was with the blue-collar worker. Then the focus began to shift to foremen and to middle management. Now it's concentrated in special areas like research and development and in top management. Why? Because the 'group' style works best where nobody knows exactly and all the time what they're supposed to be doing, where there's a continuous need to change and adapt."

Democracy Works Better In Plastics

One conclusion that has been drawn from this is that management style has to be custom-designed to fit the particular characteristics of each industry. The participative approach will work best in those industries that are in the vanguard of change. A Harvard Business School study has compared high-performance companies in three related, but subtly different, fields: plastics, packaged food, and standard containers. The plastics company faced the greatest uncertainties and change in research, new products, and market developments. The food company's business was somewhat more stable, while the container company encountered little or no requirement for innovation. The three achieved good results using markedly different management styles. The plastics firm provided for wide dispersal of responsibility for major decisions, the food company for moderate decentralization of authority, and the container company operated with fairly centralized control.

Less successful enterprises in each of the three industries were also examined, and their managements were compared with those of the high-performance companies. From this part of the study, Harvard researchers Paul Lawrence and Jay Lorsch drew another conclusion: not only may each industry have its own appropriate management style, but so may the individual operations within the same company. The companies that do best are those which allow for variations among their departments and know how to take these variations into account in coordinating the whole corporate effort.

Both the sales and the research departments in a fast-moving plastics company, for example, may adopt a style that encourages employees to participate actively in departmental decision making. But in special ways the two operations still need to differ. The research worker, for example, thinks in long-range terms, focusing on results expected in two or three years. The sales executive has his sights set on results next week or next month. This different sense of time may make it hard for the two departments to understand each other. But if top management recognizes the reasons and the need for such differences, each department will do its own job better, and they can be better coordinated. On the other hand, if top management ignores the differences and insists, for example, on rigidly uniform budgeting and planning timetables, there will be a loss of effectiveness.

It seems an obvious point that sales must be allowed to operate like sales, accounting like accounting, and production like production. But as Lawrence comments, "The mark of a good idea in this field is that as soon as it is articulated, it does seem obvious. People forget that, five minutes before, it wasn't. One curse of the behavioral scientist is that anything he comes up with is going to seem that way, because anything that's good *is* obvious."

People, Too, Have Their Styles

Other behavioral scientists take the view that management style should be determined not so much by the nature of the particular business operation involved, but by the personality traits of the people themselves. There may be some tendency for certain kinds of jobs to attract certain kinds of people. But in nearly any shop or office a wide range of personality types may be observed. There is, for example, the outgoing, socially-oriented scientist as well as the supposedly more typical introverted recluse. There are mature, confident managers, and there are those who somehow fill the job despite nagging self-doubt and a consuming need for reassurance.

For a long time, personality tests seemed to offer a way to steer people into the psychologically right kind of work. Whether such testing for placement is worthwhile is now a matter of some dispute. In any case, the whole question of individual differences is often reduced to little more than an office guessing game. Will Sue cooperate with Jane? Can Dorothy stand working for Jim? Will Harry take suggestions?

The participative approach to management may be based upon a greatly oversimplified notion about people, in the view of psychologist Clare Graves of Union College in Schenectady, New York. On the basis of limited samplings, he tentatively concludes that as many as half the people in the northeastern U.S., and a larger proportion nationwide, are not and many never will be the eager-beaver workers on whom the late Douglas McGregor of M.I.T. based his "Theory Y." Only some variation of old-style authoritarian management will meet their psychological needs, Graves contends.

Graves believes he has identified seven fairly distinct personality types, although he acknowledges that many people are not "purebreds" who would fit his abstractions perfectly and that new and higher personality forms may still be evolving. At the bottom of his well-ordered hierarchy he places the childlike "autistic" personality, which requires "close care and nurturing." Next up the scale are the "animistic" type, which must be dealt with by sheer force or enticement; the "ordered" personality that responds best to a moralistic management; and the "materialistic" individual who calls for pragmatic, hard bargaining. None of these are suited for the participative kind of management.

At the top of Graves's personality ladder are the "sociocentric," the "cognitive," and the "apprehending" types of people. They are motivated, respectively, by a need for "belonging," for "information," and for an "understanding" of the total situation in which they are involved. For each of these levels some form of participative management will work. However, those at the very top, the unemotional "apprehending" individuals, must be allowed pretty much to set their own terms for work. Management can trust such people to contribute usefully only according to their own cool perception of what is needed. They will seldom take the trouble to fight authority when they disagree with it, but merely withdraw, do a passable but not excellent job, and wait for management to see things their way. In that sense, these highest-level people are probably not ideal participators.

Graves believes most adults are stuck at one level throughout their lifetimes or move up a single notch, at best. He finds, incidentally, that there can be bright or dull, mature or immature behavior at nearly all levels. The stages simply represent psychological growth toward a larger and larger awareness of the individual's relationship to society.

If a company has a mixture of personality types, as most do, it must somehow sort them out. One way would be to place participative-type managers in charge of some groups, and authoritarian managers in charge of others. Employees would then be encouraged to transfer into sections where the management style best suits them. This would hardly simplify corporate life. But companies pushing the group approach might at least avoid substituting harmful new rigidities—"participate, or else!"—for the old ones.

The Anthropological View

   Behaviorists who have been studying management problems from an anthropological viewpoint naturally stress cultural rather than individual differences. Manning Nash, of the University of Chicago's business school, for example, observes that the American emphasis on egalitarianism and performance has always tempered management style in the U.S. "No matter what your role is, if you don't perform, no one in this country will defer to you," he says. "Americans won't act unless they respect you. You couldn't have an American Charge of the Light Brigade." But try to export that attitude to a country with a more

DIAGNOSE YOUR MANAGEMENT

The chart on the next two pages is adapted from a technique developed by Rensis Likert, director of the Institute for Social Research at the University of Michigan, to help businessmen analyze the management style used by their companies. Anyone —executive or employee—can use it to diagnose his own company or division. Check the appropriate answers, using the guide marks to shade your emphasis. After the first question, for example, if your answer is "almost none," put the check in the first or second notch of the "none" box. Regard each answer as a sort of rating on a continuous scale from the left to the right of the chart. When you have answered each question, draw a line from the top to the bottom of the chart through the check marks. The result will be a profile of your management. To determine which way management style has been shifting, repeat the process for the situation as it was three, five, or ten years ago. Finally, sketch the profile you think would help your company or division to improve its performance. Likert has tried the chart on a number of business executives. Most of them rated their own companies about in the middle—embracing features of System 2 and 3. But nearly all of them also believe that companies do best when they have profiles well to the right of the chart, and worse with profiles well to the left.

		System 1 Exploitive Authoritative	System 2 Benevolent Authoritative	System 3 Consultative	System 4 Participative Group
LEADERSHIP	1. How much confidence is shown in subordinates?	None	Condescending	Substantial	Complete
	2. How free do they feel to talk to superiors about job?	Not at all	Not very	Rather free	Fully free
MOTIVATION	3. Are subordinates' ideas sought and used, if worthy?	Seldom	Sometimes	Usually	Always
	4. Is predominant use made of 1 fear, 2 threats, 3 punishment, 4 rewards, 5 involvement?	1, 2, 3, occasionally 4	4, some 3	4, some 3 and 5	5, 4, based on group set goals
	5. Where is responsibility felt for achieving organization's goals?	Mostly at top	Top and middle	Fairly general	At all levels
COMMUNICATION	6. How much communication is aimed at achieving organization's objectives?	Very little	Little	Quite a bit	A great deal
	7. What is the direction of information flow?	Downward	Mostly downward	Down and up	Down, up, and sideways
	8. How is downward communication accepted?	With suspicion	Possibly with suspicion	With caution	With an open mind
	9. How accurate is upward communication?	Often wrong	Censored for the boss	Limited accuracy	Accurate
	10. How well do superiors know problems faced by subordinates?	Know little	Some knowledge	Quite well	Very well

DECISIONS	11.	At what level are decisions formally made?	Mostly at top	Policy at top, some delegation	Broad policy at top, more delegation	Throughout but well integrated
	12.	What is the origin of technical and professional knowledge used in decision making?	Top management	Upper and middle	To a certain extent, throughout	To a great extent, throughout
	13.	Are subordinates involved in decisions related to their work?	Not at all	Occasionally consulted	Generally consulted	Fully involved
	14.	What does decision-making process contribute to motivation?	Nothing, often weakens it	Relatively little	Some contribution	Substantial contribution
GOALS	15.	How are organizational goals established?	Orders issued	Orders, some comment invited	After discussion, by orders	By group action (except in crisis)
	16.	How much covert resistance to goals is present?	Strong resistance	Moderate resistance	Some resistance at times	Little or none
CONTROL	17.	How concentrated are review and control functions?	Highly at top	Relatively highly at top	Moderate delegation to lower levels	Quite widely shared
	18.	Is there an informal organization resisting the formal one?	Yes	Usually	Sometimes	No—same goals as formal
	19.	What are cost, productivity, and other control data used for?	Policing, punishment	Reward and punishment	Reward, some self-guidance	Self-guidance, problem solving

Adapted, with permission, from The Human Organization: Its Management and Value. By Rensis Likert, published in April, 1967, by McGraw-Hill autocratic social tradition, and, in the words of Stanley Davis of Harvard, "it won't be bought and may not be workable."

Within the U.S. there are many cultural differences that might provide guides to managerial style if they could be successfully analyzed. Recent research by Lawrence and Arthur N. Turner at the Harvard Business School hints at important differences between blue-collar workers in cities and those in smaller towns, although religious and other factors fog the results. Town workers seem to seek "a relatively large amount of variety, autonomy, interaction, skill and responsibility" in their work, whereas city workers "find more simple tasks less stress-producing and more satisfying."

In managerial areas where democratic techniques *are* likely to work, the problem is how to give managers skill and practice in participation. The National Education Association's National Training Laboratories twenty years ago pioneered a way of doing this called "sensitivity training" (see "Two Weeks in a T Group," *Fortune,* August, 1961). Small groups of men, commonly drawn from the executive ranks, sit down with a professional trainer but without agenda or rule book and "see what happens." The "vacuum" draws out first one and then another participant, in a way that tends to expose in fairly short order how he comes across to others.

The technique has had many critics, few more vocal than William Gomberg of the University of Pennsylvania's Wharton School. Renewing his assault recently, he called the "training" groups "titillating therapy, management development's most fashionable fad." When people from the same company are in the group, he argues, the whole exercise is an invasion of privacy, an abuse of the therapeutic technique to help the company, not the individual. For top executives in such groups, Gomberg and others contend, the technique offers mainly a catharsis for their loneliness or insecurity.

"Psyching Out The Boss"

Undoubtedly the T group can be abused, intentionally or otherwise. But today's sensitivity trainers are trying to make sure the experience leads to useful results for both the individual and his firm. They realize that early groups, made up of total strangers gathered at some remote "cultural island," often gave the executive little notion of how to apply his new knowledge back on the job. To bring more realism to the exercise, the National Training Laboratories began ten years ago to make up groups of executives and managers from the same company, but not men who had working relationships with one another. These "cousin labs" have led, in turn, to some training of actual management "families," a boss and his subordinates. At the West Coast headquarters of the T Group movement, the business school at U.C.L.A., some now call such training "task-group therapy."

Many businessmen insist T Groups have helped them. Forty-three presidents and chairmen and hundreds of lesser executives are National Training Laboratories alumni. U.C.L.A. is besieged by applicants, and many are turned away.

Sensitivity training is supposed to help most in business situations where there is a great deal of uncertainty, as there is in the training sessions themselves. In such situations in the corporate setting there is sometimes a tendency for executives to withdraw, to defer action, to play a kind of game with other people in the organization to see who will climb out on a limb first. A chief ploy is "psyching out the boss," which means trying to anticipate the way the winds of ultimate decision will blow and to set course accordingly.

The aim of sensitivity training is to stop all this, to get the executive's nerve up so that he faces facts, or, in the words of U.C.L.A.'s James V. Clark, to "lay bare the stress and strain faster and get a resolution of the problem." In that limited sense, such therapy could well serve any style of management. In Clark's view, this kind of training, early in the game, might save many a company a costly detour on the road to company-wide "democracy." He cites the experience of Non-Linear Systems, Inc. of Del Mar, California, a manufacturer of such electronic gear as digital voltmeters and data-logging equipment and an important supplier to aerospace contractors. The company is headed by Andrew Kay, a leading champion of the participative style. At the lower levels, Kay's application of participative concepts worked well. He gave workers responsibility for "the whole black box," instead of for pieces of his complex finished products. Because it was still a box, with some definite boundaries, the workers seized the new opportunity without fear or hesitation. The psychological magic of meaningful work, as opposed to the hopelessly specialized chore, took hold. Productivity rose.

Vice Presidents In Midair

But at the executive level, Kay moved too quickly, failing to prepare his executives for broad and undefined responsibilities—or failing to choose men better suited for the challenge. One vice president was put in charge of "innovation." Suspended in midair, without the support of departments or functional groups and lacking even so much as a job description, most of the V.P.'s became passive and incapable of making decisions. "They lost touch with reality—including the reality of the market," recalls Clark. When the industry suffered a general slump and new competition entered the field, Non-Linear wasn't ready. Sales dropped 16 percent, according to Kay. In time he realized he was surrounded with dependent men, untrained to participate in the fashion he had peremptorily commanded. He trimmed his executive group and expects to set a new sales record this year.

Sheldon Davis of TRW Systems in Redondo Beach, California, blames the behavioral scientists themselves for breakdowns like Non-Linear's. Too often, he argues, "their messages come out sounding soft and easy, as if what we are trying to do is build happy teams of employees who feel 'good' about things, rather than saying we're trying to build effective organizations with groups that function well and that can zero in quickly on their problems and deal with them rationally."

To Davis, participation should mean "tough, open exchange," focused on the problem, not the organizational chart. Old-style managers who simply dictate a solution are wrong, he argues, and so are those new-style managers who think the idea is simply to go along with a subordinate's proposals if they're earnestly offered. Neither approach taps the full potential of the executive group. When problems are faced squarely, Davis believes, the boss—who should remain boss—gets the best solution because all relevant factors are thoroughly considered. And because everyone has contributed to the solution and feels responsible for it, it is also the solution most likely to be carried out.

One of the most useful new developments in the behavioral study of management is a fresh emphasis on collaboration with technology. In the early days of the human-relations movement in industry, technology was often regarded as "the enemy," the source of the personal and social problems that the psychologists were trying to treat. But from the beginning, some social scientists wanted to move right in and help fashion machines and industrial processes so as to reduce or eliminate their supposedly anti-human effects. Today this concept is more than mere talk. The idea is to develop so-called "socio-technical" systems that permit man and technology *together* to produce the best performance.

Some early experimentation in the British coal mines, by London's Tavistock Institute, as well as scattered work in this country and in Scandinavia, have already demonstrated practical results from such a collaboration. Tavistock found that an attempt to apply specialized factory-style technology to coal mining had isolated the miners from one another. They missed the sense of group support and self-direction that had helped them cope with uncertainty and danger deep in the coal faces. Productivity suffered. In this case, Tavistock's solution was to redesign the new system so that men could still work in groups.

In the U.S. a manufacturer of small household appliances installed some highly sophisticated new technical processes that put the company well in the front of its field. But the engineers had broken down the jobs to such an extent that workers were getting no satisfaction out of their performance and productivity declined. Costs went up and, in the end, some of the new machinery had to be scrapped.

Some technologists seem more than ready to welcome a partnership with the human-relations expert. Louis Davis, a professor of engineering, has joined the U.C.L.A. business-school faculty to lead a six-man socio-technical research group that includes several behaviorists. Among them is Eric Trist, a highly respected psychologist from the Tavistock Institute. Davis hopes today's collaboration will lead in time to a new breed of experts knowledgeable in both the engineering and the social disciplines.

"It's Time We Stopped Building Rival Dictionaries"

The importance of time, the nature of the task, the differences within a large organization, the nature of the people, the cultural setting, the psychological preparation of management, the relationship to technology—all these and other variables are making the search for effective managerial style more and more complex. But the growing recognition of these complexities has drained the human-relations movement of much of its antagonism toward the "super-rationalism" of management science. Humanists must be more systematic and rational if they are to make some useful sense of the scattered and half-tested concepts they have thus far developed, and put their new theories to a real test.

A number of behaviorists believe it is well past time to bury the hatchet and collaborate in earnest with the mathematicians and economists. Some business schools and commercial consulting groups are already realigning their staffs to encourage such work. It won't be easy. Most "systems" thinkers are preoccupied with bringing all the relevant knowledge to bear on a management problem in a systematic way, seeking the theoretically "best" solution. Most behaviorists have tended to assume that the solution which is *most likely to be carried out* is the best one, hence their focus on involving lots of people in the decision making so that they will follow through. Where the "experts" who shape decisions are also in charge of getting the job done, the two approaches sometimes blend, in practice. But in many organizations, it is a long, long road from a creative and imaginative decision to actual performance. A general theory of management must show how to build systematic expertise into a style that is also well suited to people.

The rapprochement among management theorists has a distinguished herald, Fritz J. Roethlisberger of Harvard Business School, one of the human-relations pioneers who first disclosed the potential of the "small group" in industrial experiments forty years ago. He laughs quickly at any suggestion that a unified approach will come easily. "But after all, we are all looking at the same thing," he says. "It's time we stopped building rival dictionaries and learned to make some sentences that really say something."

Today's Problems with Tomorrow's Organizations

CHRIS ARGYRIS

There is a revolution brewing in the introduction of new organizational forms to complement or to replace the more traditional pyramidal form. I believe, on the basis of some recent research, that the new forms are basically sound. However, because of the methods used to introduce them and because of those used to maintain them, many of the unintended self-defeating consequences of the older structures are re-appearing.

Two major causes for this revolution are the new requirements for organizational survival in an increasingly competitive environment and the new administrative and information technology available to deal with complexity. Wallace (1963) summarizes these requirements as:

(1) the technological revolution (complexity and variety of products, new materials and processes, and the effects of massive research),

(2) competition and the profit squeeze (saturated markets, inflation of wage and material costs, production efficiency),

(3) the high cost of marketing, and

(4) the unpredictability of consumer demands (due to high discretionary income, wide range of choices available, and shifting tastes).

To make matters more difficult, the costs of new products are increasing while their life expectancy is decreasing.

Requirements of Tomorrow's Organizations

In order to meet these challenges, modern organizations need:

(1) much more creative planning,

(2) the development of valid and useful knowledge about new products and new processes,

Reprinted by permission of author and publisher. From the *Journal of Management Studies*, Vol. 4, No. 1, Feb., 1967, pp. 31-55.

(3) increased concerted and cooperative action with internalized long-range commitment by all involved, and

(4) increased understanding of criteria for effectiveness that meet the challenges of complexity.

These requirements, in turn, depend upon:

(1) continuous and open access between individuals and groups,

(2) free, reliable communication, where

(3) interdependence is the foundation for individual and departmental cohesiveness and

(4) trust, risk-taking, and helping each other is prevalent, so that

(5) conflict is identified and managed in such a way that the destructive win-lose stances with their accompanying polarization of views are minimized and effective problem-solving is maximized.

These conditions, in turn, require individuals who:

(1) do not fear stating their complete views,

(2) are capable of creating groups that maximize the unique contributions of each individual,

(3) value and seek to integrate their contributions into a creative total, final contribution,

(4) rather than needing to be individually rewarded for their contributions, thus

(5) finding the search for valid knowledge and the development of the best possible solution intrinsically satisfying.

Unfortunately these conditions are difficult to create. Elsewhere I have tried to show that the traditional pyramidal structure and managerial controls tend to place individuals and departments in constant interdepartmental warfare, where win-lose competition creates polarized stances, that tend to get resolved by the superior making the decisions, thereby creating a dependence upon him. Also, there is a tendency toward conformity, mistrust, and lack of risk-taking among the peers that results in focusing upon individual survival, requiring the seeking out of the scarce rewards, identifying with successful ventures (be a hero), and being careful to avoid being blamed for or identified with a failure, thereby becoming a bum. All these adaptive behaviors tend to induce low interpersonal competence and can lead the organization, over the long run, to become rigid, sticky, less innovative, resulting in less than effective decisions with even less internal commitment to the decisions on the part of those involved.

Some people have experimented by structuring the organization in such a way that people representing the major functions (marketing, engineering, manufacturing, and finance) are coerced to work together. Unfortunately, the pyramidal structure does not lend itself to such a strategy. As Wallace points out, the difficulty is that typically each function approaches the business problems inherent in the product from a somewhat different point of view: marketing wants a good product at a low price; production, a product that is easily produced; engineering, a product that outclasses—engineering wise—all other products, and so on. None of these stances tends to lead to the resolution of conflicting ideas into a decision that tends to integrate the best of each view.

THE MATRIX ORGANIZATION

One of the most promising strategies to induce co-operation and integration of effort on crucial business problems is the development of project teams and the matrix organization. These administrative innovations were created initially to solve the complex problems of coordination and scheduling of large defense projects. They have been adapted and used by many other organizations because of their potential promise. The future role of the team approach and matrix organization is, in my opinion, an important one for administration.

A project team is created to solve a particular problem. It is composed of people representing all the relevant managerial functions (e.g., marketing, manufacturing, engineering, and finance). Each member is given equal responsibility and power to solve the problem. The members are expected to work as a cohesive unit. Once the problem is solved, the team is given a new assignment or disbanded. If the problem is a recurring one, the team remains active. In many cases, especially in the defense programs, the project manager is given full authority and responsibility for the completion of the project including rewarding and penalizing the members of the team. An organization may have many teams. This results in an organization that looks like a matrix; hence the title of matrix organization.

Representatives of	Project 1	Project 2	Project 3
Manufacturing			
Engineering			
Marketing			
Finance			
	Team 1	Team 2	Team 3

How effective are the project teams and the matrix organizations? In order to begin to answer that question, I have been conducting some research in nine large organizations utilizing a matrix organization structure. In preliminary interviews the executives reported that the matrix organization and team approach made sense, but that they found them very difficult to put into actual practice. People still seemed to polarize issues, resisted exploring ideas thoroughly, mistrusted each other's behavior, focused on trying to protect one's own function, over-emphasized simplified criteria of success (e.g., figures on sales), worked too much on day-to-day operations and short-term planning, engaged in the routine decisions rather than focus more on the long-range risky decisions, and emphasized survival more than the integration of effort into a truly accepted decision.

Others found fault with the team approach for not providing individuals enough opportunity to get recognition in their own functional departments for their performance on the team. Still others insisted that individuals sought to be personally identified with a particular accomplishment; that it wasn't satisfying for them to know that their group (and not they) obtained the reward. Finally, some said that during their meetings the teams got bogged down in focusing on the negative, i.e., what had not been accomplished.

Why are these new administrative structures and strategies having this trouble? I do *not* believe the concept of the matrix organization is inherently invalid. I believe the answer lies in the everyday *behavior styles that the managers have developed, in the past, to survive and to succeed within the traditional pyramidal organization.* The behavior styles needed for the effective use of the matrix organization are, I believe, very different. Also, the group dynamics that are effective in the pyramidal structure are different from those that will be effective in the matrix organization. Thus I do not agree that the comments above are 'natural' for all people. They are 'natural' for people living under the pyramidal concept. For example, groups *can* be created where individuals gain success from seeing integrated decisions; where recognition *does* come more from success and less from compliments from others, where overcoming barriers and correcting faults and failures are not perceived as negative.

A second important cause for the ineffectiveness of the matrix type organization lies in the very processes that have given it birth. Again, the difficulty has been that the birth processes used were more applicable to the pyramidal than to the matrix organization. In short, I am suggesting that a basic problem has been that a new form of organization has been introduced in such a way as to make difficulties inevitable and that the leadership styles that the executives use to administer the matrix organization, on the whole, compound the felony. In order to illustrate my point I should like to take one of these nine studies and discuss it in some detail. The case that I have selected to discuss approximates the other eight. The variance among the cases was not high. More importantly, the establishment of a project and program approach had the most careful thought and analytical competence brought to bear on it by the top management. It is a study of a multi-million-dollar organization that decided to reorganize its *product planning* and *program review* activities into a team approach which resulted in a matrix organization. These two activities have been the ones most frequently organized into a matrix organization. The study lasted about one year. I interviewed all the top executives involved (25), asked them to complete questionnaires, and observed, taped, and analyzed nearly 35 meetings of the teams, ranging from 45 minutes to 2½ hours in length.

PRODUCT PLANNING AND PROGRAM REVIEWS

The responsibility of product planning program reviews was to collect and integrate, and maintain up to date information of the progress of any given activity in the organization. Under this concept, the top men could go to one source to get complete information on the organization's present plans, progress against plans, and so on. The staff group had no authority to order any of the line executives. It was their task to analyze what the problems were and to get from the line executives their plans as to how they were to be solved. If the line executives were unable to agree then the problem was taken to the chief executive for his decision. In the manual of this company there existed a sentence which stated, ". . . the president retains the authority for final decisions and can ordinarily expect that his product planning staff will achieve the agreement of all other departments before plans are presented." Still later, "Product planning provides team leadership to a team made up of appropriate, fully responsibly representatives of the (line) departments. The Product Planner as team leader encourages, challenges, and insists upon mature, complete and competent coverage by these representatives. Encouragement of better communication between departments is necessary and vital."

The assumption behind this theory was that if objectives and critical paths to these objectives were defined clearly, people would tend to cooperate to achieve these objectives according to the best schedule that they could devise. However, in practice, the theory was difficult to apply. Why? Let us first take a look at the processes by which these new concepts were introduced.

The management strategy for implementing this new program was primarily one of pushing, persuading, and ordering. The objective was to overcome the forces in the organization that were resisting change thereby pushing the level of effectiveness upward. However, the way this was done added, unintentionally, to the resisting forces. For example, 76 percent of the subordinates interpreted the processes of a small elite group planning the changes and then management unilaterally installing the activities by persuading the people to accept them, as implying that they (subordinates) had not been competent in the past and that they could not be trusted in making changes. These feelings were strengthened by the fact that the new activities required greater control over subordinates, more detailed planning, and more concrete commitments which could get the subordinate in trouble if they did not fulfill them. These activities of fear and mistrust still exist. For example:

> Sometimes I wonder if the real impact of program reviews isn't to teach people that we don't trust them. I think that the top people have got to have faith in the people, and eliminate some of these constant and repetitive type of meetings, just to check being checked. I think we can get management to get themselves pretty well informed just through a nominal report type of thing, rather than all this paper work that we have.

The increasing lack of cooperation, hostility, resistance to meeting program plans, were recognized by the people responsible for the activities. They responded by making the controls even tighter. They asked for more detailed reports, for a wider distribution of minutes, and they used the minutes as evidence that agreements were arrived at that were binding. But again the impact was not completely what was expected. For example:

'Do we need these complete minutes? We still have a number of people in the organization who feel that they have to document everything in terms of a letter or memo. To me this is an indication of fear.'

'The more trouble the programs got into the more paper work that we had to complete.'

It was not long before the completion of the paper work became an end in itself. Seventy-one percent of the middle managers reported that the maintenance of the product planning and program review paper flow became as crucial as accomplishing the line responsibility assigned to each group. For example:

'I'm afraid that we program the most minute things and the more we program, the less work we get done. I have tried to get this across to the president, but have not been very successful.'

'One problem I find is the amount of paper work that this system generates. I dare say out of the five-day week it would take you three quarters of a day or a day of your week to just keep up with the paper work. All of the paper work you get does not affect you, but you have to go through it to find out what does and what does not.'

'In all honesty I think we waste too damn much time around here. These program reviews are especially costly in time. Why one of the fellows the other day said that he received and sends out approximately 50 thousand pieces of paper a month.'

The final quotation illustrates the next problem that arose. Since each individual had his regular job to accomplish in addition to his role as product planning and program reviews, the load became very heavy. *The executives increasingly felt overworked and overloaded with activities that were not leading to increased effectiveness (83 percent).* For example:

'I believe -- held a scheduling type meeting, and they do call ordinary meetings, and then all the vice presidents call their people together for a meeting, so that one little meeting at the divisional level has a heck of a lot of man hours tied up into it for the background.'

'The number of jobs to be done. The sheer volume that has to be turned out. Sometimes you feel as though you are on a treadmill and you can't get off it because no matter what jobs you can see getting accomplished, there are so many more ahead of you that you know you are behind schedule, and it seems to drive you crazy at times. Everyone has the same feelings.'

In spite of these difficulties the level of effectiveness eventually stabilized. But now the resisting forces became much stronger. Also the level of organizational pressure rose.

Most of the lower level managers reported that they did *not* like to be associated with the restraining activities, because they saw such alliance as an indication of disloyalty. I believe that one way to resolve these dissonant feelings about themselves was to strengthen their personal opinions about the negativeness of the program by finding faults with it and by knowingly (and unknowingly) acting so as to make it less effective.

Another mode of adaptation was to withdraw and let the upper levels become responsible for the successful administration of the program. (This is their baby—let them make it work.) At the same time much hostility could be released safely by constant joking about 'everything is programmed.' For example, girls were asked had they programmed their sex life; men were asked if they had defined the critical path to the men's toilet; etc.

These attitudes threatened the upper levels. They saw them as suggesting that the managers were not as loyal and committed as they should be. The executives reacted by involving the potential wrath of the president. (He really means business—let's climb on board.) Soon the president found himself in the position of being cited as the reason why the programs may not be questioned. Also, his immediate subordinates encouraged him to speak out forcefully on the importance of these functions. The president began to feel that he must defend the programs because if he did not, the restraining forces may begin to overcome the management pressure for change. For example:

'Make no mistake about it, this is the president's baby. Have you ever tried to talk to him about it? He listens for a few minutes and then soon lets you know that he isn't going to tolerate much question.'

'No, we have pretty much consoled ourselves to the fact that the president is really behind this, and you might just as well forget it. You are entitled to a personal opinion, of course, but beyond that, you better not take any action.'

The increasing number of control activities and the increasing feelings of pressure led the subordinates to feel that product planning and program reviews had become dominant in the organization. They unknowingly or knowingly placed less attention upon their original line function activities. This reaction increased the probability that failures would occur, which increased the pressures from the president and in turn his staff people, which infuriated the line managers, and the loop was closed. The top management forces tended to increase, the middle and lower management resistance also tended to increase (even though such action may have made them feel a sense of disloyalty), the tension and pressures increased, and the effectiveness of the program was at a lower level than was potentially possible.

To make the situation more difficult, the majority of the participants reported that, in addition to the process of introduction being a dissatisfying one, they also reported overall dissatisfaction with the way the programs were being carried out. For example, the meetings tended: to suppress individuality, polarize issues into win-lose stances, censor bad news to the top and immobilize the groups with unimportant issues.

Overall Dissatisfaction with Small Group Meetings

Dissatisfaction was found to exist with the product planning and program review meetings. The dissatisfactions increased as one went down the chain of command. Thus 64 percent of the top executives and 83 percent of the middle managers expressed dissatisfaction with the group meetings.

'These committees are not the best way to administer an organization. We tend to make little problems into big ones and ignore the nasty ones. We also eat up a lot of time. People don't come in to really listen; they come in to win and fight not to lose.'

'I think the simple fact is even now there is probably less true acceptance of the product planning function than there was. And I think in truth there is quite fundamental and sincere nonacceptance of the role of planning in the function, not the general idea of −−, 'I've talked to people about this quite a bit.'

Why is that?

'Because the fact remains that we do have a schedule, and someone is after them for their answer at that point. And I guess that's tough for most of us to accept. Maybe this game of having an objective and planning their work accordingly and say what you are going to do. Management is flexible, you're so right. They know we run a high risk here, and the top management never beat them over the back for this kind of stuff.'

Suppressing Individuality

The members reported that in practice, the groups functioned so that individuality was not optimized; conformity and non-risktaking predominated (71 percent). Playing it relatively safe seemed to be a common activity. For example:

During a heated session about program reviews A accused B of being a coward for not standing up for his view. A replied 'Listen mister, when you have to live with these people as I do, then you can talk. If I really stuck to my views I'd be hated by everyone—and I'd come to hate myself.'

'Yes, I think the choice that we have been asked to make between no decision and one not so good is a negative choice. Most of the time it is an 11th-hour thing that they arrive at. You either can take it this way or you won't have it for another six months.'

What prevents a person from sort of digging in and saying no, I don't want anything else?

'Well, there is a lot of pressure. We've got commitments made to the management where we charge a certain amount of dollars for the dollars they have allowed us to invest in this business.'

Polarizing Issues

At the lower levels, there was a good deal more heated argument which caused the issues to be polarized and people felt that they were not being heard. This tended to lead to a decrease in the faith in the group's processes and, at the same time, increased the probability that people would tend to come to the meetings with prepared positions (83 percent). For example:

'We have a great deal of jockeying for position.'

'There are certain things that people are not willing to stick their necks out about. Particularly when it comes to a new program. When it comes to a new program everyone has preconceived positions, and they adhere to them.'

'I think at times people will take an extreme position one time, and another time be very compromising. To take the -- committee as an example, there are occasions where they do not agree and they say, "Too bad we couldn't agree, we'll set up a meeting at the next level." '

Censoring Bad News to the Top

Another major problem was that some of the more difficult issues developed at the lower levels were watered down by the time they were transmitted to the top. People had learned not to describe to their superiors the complete differences in views and the difficulties in discussing the issues in as strong terms as they experience them. (71 percent).

'By the way, there is an awful lot of time spent at the lower level and people getting information ready to beat the people at the upper level. And I would say in all honesty that we don't give all the information to the people on top. If we do present them with all the problems it would probably bring this place to a screeching halt.'

'When you have an overly protected meeting the people upstairs don't really get the facts. For example, you soon learn that in a review you take all the things out that might be arbitrary or that might raise difficulties with somebody else.'

Immobilizing the Group with Unimportant Details

Still another frequently reported problem was the immobilization of the group with countless small decisions. (63 percent). Some department representatives brought everything to the meetings partially to make certain that the program review group took the responsibility for all activities. Other department representatives raised many issues when they were upset with the direction a particular decision was taking or when they wished to delay the making of a decision until further data could be obtained. For example:

'Some people also don't mind flooding the committee with agenda items. And once there is an item on the agenda the board is committed to study it, whether it is important or not. I think it can be an awful expense of money and time.'

'If you looked at these minutes of our meetings, and you haven't attended any yet, of course, the number of topics we take up is fantastic, and to the point where we feel that too many people aren't deciding at lower levels, and bucking it is up to us.'

The members of a review group could postpone action or prevent themselves (and their department) from being held responsible for a decision by asking the group to make it. This was guaranteed to take time since those in the group who did not specialize in that particular technical area had to be briefed.

To summarize, the product planning and program review committees were viewed as plagued with ineffectiveness and win-lose dynamics. An executive who kept a count of how people described these committees concluded that the two most frequent categorizations were 'Committee management at its worse' and 'Moscow delegates' (i.e. delegates who couldn't make a contribution without checking with their department).

The same managers freely admitted that they could not see any resolution, 'any time you run a company by a committee, you'll always have trouble', or 'it's human nature for people to lie and fight when they believe they are being exposed.' Such pessimistic diagnoses will not lead to action for correcting the situation. On the contrary, such diagnoses probably provide ideal rationalization why 'things cannot be changed' and why they can go on feeling and behaving as they do.

As in the problems presented in the previous section, management's reaction was not to deal with the issues openly. More subtle and covertly controlling actions were typically taken. Meetings were scheduled with greater precision, presentations were made both with viewgraph and written script, and even more detailed minutes were taken. The hope was that with tighter outside controls, the groups would tend to operate more effectively. If we may judge from the comments reported above as well as from the observations, the group dynamics have not been altered—indeed, one could argue with some justification that the group defenses are becoming stronger. Thus we conclude again that although the members are aware that the relative ineffectiveness of the group is a crucial problem, they are not able to solve the problems. Moreover, most of the action taken actually helps to increase the members feeling of being unduly controlled and mistrusted.

WHY DID THE PROBLEMS ARISE?

The explanations for problems like these are multiple and complicated. One way to begin to organize our thoughts is to view the problems as arising from a long causal chain of actions where one action causes several others, which in turn, breeds further actions, etc. I believe that at the beginning of this complicated causal chain lie the basic values or assumptions that executives have learned to hold about how to organize human effort effectively. These values, once internalized, act as commands to coerce the executives to behave in specific ways when they meet to solve problems.

Elsewhere I have shown that executives tend to hold three basic values about effective human relationships within organizations. They are:

1. Get the job done. We are here to manufacture shoes, that is our business, those are the important human relationships; if you have anything that can influence those human relationships, fine.

2. Be rational and logical and communicate clearly. Effectiveness *decreases* as behavior becomes more emotional. 'Gentlemen, let's get back to the facts,' is the classic conference table phrase, or in other words, if you want to be effective, be rational, be clear. If you want to be ineffective, focus on the emotional and interpersonal.

3. People work best under carefully defined direction, authority and control, governed by appropriate rewards and penalties that emphasize rational behavior and achievement of the objective.

In Figure 1, I should like to illustrate what I believe may be one underlying causal chain causing the problems described above. Let us assume that an organization, at any given point in time, may be described as having a particular level of effectiveness; that there are forces pushing upward to increase the effectiveness (e.g. top management); and that, since the level is somewhat stable, there are forces pushing downward resisting or restraining the level from going higher.[1] A balance of forces exists.

---

1. The model is taken from Kurt Lewin's concept of quasi-stationary equilibria; 'Frontiers in Group Dynamics', *Human Relations*, Vol. 1, No. 1 and No. 2, 1947, pp. 2-38. For the readers interested in organization theory, I mean to imply that people holding the three values above will always tend to create the problems originally depicted in Lewin's model. I am suggesting an explanation to Lewin's question as to why he found change activities in our society tended to take one form.

FIGURE 1

Causal Chain in Organizational Human Relations Difficulties

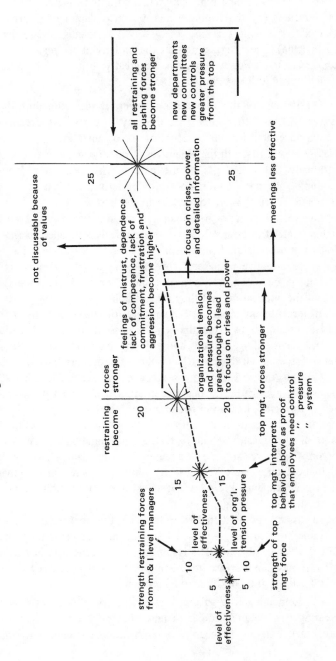

Now, let us assume that management wants to increase the level of effectiveness (by developing a new product planning and program review activities as in this case, or by any other change the reader wants to imagine). I am suggesting that the underlying *strategy* for, and the *processes of change* will tend to be greatly influenced by values the executives hold. For example:

(1) Because of the emphasis on objectives and rationality, the executives will tend to assume that the way to get a new organizational activity accepted by the members of the organization is to show them clearly how it fits with the objectives of the organization and to explain rationally the advantages of the new activity over the old one. For example, 'We need tighter controls' 'effectiveness must be increased,' 'I'm sure all of us want to manage in the best way available,' 'we must always remain alert for new management innovations.' As seen by the subordinates this means that management feels compelled to sell them a bill of goods; an implication that they resent. They see little need (if they are effective managers) for someone to tell them effectiveness should be increased, new concepts should be tried, etc. Indeed, many resent the implication that they are not doing this already.

In terms of our diagram, the strategy for change is to overcome the restraining forces by strengthening the pushing forces. This is done by management selling, pushing, and ordering. As we can see, at the second set of forces in our diagram, the level of effectiveness does increase.

(2) But the resisting forces are also increased. The resistance increases because of (a) the negative interpersonal impact the necessity to sell the program had upon the managers, (b) the mistrust and condemnation of the subordinates implied by the new program, (c) the inhibition of the questions and fears the subordinates wished to express *before* they were 'sold', (d) the feeling of being manipulated by the fact that the changes were kept a secret while they were being planned, and (e) the dependence and submissiveness caused by the unilateral management strategy.

(3) As can be predicted from knowing that management is uncomfortable in discussing negative feelings openly, the restraining forces are not dealt with directly. The result so far, is an increase in the level of effectiveness, an increase in resisting forces, and an increase in what we might call the gross organizational tension level.

(4) Remaining true to their values the top executives respond by creating new rational forces (a new sales pitch on the values of the program); bringing to bear new controls, and issuing new orders to

overcome the resistance. This tends to coerce the subordinates to suppress their confusion, feelings of distrust, and tension related to the new program, especially when interacting with the superiors. However, these feelings and tensions cannot be suppressed forever. They may erupt during the meetings that are part of the new change activities, thereby guaranteeing the ineffectiveness of these meetings.

(5) The increased management pressure, the increase in controls through paper work, the overload of work, all act to increase the forces pushing the level of effectiveness upward. The mistrust, tension, ineffective meetings (in our case of product planning and program reviews), the willingness on the part of lower level management to make the top responsible for the change (this is their baby) become examples of how the restraining forces are increased. The organizational tension also increases. This, in turn, stimulates management to develop new controls, check points, new courses to explain the importance of the program. These actions further increase the upward forces, which, in turn, increases the resisting forces, which in turn increases the organizational tension. The loop is now closed.

At some point the difficulties and tensions reach a breaking point among the members. The top executives usually sense this and typically call for a one or two day meeting away from home base 'to take out the kinks in the program.' In my experience most of these meetings were not very effective because the subordinates feared bringing out their real feelings and the true difficulties. One interesting sign that the true problems did not come out in these meetings was the degree to which the participants assigned the causes of their problems to conditions that were typical under the pyramidal organizational structure. For example, people may spend time trying to find out who was the *one* person responsible for decision making; they craved identification of their individual contribution; they competed in win-lose battles.

The difficulties with these meetings is illustrated in the example below. Three years after the reorganization plan went into effect developing a team approach, marketing and manufacturing were still having difficulties defining their roles and responsibilities. Manufacturing doubted that it needed marketing and *vice versa*. (If I included all the data we would see that engineering also had its doubts). In reading the example, it is useful to note how many of the problems raised and the solutions suggested are typical of the traditional organizational climate and not those endemic of the matrix organization. Each group worried more about trying to show that it was truly 'the' most responsible.

There was little attempt by the participants to help each other and to try to build a cohesive team where the whole was more important than any one part. Also when personality issues were ever so gently brought out (toward the end), the leader changed the subject.

A. Just the same way that the R and D department resents it and marketing man says 'my technology manager' and he says 'my manufacturing team.'

D. You know I don't resent that at all because I talk about my marketing manager.

C. Some of us do. We're all getting over it, but at the beginning we all tended to be sensitive.

A. Rather than the marketing managers' decisions, isn't the direction of the company contingent upon the company's decisions for these market opportunities determine the direction in which our future lies?

B. I'd like to reply to that because strategy is knowing the customer. The big part of it is knowing what the hell your competition's in. If you don't know your competition, you don't really know what the hell to do and who helps you play the strategy defense. It's got to be manufacturing. They've got to know their competing existing technology. They're the people that tell you what dollars . . . they give you a good share of the judgments that you can apply to strategy.

D. An example to support your point is product X. This is a real good example because this is where the manufacturing team set, looked at all competitive economics, all known producers, all possible methods by which X could be produced, and came up with what we might call an equilibrium sales price. This is a price at which somebody could over the next ten years afford so this came out as an average sales price. Now that really established the basic strategy level, so we then compared all the methods by which we could apply ourselves to producing our requirements on this product and looked at the comparative economics of these and their performance in the in-use areas for all of the uses of the product. So all the market technology teams contributed to this area. But the prime mover in the whole thing and really the one who was developing the whole base for the decision was a manufacturing team who were drawing together all of these inputs on competitive products and competitive economics, long range planning, but the decision as it was arrived at was a completely composite decision in the different marketing areas where the products were going to be sold.

C. I don't have very much experience the way the other guys do, but I don't see how you can. There is no separation between our groups.

E. You fellows may not like this, but I really think that basically the company still sets the price beyond which profit can be made and it's the agents who are selling the goods from this company who still are responsible to maximize profit.

D. Well, what do you think this is? I can't see where we're in any conflict with manufacturing.

B. Like hell!

A. I think this is probably right and maybe this is because we don't agree with manufacturing's mandate. The whole group down there on the boondocks don't really understand what marketing's function is. That's why we're gathered around this table, to try to understand that. It's obvious that there are a lot of people that don't understand what marketing's function is because that's why we've got it on the agenda.

B. Well, maybe if we understand your point of view, maybe we can help you to understand us.

A. Manufacturing has to understand what every marketing group, how every marketing group understands their own job. If you're not going to be the same, then the manufacturing group has to understand how you understand your job and how everyone understands their job.

C. Let me ask this—maybe you can help clarify it. Suppose marketing technology's out of this thing and then just have the manufacturing team and the sales department. Could you operate on that basis? Do you need this marketing group?

A. It is a good question. The answer is probably no. We were almost doing this once before, before the reorganization, and obviously it wasn't working successfully. The thing we've got now is a good bit more successful.

B. This terminology really leaves me cold. What do you mean 'more successful'?

E. It's semantics, that's all.

B. The guys down at the boondocks now think that marketing should look at the sales department as a bunch of peddlers. These are the terms that are being thrown around.

D. I think this all helped. We understand each better, so what's the next topic? This is the thing that I want to avoid, that we bring personalities into this. It was nothing personal. It was simply a statement that you made that I was having trouble understanding.

B. Everybody's getting involved and yet the problem's not being solved. We talked about this last week. The manufacturing managers talked about this. All of us are talking and that's about all.

Some readers may wonder how typical is this situation. In my experience the confusion and conflict is quite typical. The meeting was more open than usual which permitted us to get a rich specimen of the conflict. By the way, I do hope that these observations will help top managements pause and question their belief that the best way to plan a reorganization is to appoint a top committee (with all the appropriate help) to develop a reorganization plan and then 'sell' it to the organization. The lower level managers soon hear about the meetings and see them as the first sign of mistrust. The reasons usually given for this strategy are that to get wider participation may upset people and make it more difficult to sell the new plan. In my experience people become doubly upset with the secrecy and the anxiety built up around the rumors related to the reorganization. The time necessary for getting the program truly accepted is easily doubled. (In some recent research with governmental bureaux the time is extended until the next reorganization.)

I also hope that these data will raise question with the advice that some recent theorists suggest that people's behavior can be changed by changing the organizational structure. If the data from these nine examples are valid, then we may conclude that their view is oversimplified. I would agree with them that changes in organizational structure do bring about intended changes in people's behavior. (In our figure the effectiveness level was increased.) However, they also bring about unintended behavioral changes; the restraining forces are strengthened and the organizational tension level is greatly increased. To my knowledge the proponents of this approach have never shown an example where by changing the organizational structure the restraining forces and tension levels were also not increased.

These results suggest that, in addition to organizational structural changes, one should also focus on altering the basic values of the executives so that they can develop change strategies that may minimize the unintended consequences. (One example will be discussed below.) Our approach is not to be viewed as taking sides in an argument of change in structure vs. changes in people: our view is changes in structure *through* changes in people's values. Nor does the approach imply a blanket condemnation of the change strategy illustrated in Figure I. Such a strategy may be necessary where (for whatever reason) people refuse to alter their values, to become fully involved in the change, to take on their share of creating the change. If there is a lack of time for the more involving change process then one may use the more unilateral one depicted but may consider being quite open about the possible negative consequences and asking the people to help to reduce them.

A NEW PHILOSOPHY OF ORGANIZING AND MANAGING PEOPLE

I should like, at the outset, to repeat my view that project teams and matrix organizations are fundamentally valid. I believe that they are the most effective organizational structures for decisions that are complex and risky, that require the integration of many different inputs, and that depend on the continuing, long-range commitment of everyone involved without the organization's being saddled with excess and unneeded structures. (Once the project is complete, the team can be disbanded or a new project be assigned to it.)

One of the most important first steps is to communicate to the people that the matrix organization is not a simple extension of the traditional pyramidal structure. The pyramidal structure acquires its form from the fact that as one goes up the administrative ladder (1) power and control increase, (2) the availability of information increases, (3) the degree of flexibility to act increases, (4) the scope of the decisions made and the responsibilities involved increase. Implicit in the matrix organization are almost opposite tendencies. For example, power and control are given to the individual and/or to the groups who have the technical skill to accomplish the task, no matter what their organizational level. Thus a team could be composed of five people representing all different levels of authority (on the traditional chart), who are equal. The group could be chaired by the individual with the least organizational authority. The individual or groups are given responsibility and authority to make decisions of the widest necessary scope.

If we may extrapolate to the probable matrix organization of the future, Forrester suggests that the organization will eventually eliminate the superior-subordinate relationship and substitute for it the individual self-discipline arising from self-interest created by a competitive market mechanism within the system. The individual would negotiate continuously changing relationships. Each individual would be a profit center whose objective would be to produce the most value for the least activity; who would have the freedom to terminate as well as to create new activity, who would have access to all the necessary information. The organization of the future would be rid of internal monopolies which is the usual status of most traditional departments.

Although I would agree with Forrester, I believe that the organizations of the future will be a combination of the old and the new forms of organization. I believe that the old forms are going to be more effective for the routine, non-innovative activity that requires little, if any, internal commitment by the participants. However, as the decisions become less routine, more innovative and require more commitment, the newer forms such as the matrix organizations will be more effective.

LEADERSHIP STYLE AND MATRIX ORGANIZATION

In addition to being able to differentiate clearly between the old and the new forms, the future executive must also be able to know the conditions under which he will use the different organizational forms. Moreover, he will need to become skillful in several different kinds of leadership styles, each of which is consistent with a particular form. For example, an authoritarian leadership style is more consistent with the traditional structure; a participative style with the link pin organization defined by Likert and a style that develops risk-taking and trust for the matrix organization.

If recent research is valid, then the majority of executive leadership styles conform to the traditional pyramidal style. This is not surprising since leadership styles and organizational design would naturally go together. The findings that did surprise us were (1) the degree to which the executives believed in leadership styles that were consonant with the matrix organization, and (2) the degree to which they were *unaware* that they were *not* behaving according to their ideals.

Another important first step therefore is to help executives become more aware of their actual leadership style. Unless they develop such awareness, they are not going to be able to unfreeze their old styles, develop new ones, and most importantly, switch from one style to another as the administrative situations and the organization structure used is changed. Unless the switching from one style to another can be clearly identified by the person and the receivers, confusion will result.

Another finding that surprised us about executive decision-making was how many executives focused on keeping people 'happy'. Indeed, the most frequently cited reason for not being open with another was the fear that it might upset the receiver (and thus upset the sender). The most frequently cited reason for not bringing two groups together who are locked in interdepartmental warfare was that it would simply 'involve personalities and nothing but harm could come of it.' Although the executives that we studied were happiness-oriented in their behavior, they were not in their attitudes. They believed in strong leadership that could call a spade a spade and let the chips fall where they may. Again according to the observations, the spades were called spades and the chips placed on the line, but in private settings where few could be witnesses, or by such deft and diplomatic processes that few people, including the targets, were aware of what was happening. I cannot refrain from adding that there seemed to be a strong correlation between those executives who were critical of the field of 'human relations' as one whose objective was to make people happy and the degree of their blindness to the fact that they tended to do the very same thing when they were actually leading.

THE MANAGEMENT OF TENSION

Executives in the matrix organization will also need to learn, if I may be permitted to oversimplify, that there is productive and unproductive or crippling tension. The unproductive or crippling tension is tension that a person experiences but which he cannot control. The reason he cannot control the tension may be external (pressure from his superior) or internal (inability to control his own demands on himself, plus the accompanying feelings of impatience and guilt aimed at himself).

Productive tension is that tension that the individual can control and which comes from accepting new challenges, taking risks, expanding one's competencies, etc. These are the very qualities that are central to the matrix organization. Thus the executive of the future will have to learn how to define internal environments that challenge people, stretch their aspirations realistically, and help them face interpersonal reality. Some examples are financial controls that reward people for risk-taking; organizational situations that are optimally undermanned; incentive systems that reward excellence (not average performance), work that is designed to use people's complex abilities. To put this another way, we need to develop competence in manipulating the environment but not the people. (They should have the freedom and responsibility to choose if they will enter the new environment).

THE MANAGEMENT OF INTERGROUP CONFLICT

The matrix organization is composed of teams which in turn are populated by representatives of the traditional line functions. As we have seen, this leads to much intergroup conflict within the team as well as between teams.

Instead of trying to stamp out intergroup conflict as bad and disloyal, the executives need to learn how to manage it so that the constructive aspects are emphasized and the destructive aspects are de-emphasized. This means that the organization needs to put on the table for diagnosis the interdepartmental fires, the incidents of throwing the dead cat over into the other department's yard, the polarized competitive warfare where success is defined by the participants in terms of which side won rather than the contribution to the whole. The executives will have to learn how (1) to bring the groups together, (2) where each discusses and seeks, in private, to agree on its views and attitudes toward the other and toward self, (3) then the representatives of both groups talk together in the presence of the other group members, followed by (4) private discussion to establish the way they are perceived by others in order (5) to develop (through representatives) an understanding of the discrepancy between their and other's views.

THE EXECUTIVE EDUCATIONAL ACTIVITIES

Most organizations send their executives to university executive programs or to internal executive programs usually designed following the concept of the university. I do not want to get into philosophical discussions about the nature of university education at this point. I would like to point out, however, that *there may be a discrepancy between the characteristics of university education and the needs of the matrix organization.*

The university has typically assumed that learning (1) is for the individual, (2) occurs when it is given, (3) is tested by contrived examinations of the knowledge acquired, (4) need not be relevant to any immediate problem, (5) should be designed and controlled by the educator; it is the task of the educator to define the problems, develop ways to solve them and define the criteria for evaluation who passes and who does not. The matrix organizations require education that (1) focuses on individuals in team systems and (2) it occurs where the problem is located, (3) is learned by the use of actual problems, and (4) is tested by the effectiveness of the actual results, and (5) is controlled by those participating in the problem (aided by the educator as a consultant).

Executive education in the matrix organization will focus on system effectiveness. This means that the central educational department will now become an organizational development activity. It will have systems as its clients. A small team of consultants will enter the system and develop a diagnosis of its human and technical effectiveness. These data will then be fed back to representatives at all levels of the system to generate, at the grass-roots level, action recommendations. A steering committee composed of representatives of the client system and the organizational development will then prepare a long-range educational program designed to increase the immediate as well as the long-range effectiveness of the system.

Classes may then be held at the plant location or at a central facility, depending upon the resources needed, the time available, the availability of the 'students,' as well as the faculty. Teams and not disconnected individuals will study together for the majority of technical and management subjects. These teams will be actual working teams. This will place pressure on the faculty to develop learning that is valid for the real problems of the team and motivate the students to learn, since it is their problems upon which the education is focusing.

To put this another way, education will be for organizational and system diagnosis, renewal and effectiveness. It will be held with groups, subject material, and faculty that are organic to the organization's problem. One of the dangers of this education is the possibility that it will focus on the trivial, short-range problems. The quality control in this area will depend partially on the diagnostic competence of the faculty. In defining the problem they can help the organization to get to the underlying and basic causes. The students can also help by being alert to the validity of the education that is being offered to them.

Some critics wonder if teams of people working together can be pulled away from work. The answer, in my experience, is affirmative. The fear, for example, that the company will be in trouble if the top team leaves for a week, has been quietly exploded in several cases. The explosions have been quiet lest, as one president put it, 'it was learned how well things ran while the top management was away.'

More importantly, this new type of education is central to the work of the system. Thus, the team is not being pulled away from work. Indeed, in many cases, it is pulled away *in order to work*. Systems, like cars, need to have their organizational hoods opened and the motor checked and tuned. Unless this maintenance work is done, the system will deteriorate as certainly as does an automobile.

Finally, the concern of being away physically from the location should be matched with the concern about the number of hours being consumed needlessly while at work. In the studies listed previously, I have found that as many as half the meetings and as much as three quarters of the time spent at meetings are not productive and worse than unnecessary.

ORGANIZATIONAL CHANGE

Anyone who has planned major organizational change knows (1) how difficult it is to foresee accurately all the major problems involved, (2) the enormous amount of time needed to iron out the kinks and get people to accept the change, (3) the apparent lack of internal commitment on the part of many to help make the plan work, manifested partly (4) by people at all levels resisting taking the initiative to make modifications that they see are necessary so that the new plan can work. In preparing this article, I reviewed my notes from thirty two major re-organizations in large organizations in which I played some consulting and research role. I did not find one that could be labeled as fully completed and integrated three years after the change had been announced (and in many cases had gone through several revisions). That is, after three years there were still many people fighting, ignoring, questioning, resisting, blaming, the re-organization without feeling a strong obligation personally to correct the situation.

As I mentioned above, I believe the reasons for this long delay are embedded in the change strategy typically used by management. To refer to the diagram, the basic strategy has been for the top management to take the responsibility to overcome and outguess the resistance to change. This strategy does tend to succeed because management works very hard, applies pressure, and if necessary knocks a few heads together (or eliminates some). However, as we have seen, the strategy creates resisting forces that are costly to the organization's effectiveness, to its long run viability and flexibility, as well as to the people at all levels.

Reducing the Resisting Forces

What would happen if management experimented with the strategy of reducing the restraining forces by involving, at least, the management employees at all levels in the diagnosis, design, and execution of the change program? For example, in one organization a plan of reorganization was begun by getting all levels involved in diagnosing the present problems of the organizations. Groups were formed (which met only twice for several hours each time) to diagnose the effectiveness of the present organization. These groups were initially composed of people from various functions but holding positions of about equal level. Each group brain-stormed as much as it desired to get out the problems. They were not asked to suggest solutions at this time because no one group would have a total picture of the organization, and therefore its recommendations could be incomplete and misleading, with the added danger of each group becoming attached to their suggestions. Finally, people tend to be hesitant about enumerating a problem if they are asked for solutions and do not have any.

The results of these diagnostic sessions were fed to a top level steering committee which contained representatives of all the major managerial levels. This committee had the diagnoses collated, analyzed, and developed into an integrated picture. Wherever they found holes and inconsistencies, in the diagnoses they made a note of them. Eventually they had compiled a lengthy list of major questions to be answered before the overall diagnosis could be accepted as valid. These questions were fed to small task forces whose composition was specifically designed to be able to answer the questions. Thus, in this phase, the groups were composed of managerial personnel from many functions and levels who were relevant to the question being asked. These task forces were disbanded as soon as they provided the answers to the questions.

In the third phase the steering committee tried to develop a new organizational structure. In achieving this objective the steering committee began, for the first time, to suggest arrangements of individuals and groups tasks that could be threatening to various interests. This led to the members becoming more involved, cautious, and at times, defensive. Members who, up to this point, had felt free to be objective were beginning to feel themselves slipping into the role of protecting the groups toward which they had the closest attachment.

At this point, the task force went to the education group and asked for a course in such subjects as how to deal with intergroup rivalries and issues; with emotionality in groups, and with hidden agendas. This course was quickly but carefully planned. The steering committee members reported that it was a great help to them. It was especially helpful in welding them into a more fully functioning, open confronting of issues and risk taking. They also reported that as the members' confidence and trust in their group increased, the more willing they were to invite, at the appropriate time, members of departments whose future roles were being discussed so that the problems could be discussed and solved jointly.

The fourth phase was the preparation of a final plan. It was fully discussed with the top executives, then discussed systematically with key representatives of all the departments. Alterations were invited and carefully considered. Two members of the steering committee were members of top management who had authority to represent the top in approving most changes.

During the fifth phase two kinds of data were collected. First a questionnaire was sent to all who had participated, asking them for any individual comments about the plan as well as any comments about the effectiveness of the process of change to date. This diagnosis uncovered, in several cases, new ideas to be considered as well as several suggestions to be re-examined because individuals felt that they had been pushed through by a small but powerful clique.

The final plan was then drawn up with a specific time table (which had been discussed and accepted by people below). The top management, with the help of the steering committee, then put the new organizational plan into action. These phases took nearly seventeen months. However, once the plan became policy (1) the resisting forces and the tensions were much lower than expected on the basis of previous experience, (2) wherever they existed there were organizational mechanisms already established and working to resolve them, (3) the internal commitment to the new policy was high (It is ours, not theirs.) and thus (4) changes were made as they became necessary without much fanfare or difficulty.

One of the most important outcomes of this type of change strategy was that it provided a living educational experience for individuals and groups on how to work together; on how to develop internal commitment among the members of the organization, and how to reduce the unnecessary and destructive win-lose rivalries. Thus the change program became an opportunity for education at all levels. The result was that a new system had been created which could be used for future changes and to increase the capacity of the organization to learn.

Even with these results, I have encountered some managers who wonder if an organization can take this much time for changing organizational structure. In my experience, although time is a critical factor, it is a false issue. Time will be taken, whether management is aware of it or not, by people to ask all the questions, make all the politically necessary moves, develop all the protective devices, and create all the organizational escape hatches that they feel are necessary. The real issue is whether the time will be used constructively and effectively so that the organization can learn from its experiences, thereby increasing its competence in becoming a problem-solving system.

REFERENCES

Wallace, W. L., 'The Winchester-Western Division Concept of Product Planning', Olin Mathieson Chemical Corporation, January 1963.

Action Steps and Interventions

This section explores techniques for development and change as alternatives to the traditional unilateral decision-making approaches. The experiences of some organizations which have adopted applied behavioral science models are included to help provide a feel for the utilization of the concepts.

Emerging Criteria for Organization Development

GORDON L. LIPPITT

The development of greater numbers of more competent managers, and their successful management of human resources, has been made urgently necessary for business, industry, and government by technological advancements.

The fewer-than-needed graduates of our institutions of higher learning—who may be potentially qualified to manage in an area where efficient systems, adequate planning and ever more complex machines are commonplace—are often too soon obsolescent in the continuing knowledge explosion of today's society. It is for this reason that the initiation, nurture, evaluation and updating of management development systems are receiving increased attention. Many different types of organizations, public and private, are now developing programs that will strive to assure the development of new managers and the renewal of experienced managers. For this reason, a start must be made toward devising criteria by which these organizations may guide themselves in the difficult but essential work upon which they are embarked.

That the continuous development of all managers is a problem with wide implications is now generally recognized. Once an area of special interest thought to have intangible practical value, organizations today are hiring staffs, sponsoring research and bringing in consultants in this area which was once thought to have little practical value. But the numerous approaches, questionable theories and variable practices have caused many people to look upon management development as a quagmire of confusion—which, in the absence of bench marks, it well may be.

As much as nine years ago, one experienced practitioner observed: "Thus far, we have proceeded from an initial need—the need to increase the supply and improve the performance of managers. From this need, we have gone directly to the mechanics of application, using at first such tools as were available. In the process, two things have happened: (1) We have refined and added to these tools, until now there is a considerable array of fine techniques, methods, and 'programs' for doing the job of management development; and (2) in the course of using these tools, we have amassed a considerable body of experience with the developmental process. *But we have not extracted from that experience such standards and guides as are needed to help us discipline and organize our application of these tools.* As a consequence, we continue to fall easy prey to the fad of the moment, the gimmick peddler, and the charlatan.

Right Methods, Wrong Use

It might be said, in addition, that organizations often are frustrated in their desire for management development by the inappropriate use of otherwise sound developmental methods.

Since then, from the panoply of approaches, certain basic criteria have emerged that seem applicable to the latest and less empirical aspects of action research and planned change as opposed to pure research in behavioral science. Current synthesis can be isolated by tracing the trend of management development through some of its accumulative phases from the relatively artless to the present diagnostic and manipulative.

Anthropologists and social scientists might not argue with the hypothesis that management development was first vicarious, but that progression toward acceptance of commercial and social values, and the economic manifestation of family enterprise, led to what is now known as "on-the-job experience." The latter, in its original form, was concerned with inculcating by understudy and inbred imitation those skills and traits that an incumbent manager considered essential in anyone destined to follow in his footsteps. The process was explicit and allowed not at all for organizational change in keeping with environmental change. In its modern form, the understudy learns not only by observing and adapting, but also by questioning, assisting, initiating, and assuming a measure of responsibility in carrying out, in a narrow field of endeavor, pre-planned tasks that are progressively more difficult. Almost half a century ago, this method began to be overtaken by technology, and management itself struggled into a dawn that lighted it as a profession in its own right.

Apprenticeship, job rotation and performance appraisal—historical and still fundamental to management development in military services —became productive innovations in business and industry about 30 years ago. Men who demonstrated management potential were named

1. Bennett, Willard. *An Integrated Approach to Management Development,* Personnel Series, No. 171, American Management Association, New York, 1957, pp. 30-31. Author's italics.

to junior management boards. Here they had an opportunity to participate with a group in making recommendations to a senior board and
each participant was able to see his own role in a broader context. One
of the liabilities incurred in this system, as an outgrowth of having scant
means of pre-evaluation or post-evaluation, was the tendency to groom
"crown princes," whether or not they were truly qualified for higher
management responsibilities.

In Search of Development

About 20 years ago, competition from youthful oncomers and con-
current pressure of assumed requirements for wider cultural understanding forced incumbent executives back to school for education
promising to provide learning outside a narrow technical specialty and
outside their organizational affiliations. While none of this effort was
altogether wasted, much of it may have been disoriented and topically
misdirected as far as individual management capabilities were concerned. Sometimes participation in professional organizations, civic and
community groups, reading and lecture programs, gradually gave way to
more pertinent economic, environmental and political studies. At this
point, top organization executives in both government and industry
recognized the probability that their investment of money and the man
hours of subordinate employees might well return dividends in management development. In an overt attempt, rationalized as a means to
preserve and strengthen the "free enterprise system," management endorsed the liberal arts adult education movement that stresses the
management-directed broadening of the horizons of executives and
prospective executives as responsible performers in the 20th century.

As beneficial as this concept was and is, the science of management
soon demanded more specific knowledge and skills, and a greater conceptual understanding of the relationship between the trainee's organization and the controlling aspects of the world in which it exists.
Philosophic and cultural achievements alone did not meet the need for
such managerial skills as decision making, planning, and fiscal management, or the imperatives of communication such as faster reading and
improved writing abilities, effective public speaking and group leadership. With computers coming into general use, data process systems
analysis, information retrieval, operations research, and scheduling
methods such as PERT crowded in upon management. Starting late in
the Fifties, keeping abreast of the state-of-the-art in management became a critical concern. Many organizations, lacking professional guid-

ance and any rationale by which to identify their own requirements, assess the appropriateness of various approaches to training and education for their executives, or measure the results that might be obtained, launched themselves into management development somewhat blindly.

All-Level Implementation

At about the same time, research both within and without the organizational structures, and the pursuit of environmental influences and essential management skills, brought to the forefront in some organizations the need for the executive to better know himself. This led to laboratory training, with all its variations and debates, and psychological counseling, personality assessments and medical examinations, and thus to an even greater call for meaningful criteria.

Within the last five years, the trend has been toward *both* individual executive growth and management team-building through the problem-solving process and "management by objectives." This trend reflects a value system that requires heuristic implementation at all executive levels rather than the more common and, paradoxically, hidebound and piecemeal approach to management development. Today, the progression of methodology, greatly enriched by experience and knowledge derived from the many disciplines contributing to behavioral science, has very nearly circled back upon itself so as to be once more treading in an area not unlike the earlier, even ancient concept of developing situationally-oriented abilities in the individual manager. There is, therefore, an urgent necessity to determine on a man-to-man basis whether the application of tailored management development results in learning that is congruent to the organizational circumstances in which it is to be used.

These succeeding trends in management development reveal a poverty of fundamental guidelines that organizations can now fit to patterns of work and relationship, structure, technology, and administration that promise some of the most significant changes in our society.

Twelve criteria are here suggested to assist in evaluating any contemplated plan for management and organization development:

1. *Is it based on an articulated value system in which the purposes of an organization are clearly related to the public it serves?*
The management of any organization should identify and express the values it espouses and manifests. When this is done satisfactorily, it can

then undertake management development with a competent awareness that change or reinforcement of attitudes, skills and knowledge probably will affect these values, and it will be in a position to control the degree and manner in which new values are inculcated, or old ones modified.

However, if study reveals that an organization's value system is the result of dogmatic, authoritarian attitudes rather than rational adjustments, the inability of its present management to keep pace with a changing world may render useless whatever management development takes place in the individual employee.

2. *Does it take into account essential needs at the present state of organizational development?*
An organization develops differing needs for managerial leadership, depending upon the stage of growth at which it finds itself. A small organization trying to establish itself may need a few dynamic and autonomous executives who behave autocratically in defined spheres of responsibility. A large organization with multi-regional offices may need executives who can coordinate and communicate through others. A well-established corporation with years of success behind it may well want its executives to concentrate on community and other external relations that can contribute to larger service goals. These differences need to be continually assessed in establishing and executing the objectives of management development programs.

3. *Is it based on the realities of future change?*
Tomorrow's managerial existence in a rapidly-changing industrial governmental complex requires that today's executives be highly adaptive, and that the managers they develop be creative, tolerant of ambiguity and capable of timely self-adjustment. A practical awareness of the probable organization of tomorrow, in the near and distant future, should be maintained by those who plan the development of future leaders.

4. *Is it based on well-defined organizational objectives?*
Management by objectives has been thoroughly propounded in the management literature of the past ten years. Management development plans should translate into individual and work unit objectives, because success in human endeavor is inevitably related to meaningful achievement of personal and group goals. Individuals and groups involved in a process of management development need to know and understand

their goals, and to have knowledge of the criteria used to evaluate desirable change in their performance.

5. *Is it predicated on examples of successful and unsuccessful executive performance in other organizational systems?*

Management thinking is frequently limited by the reluctance of controlling executives, and those on whom they may rely for management development, to establish criteria for effective executive performance, both positive and negative. There is no single standard. The kind of managerial performance required in a large steel company may be quite different from that required in a large government agency. Skills of entrepreneurship needed in a small clothing company may differ remarkably from those essential in a small research and development firm. A well-conceived management development program will be based on the most thorough information possible as to the kinds of managerial characteristics and capabilities needed at each desk in that particular organization.

There is a need, too, to avoid managerial provincialism in the development of new managers. Because no organization exists in a vacuum, and because other organizations constantly, subtly bring their influences to bear on whatever value system may be endorsed, it is important that the way things are done outside the organization be not only unsuppressed but explored and evaluated as an avenue toward creating sophistication and balance in the judgments of the individual manager.

6. *Is it designed to change or reinforce individual attitudes as well as to develop applicable skills and knowledge?*

If management development contributes only the acquisition of new knowledge or skills, there may be no substantive change in performance—because so limited a contribution provides no foundation of attitude re-formation in the actual practice of new behavioral patterns by the individual. The most meaningful aspect of personal change resulting from a management development process is the examination and alteration of attitudes within the organization.

7. *Is it in all respects specifically designed for the particular organization, group or individual?*

There probably will never be such a thing as a universally applicable management development program. Canned or packaged management training which emphasizes one skill or another may be of questionable benefit unless it is quite obvious that such skills can be appropriately woven into the fabric of a larger, well-rounded management development plan that considers multiple organizational needs and that precisely fits the organization and the groups and individuals in it.

8. *Is it to be professionally created and implemented?*

Any program for developing mature, effective managers should make use of all that is known about learning processes and theory, educational methods, group and organizational behavior, and similar fields of knowledge. Whether guidance comes from within or without the organization, professional planning, designing and implementation are vital; more damage than good can be wreaked in this complex field by the inexperienced and unknowledgeable.

9. *Is it supported by the leadership practices and climate of the organization?*

Productive management development almost invariably means that desirable change will be effected in both individual and organizational practices. Reinforcement and follow-up are essential to freezing and maintaining management learning at new levels. Two major factors must be present: the behavior of senior executives should manifest support for and belief in the development program instituted for junior executives so as to establish a climate in which achievement is possible, and desired change in performance should be equitably rewarded by promotion or increase in pay, or by some other concrete indication that a goal has been reached and the fact is appreciated.

10. *Does it provide for evaluation in terms of long-range organizational goals?*

The future effect of a management development program, as well as its immediate results, should be studied by an organization as its needs change. A "happiness ratio" can, and usually is, easily obtained from the comments and testimonials of individuals who have participated in such a program, but available research methodology for assessment at a deeper level should be used to determine the absolute effect upon organizational, group and individual behavior. There is a danger that without the guidance of such deeper analysis, a management development program may prove to be culturally superficial rather than meaningfully developmental in terms of management.

Moreover, the means of evaluating short- and long-range objectives should be devised in advance. Objectives then found not to be compatible with achievement measurement probably will also be found not worth the expense and effort necessary to gain them.

11. *Is it designed ultimately to strengthen rather than weaken the individual's desire to remain employed by the organization?*
For a number of reasons, a badly handled management development program can—and has—resulted in abnormal personnel turnover. This includes both those it makes unhappy, and those who come to think they are good enough to move elsewhere for the money.

12. *Is it designed to produce greater capabilities in initiative and creativity in the individual?*
It is possible that a poorly designed program, or a misdirected one, could damage an organization's future by inadvertently creating solidified resistance to any further progress or change. This would be a result of "freezing" too hard.

Summary

The present-day approach to management development no longer considers the individual apart from his organization or the community in which he lives. As a result of a historic trend away from the purely mechanistic, the directed development of managerial leadership in the individual is now flexibly oriented to specific managerial tasks and values in a known organizational climate. Self-understanding and productive relations with others are integrated with an ability to apply a variety of methods and solutions, as well as skills and knowledge, to managerial problems that are themselves multi-faceted.

In the future, those who assume the responsibility for the development of managers will be judged by their over-all contribution to an organizational management team. Such judgments are best made in the light of parallel performance criteria, applicable on the one hand to the achievements of the individual and, on the other hand, to the intentions of the organization.

Management Issues in Organization Development

WILLIAM B. EDDY

The training function in business and public organizations has gained almost as much acceptance as has the field of education in American society. Yet organizational training is currently in a state of uncertainty and re-examination. It is common to find major discrepancies between the training director's aspirations and level of accomplishment, between the training curriculum and behavior change, and between program goals and organizational outcomes. A part of the difficulty involves attempts to move from a traditional personnel training function toward broader programs of organization development and change.

This paper examines some of the characteristics of organization development programs, as contrasted with more traditional efforts, and some of the issues which these new kinds of programs raise for management.

Traditionally, the training function in organizations has been viewed primarily as a segment of the operation designed to upgrade the skill levels of employees, both at the beginning of their employment and later as they changed roles or as new work methods were introduced. Upper level managers were rarely involved in the training programs. This view began to change with the appearance of "executive development programs" sponsored by universities, the American Management Association, and other groups. The focus at this stage, however, was still primarily upon individual growth in special areas of competence, so that the individual could make a more significant contribution to the organization by exerting better judgment, making better decisions, bringing more knowledge to bear on problems, or dealing with people more diplomatically.

This philosophy of training is currently being re-examined. The potentials of training, or management development, or organization development, as instruments for changing not only individual com-

Note: The author is indebted to Seymour Levy, James Crabtree and Thomas Lukens for their stimulating and helpful comments.

ponents, but also the climate and operation of the entire organizational system, are being explored.

ORGANIZATIONS AS SOCIAL SYSTEMS

Before examining these efforts and their rationale, it may be useful to review some of the characteristics and implications of earlier practices in training. Many organizations were built upon the principles of bureaucratic structure and administrative management. The goal of the manager was to set up the organization as a rational, efficient system with rules, procedures, and authority to hold the system together and direct the work behavior of employees. Employees were viewed largely as individual components who bartered their job skills and energies in return for wages. Training was primarily on-the-job and was oriented toward bringing the level of technical skill performance up to acceptable standards. Preparation for management came through achievement of technical skills plus experience.

As more and more researchers became interested in the processes of organization and management, as the practice of management became better understood, and as the direction of more and more organizations was taken over by professional managers, the concept of the organization began to change—and with it the concept of training. Beginning with such projects as the Hawthorne Western Electric studies,[2] it became clear that for purposes of understanding and dealing with the behavior of employees, it is more useful and valid to view the organization as a "social system" than as a set of technical skills directed by rational rules. The factors which frequently make the difference in the total performance and effectiveness of the organization include not only the individual skill levels or work methods, but also the overall functioning of the organization as a series of interdependent parts. Some characteristics which often influence performance include the quality of communication in all directions, clarity and acceptance of individual and organizational objectives and goals, cooperation among laterally-related units, trust level, distribution and use of power, effectiveness in resolving intraorganizational conflict, and adaptability to change. These findings influenced organizations to shift a part of their training focus to the skill areas that have to do with effective human relationships and team conditions. Thus, many programs in leadership, human relations, motivation and group dynamics have been developed. The problem with these programs is that they do not deal effectively with the system, but again, work with individuals and hope that their behavior will influence or contribute to the overall situation. Follow-up research has demonstrated that this occurrence is somewhat unlikely to happen. Job performance is a result not only of individual competence, but also of the "social role" of the employee as he operates within a framework of authority relationships, collaborative relationships and communication patterns. Individuals who are taught new ideas or attitudes about organizational behavior outside the context of their own job often find it difficult and sometimes threatening to try to implement these new behaviors in the work setting. Thus, the focus has begun to shift toward organizational sub-units rather than individuals as the objects of training effort.

This organizational focus has enouraged training directors and consultants to look for new approaches to training and development. The traditional classroom techniques for transferring knowledge remain useful, but do not provide the entire answer because they are not attuned to the need to bring about changes in social system behavior. Likewise, training methods based on individual learnings, separate and independent from the learnings of other members of the unit (as seen in the university classroom), have not proven particularly useful, because it is not the individual learnings, but the shared learnings, attitudes, and feelings that provide a basis for productive cooperation.

Another impetus for the search for new approaches to organizational training has been the recognition of a series of new, or at least newly recognized, conditions confronting organizations. These have been described in detail by Bennis (1966) and others. Technology is advancing so rapidly that older more rigid organizational forms are sorely taxed. New approaches, such as project management, place a premium on such skill areas as rapid adaptation to change, teamwork, and temporary system (committee and task force) formation. Emerging societal values and the rise of professionalism influence employees to be less willing to be excluded from participation in goal setting and decision-making. Complex products or functions require the pooling of varied technical resources into workable units. These and other developments have spurred the search for techniques useful in changing not only individual skill levels, but also the process of the organization.

THE ORGANIZATIONAL DEVELOPMENT PROCESS

As the need to devise new ways of improving human effectiveness in organizations has become pressing, training directors, consultants and social scientists have looked for educational approaches which are able to intervene at the system level. Ideas from the social psychology of attitude and social system change, group dynamics techniques, consulting and change agent skills, counselling, and personality theory currently form the nucleus of the field called Organization Development or O.D. The term refers to no formal set of techniques – there are none–but to a general point of view which may be implemented in a variety of ways.

Case descriptions of organizational development programs and their rationale and methodology are beginning to appear. Events at Union Carbide (Burck, 1965), TRW Systems (Davis, 1967), Harwood Manufacturing Company (Marrow, Bowers & Seashore, 1967), and Esso Standard (Buchanan, 1962) along with organizations studied by Argyris (1962), Mann (1957) and others have been documented. Warren Bennis, Gordon Lippitt, Floyd Mann, Chris Argyris, Edgar Schein, and Robert Blake and Jane Mouton are among those who have contributed to the literature in this field. Some of the common characteristics of many O.D. programs are listed.

1. They focus on the total organization or natural sub-organizational groupings (work units, teams, management levels) rather than individual employees as the object of training.

2. They emphasize experiential learning techniques (role playing, problem solving exercises, T Groups) in addition to traditional lecture methods.

3. Their subject matter includes real problems and events that exist in the organization and often in the training group, rather than hypothetical cases or examples. Often there is gathering and analysis of organizational data–either formally or informally.

4. Emphasis is placed upon competence in interpersonnel relationships rather than upon task skills. Much of the content and method is based on the behavioral sciences rather than upon administrative management theory, operations research, or personnel techniques– although these may be included as part of the program. The methodologies of the National Training Laboratories, managerial grid training, survey-feedback techniques and industrial psychology are often used.

5. Goals frequently have to do with developing group behavioral competence in areas such as communication, decision making, and problem solving, rather than understanding and retention of principles and theories. The trainer often sees himself more as consultant or change agent than expert-teacher.

6. They are frequently anchored in a humanistic value system which is committed to integrating individual needs and management goals,

maximizing opportunity for human growth and development, and encouraging more open, authentic human relationships.

7. They are not intended to refute the traditional structural-functional conception of the organization, but to help remedy some of its major dysfunctions.

Many training directors and managers are aware of the increasing interest in organization development programs and would like to try them. However, they frequently run into significant difficulty in convincing top management of the value of this approach and in developing financial and policy support. Thus, many O.D. efforts never get off the ground, while others get watered down to impotent proportions. A part of this circumstance is doubtless due to unfamiliarity or lack of appreciation of the problem by managers—as is often asserted. But another significant part is probably due to more subtle forces. While traditional training was assumed to deal primarily with relatively "safe" areas of technical job skills, O.D. evokes the specters of *influence* and *change*. It deals not only with *how* a particular individual does a job, but puts that job in its context in the total organizational system and claims as its legitimate domain the confrontation of such questions as *why* the job is

EXHIBIT A
A Comparison of Traditional Training and Organization Development

Dimension	Traditional Training	Organization Development
Unit of focus	The individual	Groups—teams or work units
Content of training	Technical and administrative skills	Interpersonal and group membership competence
Target Subjects	Primarily first line employees and supervisors, Managers trained outside organization	All levels, frequent initial intervention with upper management in-house
Conception of learning process	Cognitive and rational	Cognitive, rational, and emotional-motivational
Teaching style	Subject matter and teacher centered	Participant, immediate experience, and subject matter centered
Learning goals	Rationality and efficiency	Awareness and adaptation
View of Organization	Discrete functional skill units	Social system

structured as it is, organizational policy that relates to that job, and the behavior of other people who relate to that job—including managers. In other words, it brings organizational members at all levels in on issues that heretofore were considered to be the exclusive province of top management. Furthermore, it legitimizes the opportunity for employees to react openly to aspects of the social system which impinge upon them, and to attempt counter-influence in order to change organizational forces surrounding their roles.

It may be useful to compare the foregoing description of organization development with "management development", as the term is currently used. Management development, as described by House (1967), refers to "any attempt to improve current or future managerial performance by imparting information, conditioning attitudes, or increasing skills. Hence, management development includes such efforts as on-the-job coaching, counseling, classroom training, job rotation, selected readings, planned experience, and assignment to understudy positions." (p.13) The focus is primarily upon the manager and his behavior. The major contribution of current books and programs related to management development is that of presenting a more sophisticated and complete approach to training in the skill areas related to management. Such programs may be a major component of an organizational development effort.

PROBLEMS AND ISSUES IN IMPLEMENTATION

Organizations considering embarking on O.D. programs should seriously review their development needs, possible impacts of such programs upon the organization, their readiness for self-examination and change, and the willingness of management to open up organizational issues which may be affecting employees' performance. Below are listed some points worthy of consideration by organizations contemplating a broad development program.

1. Significant development programs are rarely successful without continued *active* support and involvement from top management. Total responsibility cannot be vested in a middle level staff person. Upper managers must be involved in formulating training goals, must participate in the training themselves, and must reinforce the behaviors sought after in training in their everyday managerial behaviors. They should also be involved in the evaluation of training.

2. The goal and probable impact of a development program is *change*—and to change the thoughts and feelings of members of the

organization will likely result in changes in their behavior, relationships, and attitudes about the organization. Outcomes of O.D. may challenge and call into question existing policies, structure, and managerial performance.

3. Training cannot realistically be expected to solve all the "people problems" of an organization, and attempts to raise morale, develop loyalty, or "sell the company" through training may be risky at best.

4. The outcomes of training will be influenced by the total organization system. The "climate" of the organization may encourage and reinforce changes aimed at in the training, or it may make these changes impossible and frustrate the trainees. The organization must be willing to look at its climate to see if it fosters development, growth, and change.

5. The organization must be willing to accept the fact that some of the people in whom it invests training resources may leave the organization and utilize their learning elsewhere. This possibility has kept more than one organization from instituting a significant development program.

6. There is evidence to suggest that underlying the substance of many discussions that take place in training sessions are basic employee concerns about such factors as interpersonal relationships, status, and career potential. Many consultants who are involved in development programs try to build into the programs the possibility for these basic concerns to be legitimized and dealt with in the training situation. It is not realistic in organization development to expect to "keep feelings out of it", or to deal only with abstract principles.

7. The relatively early state of development of management theory leaves us with differing opinions about successful management approaches and with no right or wrong answers or no magic keys to success. No training or development program can provide quick and easy solutions which can be readily implemented tomorrow.

8. Some organizations make the mistake of confusing development programs with show business. For example, the training director may become saddled with the responsibility for attracting and holding the audience on a volunteer basis, or making programs entertaining or "satisfying" as rated by participants. While participant feedback is an important aspect of a development program, the organization has no more responsibility to entertain its employees in training sessions than it does in budget conferences or planning meetings. The onus should be just as much on the participants as it is on the trainer to create conditions for productive learning, and the appropriate criterion is more

effective managerial behavior—not satisfaction.

If a decision is made to pursue an organizational development program, its success can be enhanced by building it into the management process. It may be useful to establish a permanent advisory group made up of management personnel from various parts of the organization. This group can work with the designated staff person or department in formulating, implementing and evaluating the program. And the advisory group can participate in the development of a comprehensive long-range plan for the program and can periodically review and revise the program, if necessary.

Probably the second most difficult aspect of implementing an O.D. program—after getting the organization to accept and integrate the concept—is to locate training resources. If the training department carries the responsibility for implementation, some readjustments may be necessary. One area of readjustment may be the attitudes and skills of the training staff itself. Staff members whose experience and attitudes indicate a role of teacher, audio-visual expert, or administrator of skill training classes may need a considerable amount of re-training themselves in order to perform roles more akin to change agents in the management process.

Another area of readjustment relates to the way the trainer is perceived by other members of the organization. The roles of many training directors are viewed as roles of relatively low power whose legitimate domain does not include managerial behavior and organizational operation. As long as these perceptions exist, whether they be valid or invalid, the incumbent will have difficulty administering an O.D. program.

A well-reasoned training and development program can often utilize a combination of internal and external resources. Few companies can accumulate a large and well-qualified staff of trainers to meet all needs. Yet a willy-nilly mix of visiting speakers, professional meetings, and canned programs will probably not be effective. Depending on the size and characteristics of the organizations, some programs that are recurrent and specific to the organization, such as supervisory training, can often be best handled in-house. Other programs can be developed out of regular visits by consultants, planned attendance at university or professional society conferences and management study seminars, and with regular reinforcement on the job through meetings, reports, etc. The distinguishing characteristic of most O.D. programs is a series of sessions for teams of employees in which consultants (either internally or externally based) assist participants in combining training with problem-solving and planning. No available program can realistically expect to meet all training needs. Most packages are based on certain premises and aimed at certain problem areas. They should be used to deal with certain organization problems or in tandem with other training approaches.[1]

In summary, moving from a traditional skill training program to a program of organization development may well mean that the organization has to deal with issues which are easy to ignore or avoid but crucial to the success of the program. These issues have to do with the emphasis to be placed on the development program and the resources to be devoted to it, with the implications of the program in regard to basic and sometimes uncomfortable issues such as influence, with change in behavior and attitude, and with the roles and competencies of the staff of the program. Unless these issues are confronted and dealt with, the organization is likely to find that it is extremely difficult to sustain a meaningful development program.

1. A discussion of the application of several O.D. programs can be found in *What's Wrong With Work?* New York: National Association of Manufacturers, 1967.

REFERENCES

Argyris, C., *Interpersonal Competence and Organizational Effectiveness*, (Homewood, Illinois: Dorsey-Irwin, 1962.)

Bennis, W. G., *Changing Organizations*, (New York: McGraw-Hill, 1966.)

Buchanan, P. C., "Training Laboratories in Organization Development" in *Issues in Human Relations Training*, I. R. Weschler & E. H. Schein (eds.) (Washington, D.C., NTL Institute, 1962.)

Burck, G., "Union Carbide's Patient Schemers," *Fortune Magazine*, (December, 1965.)

Davis, S. A., "An Organic Problem-Solving Method of Organizational Change," *Journal of Applied Behavioral Science*, Vol. 3, (Jan.-March, 1967)

House, R. J., *Management Development: Design, Evaluation & Implementation*, (Ann Arbor: University of Michigan, 1967.)

Mann, F. C., "Studying and Creating Change: A Means to Understanding Social Organization," in D.M. Arensberg, *et. al., Research in Industrial Human Relations*, (New York: Harper, 1957.)

Marrow, A. J., D. G. Bowers, & Stanley Seashore, *Management by Participation*, (New York: Harper, 1967.)

Roethlisberger, F. J., and W. J. Dickson, *Management and the Worker*, (Cambridge: Harvard University Press, 1939.)

T Groups for
Organizational Effectiveness

CHRIS ARGYRIS

• What causes dynamic, flexible, and enthusiastically committed executive teams to become sluggish and inflexible as time goes by? Why do they no longer enjoy the intrinsic challenge of their work, but become motivated largely by wages and executive bonus plans?

• Why do executives become conformists as a company becomes older and bigger? Why do they resist saying what they truly believe—even when it is in the best interests of the company?

• How is it possible to develop a top-management team that is constantly innovating and taking risks?

• Is it inevitable that we get things done only when we create crises, check details, arouse fears, and penalize and reward in ways that inadvertently create "heroes" and "bums" among our executive group?

Ask managers why such problems as these exist and their answers typically will be abstract and fatalistic:

- "It's inevitable in a big business."
- "Because of human nature."
- "I'll be damned if I know, but every firm has these problems."
- "They are part of the bone and fabric of the company."

Statements like these *are* true. Such problems *are* ingrained into corporate life. But in recent years there has evolved a new way of helping executives develop new inner resources which enable them to mitigate these organizational ills. I am referring to *laboratory education* or "sensitivity training" as it is sometimes called. Particularly in the form of "T Groups," it has rapidly become one of the most controversial educational experiences now available to management. Yet, as I will advocate in this article, if laboratory education is conducted competently, and if the right people attend, it can be a very powerful educational experience.

How does laboratory education remedy the problems I have mentioned? By striving to expose and modify certain values held by typical executives, values which, unless modified, serve to impair interpersonal effectiveness. These values are ingrained in the pyramidal structure of the business enterprise. The following summarizes several basic causes of management ineffectiveness as isolated by three studies (Argyris, 1962, 1960, 1964): (1) in a large corporate division — 30,000 employees, grossing $500 million per year; (2) a medium-size company — 5,000 employees, grossing in excess of $50 million per year; and (3) a small company — 300 employees.

THE PYRAMIDAL VALUES

There are certain values about effective human relationships that are inherent in the pyramidal structure of the business organization and which successful executives (understandably) seem to hold. Values are learned commands which, once internalized, coerce human behavior in specific directions. This is why an appreciation of these values is basic in understanding behavior.

What are these "pyramidal" values? I would explain them this way.

1. The important human relationships—the crucial ones—are those which are related to achieving the organization's objective, i.e., getting the job done, as for example:

"We are here to manufacture shoes, that is our business, those are the important human relationships; if you have anything that can influence those human relationships, fine."

2. Effectiveness in human relationships increases as behavior becomes more rational, logical, and clearly communicated; but effectiveness decreases as behavior becomes more emotional. Let me illustrate by citing a typical conversation:

"Have you ever been in a meeting where there is a lot of disagreement?"
"All the time."
"Have you ever been in a meeting when the disagreement got quite personal?"
"Well, yes I have, but not very often."
"What would you do if you were the leader of this group?"
"I would say, 'Gentlemen, let's get back to the fact,' or I would say, 'Gentlemen, let's keep personalities out of this.' If it really got bad, I would wish it were five o'clock so I could call if off, and then I would talk to the men individually."

3. Human relationships are most effectively motivated by carefully defined direction, authority, and control. as well as appropriate rewards and penalties that emphasize rational behavior and achievement of the objective.

If these are the values held by most executives, what are the consequences? To the extent that executives believe in these organizational values, the following changes have been found:

1. There is a decrease in receiving and giving information about executives' interpersonal impact on each other. Their interpersonal difficulties tend to be either suppressed or disguised and brought up as rational, technical, intellectual problems. As a result, they may find it difficult to develop competence in dealing with feelings and interpersonal relations. There is a corresponding decrease in their ability to own up to or be responsible for their ideas, feelings, and values. Similarly there is a dropping off of experimentation and risk-taking with new ideas and values.

2. Along with the decrease in owning, openness, risk-taking, there is an increase in the denial of feelings, in closedness to new ideas, and in the need for stability (i.e., "don't rock the boat"). As a result, executives tend to find themselves in situations where they are not adequately aware of the human problems, where they do not solve them in such a way that they remain solved without deteriorating the problem-solving process. Thus, if we define interpersonal competence as (a) being aware of human problems, (b) solving them in such a way that they remain solved without deteriorating the problem-solving process, these values serve to decrease interpersonal competence.

3. As the executives' interpersonal competence decreases, conformity, mistrust, and dependence, especially on those who are in power, increase. Decision making becomes less effective, because people withhold many of their ideas, especially those that are innovative and risky, and organizational defenses (such as management by crisis, by detail, and through fear) *increase.* So do such "protective" activities as "JIC" files (just in case the president asks), "information" meetings (to find out what the opposition is planning), and executive politicking.

If this analysis is valid, then we must alter executives' values if we are to make the system more effective. The question arises as to what changes can and should be made in these values.

But since executives are far from unknowledgeable, why have they clung to these pyramidal values? First, because they are *not necessarily wrong.* Indeed, they are a necessary part of effective human relationships. The difficulty is that alone they are not enough. By themselves they tend to lead to the above consequences. What is needed is an additional set of values for the executive to hold.

1. The important human relationships are not only those related to

achieving the organization's objectives but those related to maintaining the organization's internal system and adapting to the environment as well.

2. Human relationships increase in effectiveness as *all* the relevant behavior (rational and interpersonal) becomes conscious, discussable, and controllable. (The rationality of feelings is as crucial as that of the mind.)

3. In addition to direction, controls, and rewards and penalties, human relationships are most effectively influenced through authentic relationships, internal commitment, psychological success, and the process of confirmation.

CHANGE THROUGH EDUCATION

But how does one change an executive's values? One way is by a process of re-education. First there is an unfreezing of the old values, next the development of the new values, and finally a freezing of the new ones.

In order to begin the unfreezing process, the executives must experience the true ineffectiveness of the old values. This means they must have a "gut" experience of how incomplete the old values are. One way to achieve this is to give them a task to accomplish in situations where their power, control, and organizational influences are minimized. The ineffectiveness of the old values, if our analysis is correct, should then become apparent.

A second requirement of re-education arises from the fact that the overwhelming number of educational processes available (e.g., lecture, group discussion, and the like) are based on the pyramidal values. Each lecture or seminar at a university has clearly defined objectives and is hopefully staffed by a rational, articulate teacher who is capable of controlling, directing, and appropriately rewarding and penalizing the students. But, as I have just suggested, these represent some of the basic causes of the problems under study. The educator is in a bind. If he teaches by the traditional methods, he is utilizing the very values that he is holding up to be incomplete and ineffective.

To make matters more difficult, if the re-educational process is to be effective it is necessary to create a *culture* in which the new values can be learned, practiced, and protected until the executives feel confident in using them. Such a culture would be one which is composed of people striving to develop authentic relationships and psychological success. Briefly, authentic relationships exist when an individual can behave in such a way as to increase his self-awareness and esteem and, at the same time, provide an opportunity for others to do the same. Psychological success is the experience of realistically challenging situations that tax one's capacities. Both are key components of executive competence.

The creation of a re-educational process where the unfreezing of the old values, relearning of the new values, and refreezing of the new values under primary control of the students, embedded in a culture that is rarely found in our society, is an extremely difficult task. Yet an approach to fulfilling these requirements if offered by laboratory education.

Probably because of its novelty, laboratory education has become one of the most talked-about, experimented with, lauded, and questioned educational experiences for top executives. The interest of top executives has been so great that the National Training Laboratories* (a nonprofit educational organization which administers most of the laboratories) has had to increase the programs many fold in the past ten years.

Any educational experience that is as novel as laboratory education is destined to be controversial. And this is good because reasoned controversy can be the basis for corrections, refinements, and expansions of the process. Research (unfortunately not enough) is being conducted under the auspices of the National Training Laboratories and at various universities such as the University of California, Case Institute of Technology, Columbia, George Washington, Harvard, M.I.T., Michigan, Texas, and Yale, to name a few.

Aims of the Program

The first step in a laboratory program is to help the executives teach themselves as much about their behavior as possible. To do so they create their own laboratory in which to experiment. The strategy of an experiment begins with a dilemma. A dilemma occurs when, for a given situation, there is no sound basis for selecting among alternatives, or there is no satisfactory alternative to select, or when habitual actions are no longer effective.

What do people do when confronted with a dilemma? Their immediate reaction is to try out older methods of behaving with which

---

*Editor's note: The National Training Laboratories is now called the NTL Institute. It conducts programs for educational leaders, community planners, church leaders, and others, as well as for business executives.

they are secure, or else to seek guidance from an "expert." In this way, the anxiety so invariably associated with not knowing what to do can be avoided. In the laboratory, then, the anticipated first reactions by participants to a dilemma are to try traditional ways of responding.

Only when conventional or traditional ways of dealing with a dilemma have been tried—unsuccessfully—are conditions ripe for inventive action. Now people are ready to think, to shed old notions because they have not worked, to experiment, and to explore new ways of reacting to see if they will work. The period when old behavior is being abandoned and when new behavior has yet to be invented to replace it is an "unfrozen" period, at times having some of the aspects of a crisis. It is surrounded by uncertainty and confusion.

Fullest learning from the dilemma-invention situation occurs when two additional types of action are taken:

One is feedback, the process by which members acquaint one another with their own characteristic ways of feeling and reacting in a dilemma-invention situation. Feedback aids in evaluating the consequences of actions that have been taken as a result of the dilemma situation. By "effective" feedback I mean the kind of feedback which minimizes the probability of the receiver or sender becoming defensive and maximizes his opportunity to "own" values, feelings, and attitudes. By "own" I mean being aware of and accepting responsibility for one's behavior.

The final step in the dilemma-invention cycle is generalizing about the total sequence to get a comprehensive picture of the "common case." When this is done, people are searching to see to what extent behavior observed under laboratory conditions fits outside situations. If generalization is not attempted, the richness of dilemma-invention learning is "lost."

T for Training

The core of most laboratories is the T (for training) Group. This is most difficult to describe in a few words. Basically it is a group experience designed to provide maximum possible opportunity for the individuals to expose their behavior, give and receive feedback, experiment with new behavior, and develop everlasting awareness and acceptance of self and others. The T Group, when effective, also provides individuals with the opportunity to learn the nature of effective group functioning. They are able to learn how to develop a group that achieves specific goals with minimum possible human cost.

The T Group becomes a learning experience that most closely approximates the values of the laboratory regarding the use of leadership, rewards, penalties, and information in the development of effective groups. It is in the T Group that one learns how to diagnose his own behavior, to develop effective leadership behavior and norms for decision making that truly protect the "wild duck."

Role of Educator

In these groups, some of the learning comes from the educator, but most of it from the members interacting with each other. The "ground rules" the group establishes for feedback are important. With the help of the educator, the group usually comes to see the difference between providing help and attempting to control or punish a member; between analyzing and interpreting a member's adjustment (which is not helpful) and informing him of the impact it has on others. Typically, certain features of everyday group activity are blurred or removed. The educator, for example, does not provide the leadership which a group of "students" would normally expect. This produces a kind of "power vacuum" and a great deal of behavior which, in time, becomes the basis of learning.

There is no agenda, except as the group provides it. There are no norms of group operation (such as *Robert's Rules of Order*) except as the group decides to adopt them. For some time the experience is confusing, tension-laden, frustrating for most participants. But these conditions have been found to be conducive to learning. Naturally, some individuals learn a great deal, while others resist the whole process. It is rare, however, for an individual to end a two-week experience feeling that he has learned nothing.

Usually the T Group begins with the educator making explicit that it is designed to help human beings to explore their values and their impact on others, determine if they wish to modify their old values and develop new ones, develop awareness of how groups can inhibit as well as facilitate human growth and decision making. Thus a T Group does not begin without an objective, as far as the educator is concerned. It has a purpose, and this purpose, for the educator, is emotionally and intellectually clear.

However, the educator realizes that the purpose is, at the moment, only intellectually clear to the members. Thus, to begin, the educator will probably state that he has no specific goals in mind for the group.

Moreover, he offers no specific agenda, no regulations, no rules, and so on. The group is created so its members can determine their own leadership, goals, and rules.

There is very little that is nondirective about a T Group educator's role. He is highly concerned with growth, and he acts in ways that he hopes will enhance development. He is nondirective, however, in the sense that he does not require others to accept these conditions. As one member of the T Group, he will strive sincerely and openly to help establish a culture that can lead to increased authentic relationships and interpersonal competence.

However, he realizes that he can push those in the group just so far. If he goes too far, he will fall into the trap of masterminding their education. This is a trap in which group members might like to see him fall, since it would decrease their uncomfortableness and place him in a social system similar (in values) to their own. In other words, his silence, the lack of predefined objectives, leadership, agenda, rules, and so on, are not designed to be malicious or hurt people. True, these experiences may hurt somewhat, but the hypothesis is that the pain is "in the service of growth."

At this point, let me assume that you are a member of such a T Group, so that I can tell you what you are likely to experience.

Action and Reaction

At the outset you are likely to expect that the educator will lead you. This expectation is understandable for several reasons:

1. An educator in our culture tends to do precisely this.

2. Because of the newness of the situation, the members may also fear that they are not competent to deal with it effectively. They naturally turn to the educator for assistance. It is common in our culture that when one member of a group has more information than the others as to how to cope with the new, difficult situation, he is expected by the others, *if he cares for them,* to help them cope with the new situation. For example, if I am in a cave with ten other people who are lost and I know how to get out, it would be from their viewpoint the height of noncaring for me to fail to help them get out.

3. Finally, the members may turn to the educator because they have not as yet developed much trust for each other.

The educator may believe it is helpful, during the early stages of a T Group, to tell you that he understands why you feel dependent on him. But he will also add that he believes that learning can take place more effectively if you first develop an increasing sense of trust of one another and a feeling that you can learn from one another.

When I act as the educator for a T Group, I freely admit that silence is not typical of me and that I need to talk, to be active, to participate. In fact, I may even feel a mild hostility if I am in a situation in which I cannot participate in the way that I desire. Thus, anything you (members) can do to help me "unfreeze" by decreasing your dependence on me would be deeply appreciated. I add that I realize that this is not easy and that I will do my share.

Typically, the members begin to realize that the educator supports those individuals who show early signs of attempting to learn. This is especially true for those who show signs of being open, experimentally minded, and willing to take risks by exposing their behavior. How are these qualities recognized?

There are several cues that are helpful. First, there is the individual who is not highly upset by the initial ambiguity of the situation and who is ready to begin to learn. One sign of such an individual is one who can be open about the confusion that he is experiencing. He is able to own up to his feelings of being confused, without becoming hostile toward the educator or the others. Such an individual is willing to look at his and others' behavior under stress, diagnose it, and attempt to learn from it. Some of these individuals even raise questions about other members' insistence that the educator should get them out of the ambiguous situation.

Some members, on the other hand, react by insisting that the educator has created the ambiguity just to be hostile. You will find that the educator will encourage them to express their concern and hostility as well as help them to see the impact that this behavior (i.e., hostility) is having on him. There are two reasons for the educator's intervention: (1) to reinforce (with feelings) the fact that he is not callous about their feelings and that he is not consciously attempting to be hostile; and (2) to unfreeze others to explore their hostility toward him or toward each other. Such explorations can provide rich data for the group to diagnose and from which to learn.

Problem of Mimicking

As the group continues, some members begin to realize that the educator's behavior now may serve for what it is. That is, it may be as valid a model as the educator can manifest of how he would attempt (a) to help create an effective group, and (b) to integrate himself into that group so that he becomes as fully functioning a member as possible. The model is his; he admits owning it, but he is *not* attempting to "sell" it to others or in any way to coerce them to own it.

You may wonder if viewing the educator as a source of "model behavior" would not lead you simply to *mimic* him. Although this may be the case, we should not forget that as you begin to unfreeze your previous values and behavior, you will find yourself in the situation of throwing away the old and having nothing new that is concrete and workable. This tends to create states of vacillation, confusion, anxiety, ambivalence, and so on. These states in turn may induce you to "hang on" to the old with even greater tenacity. To begin to substitute the new behavior for the old, you will feel a need to see (1) that you can carry out the new behavior effectively and (2) that the new behavior leads to the desired results.

Under these conditions the members usually try out any bit of behavior that represents the "new." Experimentation not only is sanctioned; it is rewarded. One relatively safe way to experiment is to try out the educator's behavior. It is at this point that the individual is mimicking. And he should feel free to mimic and to talk about the mimicking and explore it openly. Mimicking is helpful if you are aware of and accept the fact that you do not *own* the behavior, for the behavior with which you are experimenting is the educator's. If the educator is not anxious about the mimicking, the member may begin safely to explore the limits of the new behavior. He may also begin to see whether or not the educator's behavior is, for him, realistic.

Individual vs. Group

At the outset the educator tends to provide that assistance which is designed to help the members to become aware of their present (usually low) potential for establishing authentic relationships, become more skillful in providing and receiving nonevaluative descriptive feedback, minimize their own and others' defensiveness, become increasingly able to experience and own up to their feelings.

Although interpersonal assistance is crucial, it is also important that the T Group not be limited to such interventions. After the members receive adequate feedback from one another as to their inability to create authentic relationships, they will tend to want to become more effective in their interpersonal relationships. It is at this point that they will need to learn that group structure and dynamics deeply influence the probability of increasing the authenticity of their interpersonal relations.

As soon as the members realize that they must become more open with those feelings that typically they have learned to hid, they will need to establish group norms to sanction the expression of these feelings. Also, if members find it difficult in the group to express their important feelings, this difficulty will tend to be compounded if they feel they must "rush" their contribution and "say something quick," lest someone else take over the communication channels. Ways must be developed by which members are able to use their share of the communication channels. Also, group norms are required that sanction silence and thought, so that members do not feel coerced to say something, before they have thought it through, out of fear that they will not have an opportunity to say anything later.

An example of the interrelationship between interpersonal and group factors may be seen in the problems of developing leadership in a group. One of the recurring problems in the early stages of a T Group is the apparent need on the part of members to appoint a leader or a chairman. Typically, this need is rationalized as a group need because "without an appointed leader a group cannot be effective."

One member said, "Look, I think the first thing we need is to elect a leader. Without a leader we are going to get nowhere fast." Another added, "Brother, you are right. Without leadership, there is chaos. People hate to take responsibility, and without a leader they will goof off."

There are several ways that your group might consider for coping with this problem, each of which provides important but different kinds of learning. One approach is to see this as a group problem. How does leadership arise and remain helpful in a group? This level of learning is important and needs to be achieved.

Another possibility is for the group members to explore the underlying assumptions expressed by those individuals who want to appoint leaders. For example, in the case illustrated above, both men began to realize that they were assuming that people "need" appointed leadership because, if left alone, they will not tend to accept responsibility. This implies a lack of confidence in and trust of people. It also implies mistrust of the people around the table. These men were suggesting that without an appointed leader the group will flounder and become chaotic.

Someone then took the initiative and suggested that their comments implied a lack of trust of the people around the table. Another individual suggested that another dimension of mistrust might also be operating. He was concerned how he would decide if he could trust the man who might be appointed as the leader. The discussion that followed illustrated to the group the double direction of the problem of trust. Not only do superiors have feelings of mistrust of subordinates, but the latter may also mistrust the former.

One of the defendants of the need for leadership then said, "Look, Mr. B. over there has been trying to say something for half an hour, and hasn't succeeded. If we had a leader, or if he himself were appointed leader temporarily, then he might get his point of view across." Several agreed with the observation. However, two added some further insightful comments. One said, "If we give Mr. B. authority, he will never have to develop his internal strength so that he can get his point across without power behind him." "Moreover," the other added, "if he does get appointed leader, the group will never have to face the problem of how it can help to create the conditions for Mr. B. to express his point of view."

Thus we see that attempting to cope with the basic problems of group membership can lead to an exploration of problems of group membership as well as requirements of effectively functioning groups.

The question of trust, therefore, is a central problem in a T Group, indeed, as it is in any group organization. If this can be resolved, then the group has taken an important step in developing authentic relationships. As the degree of trust increases, "functional leadership" will tend to arise spontaneously because individuals in a climate of mutual trust will tend to delegate leadership to those who are most competent for the subject being discussed. In doing so, they also learn an important lesson about effective leadership.

Another kind of learning that usually develops clearly is that the group will not tend to become an effective task-oriented unit without having established effective means to diagnose problems, make decisions, and so on. It is as the group becomes a decision-making unit that the members can "test" the strength and depth of their learning. The pressure and stress of decision making can help to show the degree to which authenticity is apparent rather than real. It can also provide opportunity for further learning, because the members will tend to experience new aspects of themselves as they attempt to solve problems and make decisions.

WHO LEARNS FROM T GROUP EXPERIENCES?

People who learn in T Groups seem to possess at least three attributes:

1. A relatively strong ego that is not overwhelmed by internal conflicts.
2. Defenses which are sufficiently low to allow the individual to hear what others say to him (accurately and with minimal threat to himself), without the aid of a professional scanning and filtering system (that is, the therapist, the educator).

3. The ability to communicate thoughts and feelings with minimal distortion. In other words, the operational criterion of minimal threat is that the individual does not tend to distort greatly what he or others say, nor does he tend to condemn others or himself.

This last criterion can be used in helping to select individuals for the T-Group experience. *If the individual must distort or condemn himself or others to the point that he is unable to do anything but to continue to distort the feedback that he gives and receives, then he ought not to be admitted to a T Group.*

To put this another way, T Groups, compared to therapy groups, assume a higher degree of health—not illness—that is, a higher degree of self-awareness and acceptance. This is an important point. *Individuals should not be sent to the laboratory if they are highly defensive.* Rather, the relatively healthy individuals capable of learning from others to enhance their degree of effectiveness are the kinds of individuals to be selected to attend.

FURTHER COMPONENTS

Laboratory education has other components. I have focused in detail on T Groups because of their central role. This by no means describes the total laboratory experience. For example, laboratory education is helpful in diagnosing one's organizational problems.

Diagnosing Problems. When a laboratory program is composed of a group of executives who work in the same firm, the organizational diagnostic experiences are very important. Each executive is asked to come to the laboratory with any agenda or topic that is important to him and to the organization. During the laboratory, he is asked to lead the group in a discussion of the topic. The discussion is taped and observed by the staff (with the knowledge of the members).

Once the discussion is completed, the group members listen to themselves on the tape. They analyze the interpersonal and group dynamics that occurred in the making of the decision and study how these factors influenced their decision making. Usually, they hear how they cut each other off, did not listen, manipulated, pressured, created win-lose alternatives, and so on.

Such an analysis typically leads the executives to ask such questions as: Why do we do this to each other? What do we wish to do about it, if anything?

On the basis of my experience, executives become highly involved in answering these questions. Few hold back from citing interpersonal and organizational reasons why they feel they have to behave as they do. Most deplore the fact that time must be wasted and much energy utilized in this "windmilling" behavior. It is quite frequent for someone to ask, "But if we don't like this, why don't we do something about it?"

Under these conditions, the things learned in the laboratory are intimately interrelated with the everyday "real" problems of the organization. Where this has occurred, the members do not return to the organization with the same degree of bewilderment that executives show who have gone to laboratories full of strangers. In the latter case, it is quite common for the executive to be puzzled as to how he will use what he has learned about human competence when he returns home.

Consultation Groups. Another learning experience frequently used is to break down the participants into groups of four. Sessions are held where each individual has the opportunity both to act as a consultant giving help and as an individual receiving help. The nature of help is usually related to increasing self-awareness and self-acceptance with the view of enhancing interpersonal competence.

Lectures. Research information and theories designed to help organizational learning are presented in lectures—typically at a time when it is most clearly related to the learnings that the participants are experiencing in a laboratory.

Role-Playing. As a result of the discussions at the laboratory program, many data are collected illustrating situations in which poor communications exist, objectives are not being achieved as intended, and so on. It is possible in a laboratory to role-play many of these situations, to diagnose them, to obtain new insights regarding the difficulties, as well as to develop more effective action possibilities. These can be role-played by asking the executives to play their back-home roles. For other problems, however, important learnings are gained by asking the superior to take the subordinate's role.

Developing and Testing Recommendations. In most organizations, executives acknowledge that there are long-range problems that plague an organization, but that they do not have time to analyze them thoroughly in the back-home situation (for example, effectiveness of decentralization). In a laboratory, however, time is available for them to discuss these problems thoroughly. More important, as a result of their laboratory learnings and with the assistance of the educators, they can develop new action recommendations. They can diagnose their effectiveness as a group in developing these recommendations—have they really changed; have they really enhanced their effectiveness?

Intergroup Problems. One of the central problems of organizations is the intergroup rivalries that exist among departments. If there is time in a laboratory, this topic should be dealt with. Again, it is best introduced by creating the situation where the executives compete against one another in groups under "win-lose" conditions (i.e., where only one can win and someone must lose).

CORRECTING MISUNDERSTANDINGS

Any educational activity that is as new and controversial as laboratory education is bound to have misconceptions and misunderstandings built around it. Therefore, I should like to attempt briefly to correct a few of the more commonly heard misunderstandings about laboratory education.

Laboratory methods in general, and T Groups in particular, are not a set of hidden, manipulative processes by which individuals can be "brainwashed" into thinking, believing, and feeling the way someone might want them to without realizing what is happening to them.

Central to a laboratory is openness and flexibility in the educational process. It is open in that it is continually described and discussed with the participants as well as constantly open to modification by them.

Along with the de-emphasis of rigidity and stress on flexibility, the emphasis is on teaching that kind of knowledge and helping the participants develop those kinds of skills which increase the strength and competence to question, to examine, and to modify. The objectives of a laboratory are to help an individual learn to be able to reject that which he deeply believes is inimical to his self-esteem and to his growth —and this would include, if necessary, the rejection of the laboratory experience.

A laboratory is not an educational process guided by a staff leader who is covertly in control and by some magic hides this fact from the participants.

A laboratory means that people come together and create a setting where (as is the case in any laboratory) they generate their own data for learning. This means that they are in control and that any behavior in the laboratory, including the staff member's, is fair game for analysis.

I should like to suggest the hypothesis that if anything is a threat to the participants, it is not the so-called covert control. The experience becomes painful when the participants begin to realize the scope and depth to which the staff is ready "to turn things over to them." Initially this is seen by many participants as the staff abdicating leadership. Those who truly learn come to realize that in doing this the staff is expressing, in a most genuine way, their faith in the potentiality of the participants to develop increasing competence in controlling more of their learning. As this awareness increases, the participants usually begin to see that their cry of "abdication of leadership" is more of a camouflage that hides from them how little they trusted each other and themselves and how over-protected they were in the past from being made to assume some responsibility for their learning.

The objective of laboratory education is not to suppress conflict and to get everyone to like one another.

The idea that this is the objective is so patently untrue that I am beginning to wonder if those who use it do not betray their own anxiety more than describe what goes on in a laboratory. There is no other educational process that I am aware of in which conflict is generated, respected, and cherished. Here conflict, hostility, and frustration become motivations for growth as well as food for learning. It is with these kinds of experiences that participants learn to take risks—the kinds of risks that can lead to an increase in self-esteem. As these experiences are "worked through" and the learnings internalized, participants soon begin to experience a deeper sense of self-awareness and acceptance. These, in turn, lead to an increased awareness and acceptance of others.

And this does *not* necessarily mean liking people. Self-acceptance means that individuals are aware of themselves and care so much about themselves that they open themselves to receiving and giving information (sometimes painful) about their impact on others and others' impact on them, so that they can grow and become more competent.

Laboratory education does not attempt to teach people to be callous, disrespectful of society, and to dislike those who live a less open life.

If one truly begins to accept himself, he will be less inclined to condemn nongenuineness in others, but to see it for what it is, a way of coping with a nongenuine world by a nongenuine individual.

Laboratory education is neither psychoanalysis nor intensive group therapy.

During the past several years I have been meeting with a group of psychiatrists and clinical psychologists who are trying to differentiate between group therapy and everything else. One problem we discovered is that therapists define therapy as any change. The difficulty with this definition is that it means any change is therapy.

We have concluded that it may be best to conceive of a continuum of "more" or "less" therapy. The more the group deals with unconscious motivations, uses clinical constructs, focuses on "personal past history," and is guided in these activities by the leader, the more it is therapy. Therapy is usually characterized by high proportions of these activities because the individuals who are participating are so conflicted or defensive that they are not able to learn from each other without these activities.

In my view, a T Group is—or should be—a group that contains individuals whose internal conflicts are low enough to learn by:

> Dealing with "here and now" behavior (what is going on in the room).
> Using relatively nonclinical concepts and non-clinical theory.
> Focusing on relatively conscious (or at most preconscious) material.
> Being guided increasingly less by the leader and increasingly more by each other.
> Accomplishing this in a relatively (to therapy) short time (at the moment, no more than three weeks).

This does not mean that T Groups do not, at times, get into deeper and less conscious problems. They do; and, again, they vary primarily with the staff member's biases. Usually most educators warn the group members against striving to become "two bit" psychologists.

Laboratory education does not have to be dangerous, but it must focus on feelings.

Interpersonal problems and personal feelings exist at all levels of the organization, serving to inhibit and decrease the effectiveness of the system. Does it seem to be logical (in fact, moral) for a company to say that it is not going to focus on something that people are already experiencing and feeling? The truth is that people *do* focus on interpersonal problems every hour of the day. They simply do not do it openly.

Now for the argument that the laboratory program can hurt people and is, therefore, dangerous. The facts of life are that people are being hurt every day. I do not know of any laboratory program that did, or could, create for people as much tension as they are experiencing in their everyday work relationships.

It is true that laboratory education does require people to take risks. But does anyone know of any learning that truly leads to growth which does not involve some pain and cost? The value of laboratory education is that it keeps out the people who want to learn "cheaply" and it provides the others with control over how much they wish to learn and what they want to pay for it.

The objective of laboratory education is to develop effective reality-centered leaders.

Some people have expressed concern that if an executive goes through such a learning experience, he might somehow become a weak leader. Much depends on how one defines strong leadership. If strong leadership means unilateral domination and directiveness, then the individual will tend to become "weaker." But why is such leadership strong? Indeed, as I have suggested, it may be weak. Also it tends to develop subordinates who conform, fear to take risks, and are not open, and an organization that becomes increasingly rigid and has less vitality.

Nor can one use the argument that directive leadership has worked and that is why it should remain. There are data to suggest that directive leadership can help an organization under certain conditions (e.g., for routine decisions and under extreme emergencies). But these conditions are limited. If directive leadership is effective beyond these relatively narrow conditions, it may be because of a self-fulfilling prophecy. Directive leadership creates dependence, submissiveness, and conformity. Under these conditions subordinates will tend to be afraid to use their initiative. Consequently, the superior will tend to fill in the vacuum with directive leadership. We now have a closed cycle.

The fact is that directive leaders who learn at a laboratory do not tend to throw away their directive skills. Rather, they seem to use directive leadership where and when it is appropriate. It cannot be emphasized too strongly that there is nothing in laboratory education which requires an individual to throw away a particular leadership pattern. The most laboratory education can do is help the individual see certain unintended consequences and costs of his leadership, and help him to develop other leadership styles *if* he wishes.

Change is not guaranteed as a result of attendance.

Sometimes I hear it said that laboratory education is not worthwhile, because some individuals who have attended do not change, or if they do change, it is only for a relatively short period of time.

Let me acknowledge that there is an immense gap in our knowledge about the effectiveness of a laboratory. Much research needs to be done before we know exactly what the payoff is in laboratory education. However, there are a few statements that can be made partially on the basis of research and experience and partially on the basis of theory.

One of the crucial learnings of a laboratory is related to the development of openness and trust in human relationships. These factors are not generated easily in a group. It takes much effort and risk. Those who develop trust in a group learn something very important about it. Trust cannot be issued, inspired, delegated, and transferred. It is an interpersonal factor which has to be *earned* in each relationship. This is what makes trust difficult to develop and precious to have.

Thus, it does not make very much sense to expect that suddenly an individual will act as if he can trust and can be trusted in a setting where this was never true. One executive was needled by the corporate president, who observed that he had not seen any change in the former's behavior. The executive responded, "What makes you think I feel free to change my behavior in front of you?"

This remark points up the possibility that if there is not any observable change, it could mean that the individual has not learned much. But it could also mean that he has learned a great deal, *including* the fact that he ought not to behave differently when he returns. For, it must be emphasized, laboratory education is only a partial attack on the problem of organizational effectiveness. If the changes are to become permanent, one must also change the nature of the organizational structure, managerial controls, incentive systems, reward and penalty systems, and job designs.

IMPACT ON ORGANIZATION

The impact of laboratory education on the effectiveness of an organization is extremely difficult to isolate and measure. Organizations are so complex, and their activities influenced by so many factors, that it is difficult to be precise in specifying the causes of the impact.

In one study that I conducted of the 20 top executives of a large corporate division, I did find a significant shift on the part of the experimental group toward a set of values that encouraged the executives to handle feelings and emotions, deal with problems of group maintenance, and develop greater feelings of responsibility on the part of their subordinates for the effectiveness of the organization.

As the table shows, the impact of laboratory education continued at a high level for a period in excess of six months. However, during the tenth month a fade-out began to appear. *This was studied and data were obtained to suggest that the executives had not lost their capacity to behave in a more open and trustful manner, but they had to suppress some of this learning because the corporate president and the other divisional presidents, who were not participants in the laboratory, did not understand them.*

Table I.

Before-and-After Values of 11 Executives
Who Experienced Laboratory Education

In an administrative situation, whenever possible . . .	*Before T-group*	*Six months after*
1a. The leader should translate interpersonal problems into rational intellective ones	100%	10%
1b. The leader should deal with the interpersonal problems	0	81
2a. The leader should stop emotional disagreement by redefining the rational purpose of the meeting	90	10
2b. The leader should bring out emotional disagreements and help them to be understood and resolved	6	81
3a. When strong emotions erupt, the leader should require himself and others to leave them alone and not deal with them	100	18
3b. When strong emotions erupt, the leader should require himself and offer others the opportunity to deal with them	0	82
4a. If it becomes necessary to deal with feelings, the leader should do it even if he feels he is not the best qualified	100	9
4b. The leader should encourage the most competent members	0	90
5a. The leader is completely responsible for keeping the group "on the track" during a meeting	100	0
5b. The group members as well as the leader are responsible for keeping the group "on the track"	0	100

This finding points up two important problems. Change is not going to be effective and permanent *until the total organization* accepts the new values. Also, effective change does *not* mean that the executives must lose their capacity to behave according to the pyramidal values. They do so whenever it is necessary. However, now they have an additional way to behave, and they use it whenever possible. They report that irrespective of the problem of acceptance by others, they find the pyramidal values are effective when they are dealing primarily with *routine, programed* decisions. The new values and manner of leadership seem to be best suited for decisions that are *unprogramed, innovative,* and require high commitment.

It is important to emphasize that laboratory education does *not* tell anyone what type of leadership to select. It does not urge him always to be more "democratic" or "collaborative." A successful laboratory helps the executives realize the unintended costs of the "old," develop "new" leadership behavior and philosophies, and become competent in utilizing whatever leadership style is appropriate in a given situation. A laboratory helps an individual increase his repertory of leadership skills and his freedom to choose how he will behave. If it coerces the executive, it is for him to become more *reality-centered*.

Another way of describing the impact of a laboratory program on an organization is for me to offer you excerpts from a tape of a meeting where the executives discussed the difficulties as well as successes that they were having 30 days after the program. The first part of the tape contains a discussion of examples of concrete changes which the members felt were a result of the laboratory. Here is a sample of the changes reported:

(1) Executives reported the development of a new program for certain pricing policies that could not be agreed upon before, and laid part of the success to their new ability to sense feelings.

(2) One executive stated, "We are consciously trying to change our memos. For example, we found a way to decrease the 'win-lose' feelings and 'rivalries.' "

(3) The personnel director reported a distinct improvement in the sensitivity of the line managers to the importance of personnel problems, which before the laboratory seemed to have a second-class status. He said he was especially pleased with the line executives' new awareness of the complexity of personnel problems and their willingness to spend more time on solving them.

The excerpt presented here mirrors the tone of the entire meeting. I have not purposely selected only that section in which the men praised the laboratory. If the men had criticized the laboratory, such criticism would have been included. As you may see, the researcher actually pushed the group for more negative comments.

No. 4 (after reporting that his superior, a member of the experimental group, had made a decision which should have been left to him): I was really fuming. I was angry as hell. I walked into his office and I said to myself, "No matter what the hell happens, I'm going to tell him that he cannot do that any more." Well, I told him so. I was quite emotional. You know it floored me. He looked at me and said, "You're right; I made a mistake, and I won't do that again." Well I just don't think he would have done that before.

No. 7: The most important factor in motivating people is not what you say or do; it's giving a person the opportunity to express his views and the feeling that one is seriously interested in his views. I do much less selling but it sure takes longer.

No. 2: I've had a problem. I now have a greater need for feedback than before, and I find it difficult to get. The discussion on internal commitment made much sense to me, and I try to see if I can create conditions for it.

The thing that bothers me is that I try to handle it correctly, but I don't get feedback or cues as to how well I'm doing, as I used to at the lab. The meeting is over, and you don't know whether you've scored or not. So after each meeting I've got 10 question marks. The things that before were never questions are now question marks.

You don't get feedback. You ask for something and they respond, "I know what you're trying to do." They think I've something up my sleeve. All I want is to get feedback. It was obvious to me they were all waiting for me to make the decision. But I wanted them to make it. This was their baby, and I wanted them to make it. Two days later they made it. Fine, in this case I got feedback. The point was that their decision was a severe reversal, and I realize it was difficult for them to make. But they made it. Before, I simply would have pointed out the facts, and they would have "agreed" with the reversal, but down deep inside they would have felt that they could have continued on. As it is now, it's their decision. I think they now have a greater sense of internal commitment. People are now freer to disagree.

No. 11: My list of decisions to be made is longer. I am hoping that they will make some decisions. I now know how much they wait for me.

No. 11 (after telling how he wrote a note which in effect damned No. 2 and maintained his own correctness, then reread it and realized how defensive he was): Before I wouldn't have even seen this.

No. 2: One of our most difficult jobs will be to write our feelings and to write in such a way that others can express their feelings.

No. 3: I have some difficulties in evaluating this program. What have we gotten out of this? What are we able to verbalize about what we got out of this? Do others of you have difficulty in verbalizing it?

No. 2: I have the same difficulty. I have been totally ineffective describing the experience.

No. 8: Each time I try I give a different answer.

No. 1: I don't have too much difficulty. One thing that I am certain of is that I see people more as total human beings. I see aspects of them that I had never seen before.

No. 9: I'm frustrated because I now realize the importance of face-to-face communication. I'm so far from the general managers that it is not so hot. Has anyone tried to write memos that really get feelings brought out?
  I find myself questioning much more than I ever did before I have a more questioning attitude. I take into account more factors.

No. 4: We've been talking about things as if we've slowed down a bit. We haven't. For example, remember you (No. 1) and I had a problem? I'm sure Arden House was very helpful. If I hadn't been there, my reaction to you would have been different. I would have fought you for hours.

No. 1: I know we can talk to each other more clearly. It's not a conscious way. It's spontaneous.

No. 3: I have to agree we can make some decisions much faster. For example, with No. 2 I simply used to shut up. But now I can be more open. Before the laboratory, if I had an intuitive feeling that something was wrong, but I wasn't sure, I'd keep quiet until things got so bad that then I'd have a case to go to the boss. Now I feel freer to talk about it sooner and with No. 2.
  I now feel that we are going to say exactly how we feel to anyone. You (the president), for example, don't have to worry, and, therefore, question, probe, and draw us out.

President: Yes, and today I found No. 1, who told me that he simply would not agree with me. And I said to myself, "God bless you. He really is open now."

No. 1: I agree. I would not have expressed this feeling before being in this group. It's obvious that one should but I didn't.

(No. 2 and No. 1 show real insight into how they are being manipulated by people outside and above the group. They are much more aware of the manipulative process. "This kind of manipulation is dynamite. It burns me up.")

No. 1: Yes, it's really horrible to see it and not be able to do anything about it.

No. 7: In this case it seems to me you've got to really hit hard, because you're dealing with an untrained man (laughter). . . . I think I now have a new understanding of decision making. I am now more keenly aware of the importance of getting a consensus so that the *implementation* is effective. I am not trying to say that I do this in every meeting. But I do strive more to give opportunity for consensus.

No. 1: One of the problems that I feel is that the "initiated" get confused so they don't play the game correctly. Sometimes I feel walked upon, so I get sore. This is difficult. (Many others expressed agreement.)

No. 6: Does it help to say, "I trust you?" I think it does.

No. 11: For example, No. 2, you went to a meeting where you admitted you had made a mistake. Boy, you should have heard the reaction. Boy, Mr. ———— admitted a mistake. Well, wonderful; it helped to get these guys to really feel motivated to get the job done.

No. 9: Yes, I heard that many took on a deeper feeling of responsibility to get the program on the right track.

No. 7: I'd like to come back to what No. 6 said. I used to say to people that I trusted them, that I was honest, and so on. But now I wonder if people really believe me, or if they don't begin to think if I'm not covering that I'm not honest.

No. 3: Another example which I am now aware of is the typical way we write memos. We start off: "I have confidence in your judgment to handle this question," and so on. Few more paragraphs. Then fifth paragraph reads: "Please confirm by return mail exactly what you have done and what controls have been set up."

No. 2: I agree. We do an awful lot to control people. Although I think that we're trying.

(No. 7 gave examples of how he stopped making a few phone calls to exert pressure. Others agreed.)

Researcher: Aren't there negative comments?

No. 11: We have one man who has chosen not to be here. I wonder why?

No. 3: Well, really, to me that is a sign of health in the group. He feels he would still be accepted even if he didn't come. It certainly would be easy for him to come and just sit here.

No. 1: Yes, he wouldn't go to the trouble of avoiding a meeting that you didn't think was important.

No. 3: The only negative that I can think is: "What can you tell me that actually increases effectiveness?" I am not sure, but I must agree that there is a whale of a different climate.

No. 7: Well, I'd like to develop a list of things that we feel we have gotten out of this program so far. How do others of you feel? (All agreed, "Let's try.")

(ALL GROUP MEMBERS reporting they reached the following conclusions):

(a) All of us begin to see ourselves as others see us . . . a real plus.

(b) A degree of greater confidence in oneself in meetings and in interviews. Beginning to be more comfortable with self.

(c) Greater confidence in associates. We feel more secure that you're telling what you think. . . . Greater feeling of freedom of expression to say what you really think.

(d) Individuals have a greater understanding and appreciation of viewpoint of associates.

(e) Greater appreciation of the opposite viewpoint.

(f) An awareness of what we do and others do that inhibits discussion.

(g) More effective use of our resources . . . getting more from them, and they feel this . . . patient to listen more.

(h) Meetings do not take longer and implementation is more effective. Internal commitment is greater.

(i) We have had a great realization that being only task-oriented, we will not get the best results. We must not forget worrying about the organization and the people.

(j) We get more irritated to infringement of our jobs and unique contributions.

(k) Fewer homemade crises.

No. 6: One of the difficult things about the list is that when you look at it, you wake up to the fact that you haven't really been using these principles. When you tell someone else who doesn't realize the gap between knowing something and actually doing it, he doesn't realize.

No. 7: But I think I really did learn and do care. Now when I think what I used to do, because that was the way. Today I realize that I could have had three times as much if I had known what I know now."

CONCLUSION

While I do not hold up laboratory education as a panacea to remedy all organizational problems, I do feel that six conclusions can fairly be drawn:

(1) Laboratory education is a very promising educational process. Experience to date suggests that it can help some organizations to *begin* to overcome some of their problems.

(2) Laboratory education is *not* a panacea, nor is it a process that can help every organization. Furthermore, it must be followed by changes in the organization, its policies, managerial controls, and even technology. Not all organizations can profit from it; nor do all organizations need similar amounts of it. All these factors should be carefully explored before becoming involved.

(3) Not all laboratory programs are alike. Some focus more on interpersonal learning, some on intellectual problem solving, some on small groups, some on intergroups, and some on varying combinations of all of these. Again a careful diagnosis can help one to choose the right combination for the organization, as well as the appropriate educators. Nor are all laboratory programs equally effective. The competence of the educators can vary tremendously, as well as the receptivity of those who attend. The best thing to do is to attempt to attend a laboratory program conducted by competent professionals.

(4) Openness, trust, commitment, and risk-taking grow only where the climate is supportive. A one-shot program, even at its best, can only begin the process of unfreezing the executive system. For optimum results, repeat or "booster" programs will be necessary.

(5) Although I personally believe that a laboratory program with the "natural" or actual working groups has the greatest probable payoff, it also has the greatest risk. However, one does not have to begin the process this way. There are many different ways to "seed" an organization, hoping to develop increasing trust and risk-taking. The way that will be most effective can best be ascertained by appropriate study of the executive system.

(6) Finally, if you ever talk to an individual who has had a successful experience in a laboratory, you may wonder why he seems to have difficulty in describing the experience. I still have difficulty describing this type of education to a person who is a stranger to it.

I am beginning to realize that one reason for the difficulty in communication is that the meaningfulness of a laboratory experience varies enormously with each person. Some learn much; some learn little. I find that my learning has varied with the success of the laboratory. Some can hardly wait until it is over; others wish that it would never end. Anyone who understands a laboratory realizes that all these feelings can be real and valid. Consequently, to attempt to describe a laboratory (especially a T Group) to an individual who has never experienced one is difficult because he may be one of those persons who would not have enjoyed the process at all. Therefore, an enthusiastic description may sound hollow.

Another reason why it is difficult to communicate is that the same words can have different meanings to different people. Thus one of the learnings consistently reported by people who have completed a laboratory is that trust, openness, leveling, risk-taking take on a new meaning —a meaning that they had not appreciated before the laboratory. This makes it difficult for a person who found laboratory education meaningful to describe it to another. He may want very much to communicate the new meanings of trust, risk-taking, and so on, but he knows, from his own skepticism before the laboratory, that this is a difficult undertaking and that it is not likely to succeed.

The point to all this is that the results of laboratory education are always individualistic; they reflect the individual and the organization. The best way to learn about it is to experience it for oneself.

An Organic
Problem-Solving Method
of Organizational Change

SHELDON A. DAVIS

In my opinion, behavioral science literature does not give proper emphasis to the principle of confrontation as it relates to the improvement and development of organizations. Furthermore, sensitivity training is not effectively put into a larger context as a means to an end. This paper describes an extensive organizational development effort within TRW Systems which places a heavy emphasis on confrontation and the use of sensitivity training as part of an effort to improve the culture of an organization. The improvement focuses on the quality of working relationships between interdependent individuals and groups.

A few months ago, I learned from a vice-president of a large national corporation that two of the three top executives in his company had recently participated in a Presidents' Conference on Human Behavior conducted by the National Training Laboratories. I learned further that, both before and after attending the conference, these two persons were highly committed to Theory Y notions, as described by Douglas McGregor in *The Human Side of Enterprise*. My acquaintance expressed concern, however, with the form this commitment was taking. One of these men had chaired a meeting during which he expressed his commitment to those assumptions stated by McGregor. As a concrete example of this commitment, he said that a few days earlier a key subordinate had presented some work for approval. The "boss" did not like the quality of the work and said so. The subordinate pointed out that his people had worked very hard in producing the work and were highly committed to it. The top executive said, "OK. In that case, let's go ahead."

To me, this is *not* an example of what McGregor meant. It is an example of very soft human relationships that are not task-oriented and therefore, in my opinion, are irrational. It does represent, however, a problem presented in laboratory training. How can we eliminate some of the soft, mushy, "sweetness and light" impressions that some people feel are implicit in sensitivity training?

Reprinted by permission of the author and NTL Institute for Applied Behavioral Science, associated with the National Education Association, from "An Organic Problem-Solving Method of Organizational Change," by Sheldon A. Davis, in the *Journal of Applied Behavioral Science*, Volume 3, Number 1 (January/February/March 1967), pp. 3-21.

A different approach was recently illustrated within TRW Systems.

A section head, the lowest managerial level in the organization, discovered that a certain quality control procedure for Manufacturing hampered his effectiveness. He sought to get the procedure modified, only to be told that this was impossible because it covered all of the divisions and therefore could not be modified. He was further told that a change would raise the ire of at least one general manager of another division. The section head refused to accept the explanation and personally called a meeting of the general manager identified, the manager of Manufacturing—both vice-presidents of the company, and four levels above the section head—and the director of Product Assurance. Within an hour the procedure was modified in the direction desired by the section head.

The foregoing vignettes dramatize the differences which can occur because of markedly different applications of behavioral science theories within an organization. In both instances, the individuals involved were convinced that they were using the best of behavioral science techniques. The consequence of their interpretation and application had decidedly different payoffs.

The Missing Element in Behavioral Science Literature

The values that McGregor stood for and articulated regarding organizational development have a toughness: In dealing with one another, we will be open, direct, explicit. Our feelings will be available to one another, and we will try to problem-solve rather than be defensive. These values have within them a very tough way of living—not a soft way. But, unfortunately, in much of the behavioral science literature, the messages come out sounding soft and easy, as if what we are trying to do is to build happy teams of employees who feel "good" about things, rather than saying we are trying to build effective organizations with groups who function well and can zero in quickly on their problems and deal with them rationally, in the real sense of the word. As an example of this kind of softness, I do not remember reading in any book in the field that one of the alternatives in dealing with a problem person is the possibility of discharging him.

There is no real growth—there is no real development—in the organization or in the individuals within it if they do not confront and deal directly with their problems. They can get together and share feelings, but if that is all they do, it is merely a catharsis. While this is useful, it has relatively minimal usefulness compared with what can happen if they start to relate differently within the organizational setting around task issues.

Laboratories Are Not Enough

I think one important theme of the nearly four-year organizational change effort at TRW Systems is that of using laboratory training (sensitivity training, T Grouping) clearly as a means to an end—that of putting most of our energy into on-the-job situations, real-life intergroup problems, real-life job-family situations, and dealing with them in the here-and-now. This effort has reached a point where sensitivity training, per se, represents only 10 to 15 percent of the effort in our own program. The rest of the effort, 85 to 90 percent, is in on-the-job situations, working real problems with the people who are really involved in them. This has led to some very important, profound, and positive changes in the organization and the way it does many things, including decision making, problem solving, and supervisory coaching of subordinates.

One generalization I would draw from this and similar experiences is that laboratory training in and of itself is not enough to really make the difference in an organization forcefully trying to become more rational in its processes of freeing up the untapped potential of its people and of dealing more sensibly with its own realities. Attending a strangers' laboratory or, in our case, a cousins' laboratory (that is, being in a T Group with people who are not necessarily from the same job family but are from the same company) is a very useful, important experience. Most people learn much in laboratory training, as has been well documented and discussed. However, this is not enough.

We have felt that the laboratory experience (the sensitivity training experience itself) should not be just three days or a week or whatever is spent in the off-site laboratory. As a result, we have undertaken important laboratory prework as well as postwork. The prework typically consists of an orientation session where the staff very briefly presents some of the theoretical aspects of the program and an explanation of why we do laboratories. During this time, participants in the coming laboratory can ask any kind of question, such as: Is this therapy? Is the company going to evaluate my performance? and so on.

Also, we typically hand out a questionnaire to the participants for their own use (they are not asked to turn it in). It presents questions such as: "What are the three most pressing problems you feel you pose for those who have to work with you?" It is an attempt to get the person to become introspective about his own particular work situation, to begin his articulation process within himself.

Then there is the laboratory itself. This is followed up by on-site sessions several weeks apart, perhaps one evening every other week for three or four sessions. At this time, a variety of actions are taken in an attempt to help people phase into their work situation. There is continued working in the small training groups; there can be exercises such as intergroup competition.

The laboratory is a highly intensive experience. Attitudes toward it can be extremely euphoric, and people can experience tremendous letdowns when they return to the ongoing culture—even a highly supportive one. Therefore, there is major emphasis on working in the ongoing situation in real-life job families as well as in intergroup situations and mergers, for example.

Recently, we have added to the follow-on work an opportunity for the wives of the participants to experience a micro-laboratory. This might be a 1:00 to 5:00 p.m. session on a Saturday, with a staff available, to give the wives some feel for the laboratory experience.

One of the problems many people have as a result of laboratory training is returning to their continuing organizational culture and finding it quite hostile to the values learned and to the approaches they would like to try. The notion very early in the TRW Systems effort was to focus on changes in the ongoing culture itself: the norms, values, rewards, systems, and processes. If all we did was to have a lot of people attend sensitivity training, this might indeed be useful to them as individuals, but its usefulness would be quite limited with respect to the total organization.

We have had other kinds of concerns with laboratory training. We have tried hard not to *send* people to a laboratory but to make it as voluntary as possible. People who are *sent* usually spend much of their time wondering why they were sent instead of working on relevant issues.

If we look at the processes of change itself, it is quite clear that it is not enough for an individual to gain enormous insight into his own situation, his own dynamics, and his own functioning. Granted, this will help him develop a better understanding of how groups work and of the complexity of communication processes. However, if he cannot take this understanding and turn it into action in the on-the-job situation, if he cannot find other people who are interested in trying some of the same ideas, if he cannot bring about a difference in his real life, the value of the laboratory is very severely minimized. In real life, what do we find? Typically, highly traditional methods of management and unrealistic assumptions about people (the kind of Theory X assumptions that McGregor stated). There has to be an emphasis on changing the ongoing organization. The direction has to be toward working in the organization on a day-to-day basis.

Organizational Setting and Development of Program

I should like to describe the program under way at TRW Systems as an example of this kind of effort—of a nonmechancial, organic approach to career development—the development of the careers of the individuals in the organization and the career of the organization itself, both inextricably tied.

TRW Systems currently employs about 13,300 persons. About one third are professional engineers, and half of these have advanced degrees. It is an organization with products of tremendous innovation and change. It is an organization that is highly interdependent. We have a matrix organization: there are project offices and functional areas of technical capabilities such as structures, dynamics, guidance, and control. A project office, to perform its task, must call upon capabilities and people throughout the organization. This is a highly complicated matrix of interdependencies. No one can really get his job done in this kind of system without working with others. As a result, problems of relationships, of communication, of people being effectively able to problem-solve with one another are extremely critical.

The program started at a time when the company was going through a significant change in its role—from an organization with essentially one Air Force contract for systems engineering on ballistic missile programs (Thor, Atlas, Titan, and Minuteman) to a company that would be fully competitive in the aerospace market. This has indeed happened over the past six years. We now have many contracts, many customers. Most of our work is done under fixed-price and incentive contracts; we produce hardware such as unmanned scientific satellites, propulsion engines for the Apollo mission, as well as other types of hardware. The company has become exceedingly more complex in its product lines and its mix of business.

All through this growth and diversification there has been a concern about the careers of the people in the organization, about trying to maintain certain qualities within the organization. Exhibit I was prepared in September of 1965 and is an attempt to list qualities which seem to have a direct bearing on the kind of success we have been having over the past six years. That success has been quite striking: a tremendous increase in sales, and in the number of contracts, a good record in competitions for programs in our industry, and a large increase in the number of employees.

In the middle of 1961, TRW Systems, then called Space Technology Laboratories, began to think about organizational development. At that time, Herbert Shepard, then on the faculty at Case Institute of Technology, spent a portion of the summer at TRW, including some time with key executives. The following summer he spent a month with the organization. Just prior to this visit, the director of Industrial Relations and his associate attended a laboratory conducted by the University of California at Los Angeles.

Shepard's visit and discussions centering around it led to a growing articulation of what we might want to do with respect to career development. A number of things happened in the next several months.

One was the preparation of a white paper on career development—a statement of how we might approach the subject. The paper discussed why a program was needed, assumptions to be made about employees (Theory Y), the type of organizational climate and training needed, as well as some general indications of how we might proceed.

An assumption we made was that most of the people in the organization were highly competent, very intelligent, and certainly experimental. If they could be freed up enough to look at some of their behavior, to question some of their assumptions, to look at assumptions other people were making, to try new approaches, they could, within limits, develop their own specific management theory.

The white paper was circulated to a number of key persons. Interviews were then conducted to determine possible next steps. A series of events led from this point.

One event was the first of many team development laboratories. (By team development laboratory, I mean an activity which might, for example, be a three-day off-site meeting involving a supervisor and the people who immediately report to him. The agenda for the meeting would be "How can we improve our own effectiveness?") The first team meeting involved one of the program offices in the company. It turned out to be quite successful. With this experience under our belts, we had further discussions to formulate what we wanted to do as an organization with respect to the careers of the people comprising it.

Employees within the personnel organization began attending sensitivity training laboratories such as the Arden House Management Work Conferences, conducted by National Training Laboratories.

A very significant event in the total development of this change effort occurred in May of 1963 when a group of 12 key executives attended a laboratory. Their co-trainers were Herbert Shepard, an outside consultant, and myself, a member of the TRW Systems organization.

The participants in this first laboratory were quite positive in their feedback to the director of Industrial Relations and to the president of the company, who himself was very much interested in how people were reacting to the training. The president had given support for us to be experimental: "Let's try things. If they work, continue them. If they don't, modify them, improve them, or drop them."

A consulting team evolved over time. The consultants were not used in any one-shot way but were asked to make a significant commitment of time. They have become involved with us. They have learned our culture and our problems. While our consultants are all qualified T Group trainers, most of their time is spent in on-the-job situations. There is a need to function as a team, since we are all dealing with one organization, one culture, one social system. The kind of cohesiveness that takes place during consulting team meetings has been a critical part of the program at TRW Systems.

In one sense we started at the top of the organization, and in another we did not. In the beginning, there was a shared general understanding between the president and the key people in Industrial Relations about the type of program we wanted. There were some shared values about the organization we had and wanted to maintain, build, and develop. So this was not Theory X management and Theory Y training effort. Both had a Theᵣ   Y quality.

The president and others of ᵤₑ top management team were relatively late in becoming involved in laboratory training and in applying this training to their own job families. The president of the company attended an NTL Presidents' Conference on Human Behavior early in 1965. Directly after that experience, his top team had an off-site team development meeting in March of 1965. In April 1966, they had a follow-up meeting.

Prior to this top team activity many other things had happened with a number of other people in other job families. In fact, this other activity helped us get to the point where the top management team became interested in trying to apply some of these techniques.

Since the program started, more than 500 key persons in the organization have attended sensitivity training laboratories, primarily laboratories conducted by ihe company. The staff of these laboratories is drawn from our consultants, the personnel organization, and, more recently, from skilled and interested employees in line management ·positions.

We have also conducted more than 85 team development efforts. These vary in format, but a typical one involves interviews with each of the members of the team (a job family consisting of a supervisor and his immediate subordinates) and then perhaps a three-day off-site meeting where the interview data are fed back for the groups to work with. The team ends the meeting with explicit action items. Follow-on to the off-site meeting involves implementing the many action items.

We have been devoting much effort to intergroup problems: relationships between Manufacturing and Engineering, between Product Assurance and other parts of the organization, between various interfacing elements in the engineering organizations. We have found that these efforts have a great deal of leverage. We have done some work on facilitating mergers and with key people on approaching satellite launches. The latter become very tense, tight operations where people can become extremely competitive and behave in ways which clearly get in the way of having an effective launch.

Characteristics of the Process

We "wound up" with a number of notions. We did not want to have a program that was canned but one that was experimental. We wanted participation to be voluntary rather than something that the company forced upon employees. We did not want it to be a crash program. (In our industry there are many crash programs.) We wanted the training to be highly task oriented. (If it were not relevant to making a difference on today's problems, it would not be a successful program.) We wanted to have the emphasis on experience-based learning, which implies, in a very general sense, the use of laboratory methods, of people really looking at how they are doing, examining the assumptions behind their management style, identifying alternate ways of problem solving, and making choices based on a wider range of possibilities. We wanted to be concerned with the careers of all employees, not those of key people only. We wanted to be concerned about company goals and the actual, on-the-job work environment, since this has a profound effect on the careers of people. We wanted to place the emphasis on measuring ourselves against our potential, on being quite introspective on how we were doing. So, for example, if there were an either/or situation (and there usually is not), we would rather not have someone come in and lecture on how to conduct staff meetings, but would ourselves look introspectively at the conduct of our own staff meetings. And we wanted to do continuous research on how we were faring so that it could be fed back into the program for further development.

I should like to describe what I think we have come to mean by an organic approach to organizational change within TRW Systems. There are a number of points which, at least for me, tend to describe what is meant by organic methods.

1. There is the notion that if you are interested in improving a particular culture—a particular social system—you must be able to step out of it in the sense of being very analytical about it, of understanding what is going on, by not being trapped within the culture and its own particular values. If you look at a culture from the viewpoint of its own values, you are not going to come up with anything very startling and different for it to do. You have got to be able to step out of it and say, "What really would make sense here?" This ability to step out of the culture and yet not leave it, not become alienated from it, is a very important one.

2. Optimism regarding the chances for meaningful organizational development to take place increases the psychological freedom for those trying to introduce the change. There is certainly a tremendous amount of evidence at this point that significant, even profound, changes can occur in the behavior of individuals and organizations.

3. Taking a systems engineering approach to the effort (i.e., looking at the totality of the system, dealing with fundamentals within it, considering how a change in one part affects parts elsewhere) provides an analytical approach which increases the conceptual freedom.

4. The extensive use of third-party facilitation is made with respect to interpersonal and organizational problems. A consultant who is not directly involved in an emotional sense in a situation can be useful just by that fact.

5. Direct confrontation of relevant situations in an organization is essential. If we do not confront one another, we keep the trouble within ourselves and we stay in trouble. With respect to confrontation, the whole notion of feedback is crucial. Giving persons feedback on how they are doing gives them a choice to do better. Caring plays an important part. Confronting without caring can be a rather destructive process. (See Albee's *Who's Afraid of Virginia Woolf?*) It does turn out that people in general can be very caring of one another.

6. Becoming the "other" is an important part of the organic method. This is the empathic notion that Carl Rogers and others have developed. To have a really meaningful exchange, one somehow has to look at the situation as the other sees it. For a consultant to work effectively with an organization, he has to be perceptive and under-

standing about the organization and its people from *their* point of view.

7. Dealing with the here-and-now and increasing the ability of people within the organization to do the same have a great deal of leverage. It is important in an organizational development effort to start with what is going on now within the organization and to deal with those things effectively. One of our objectives is to help the organization build its own capability, to deal with its problems as they emerge. Problems are constantly emerging in any live organization, and so our objective is *not* to end up with an organization that has no problems: that would be a very fat, dumb, and happy kind of place.

8. Multiplier planning is rather crucial in the early stages of introducing organizational change. What can we next do that will have the largest effect? There is always a wide range of alternatives and possibilities; there is never enough time, money, or energy to do all the things we might do, so we are constantly picking and choosing.

9. Fanning out is coupled with the multiplier planning aspect. It is important in an effort of this kind—if it is not to be subversive, sub rosa, hidden, squashed out—to be something that does fan out: someone does something that leads to others doing something that leads to still others doing something.

10. A person can act, then act again and then act again; or he can act, critique what he just did, then act, then critique, then act. And that is the whole notion of going back and forth between content and process, between doing the job and then looking at how we are doing it. Building that into the day-to-day culture is a major objective.

11. Finally, there is the notion of testing of choices. One always has choices within any particular situation. However, it is typically true that we do not test the choices we have. So someone might say, "Well, I really can't do that because these fellows won't let me," or "Yes, I would very much like to do the following, but I can't because of so and so." Given these limits, some choices do not get tested. One of the efforts is to get people to be aware of the various possibilities they have and to test them—not to accept the stereotypes in the situation, the sacred cows, that exist in any kind of organization, but to say, "OK, this is what makes sense to me in working that problem. This is what I want to try to do."

Underpinnings to the Effort

The principles of confrontation—that laboratory training must be seen as a means to an end, that most of the effort has to be done after people have attended the laboratory, and not in the laboratory itself—

have been central to this effort. This has affected the way we budget time, the way we spend money, the assumptions we make about what we are doing.

Another significant development in this large-scale effort has been a deliberate, successful attempt to build up the internal resources to carry out the program. Two years ago, in a sensitivity training laboratory put on by the company, there would have been a staff of six, four or five of whom were outside consultants. This situation has completely reversed itself. Today, when a T Group cousins' laboratory is conducted, four or five of the persons are from inside the organization, and only one or two are external consultants.

Furthermore, in the on-the-job aspects of the program, the effort is carried on by people within the organization, primarily individuals in Personnel and, increasingly, managers from the line organization.

A very interesting aspect of the program has focused on the question of risk taking. In my opinion, those of us engaged in this kind of work are quite often too cautious, too constrained, and not experimental enough in trying out things within the organization. We do not behave as though we fully believe the implications of McGregor's Theory Y formulation: that people are creative, that they are strong, that they are motivated, that they want to make a difference. We tend sometimes to approach them gingerly and tentatively. These are constraints more within ourselves than within others or within the situation.

Many times our consultants have reported that their experience at TRW Systems has been a very "stretching" one: they have been fully challenged; people at TRW Systems are experimental, want to try things, are saying, "OK, that was useful, what should we do next?" Much of the effort in the consulting team meetings has been to push ourselves to be more developmental, more experimental in the approaches that we take within the effort.

For example, until quite recently, many people in the field felt that laboratory training was not something one could do within a job family. It seems to me that the whole objective of sensitivity training is to develop an on-the-job culture within which we can relate to one another interpersonally just the way we do in a T Group. We at TRW want to make that transfer; we do not want the T Group to be a separate, special kind of experience. We prefer to say: "All right, let's sit down and really level with one another. Let's do this on the job, and from day to day." That is the objective. It leads to a more effective, efficient, problem-solving organization.

Working with teams in real-life situations is exactly what we are

after. Otherwise, the program can be ethereal—not particularly related
to the company's real-life situations. It cannot be "gutty" if it does not
come to grips with some of the tougher issues, pinpoint and deal with
them, and cause people to become involved and to work actively to
solve problems.

In September 1963, I put together a short paper which conceptualized several plateaus that we might be moving through as an organization in this change effort.

The first one is characterized as problem awareness—that point in
time during which there is general recognition and awareness on the
part of some people within the organization that there are crucial interdependencies which exist in order for us to function and that there are
problems due to inappropriate means of dealing with these
interdependencies.

The second plateau, the identification and freeing of key people
within the organization, is seen as consisting of two parts. The first part
is an effort to identify key people in the organization who seem to be
perceptive about the problems the company is experiencing and have a
desire to work on them. They are key people in the sense that their
efforts to deal with organizational problems could produce a multiplier
effect that would lead others to similar action.

The second part of this particular phase of the program is characterized by an effort to provide a situation that would initiate the process of freeing up these potential multipliers from the organizational
and personal constraints which, in the past, kept them from responding
effectively to their awareness of the problems. Here, the strangers' laboratories, the cousins' laboratories conducted by the company, and the
team development laboratories are seen as being especially relevant.

The third phase, or plateau, involves action steps to follow-up—
experimental steps stimulated by a participation in the various kinds of
laboratories that are taking place. These action steps have taken many
forms: a supervisor holding a team development laboratory within his
own job family; a family group diagnosing the kinds of interaction
problems it has with other parts of the organization and beginning to
resolve these problems in an open, direct manner in a search for a
creative solution rather than an avoidance compromise; two persons at
odds moving in on the problem of relating and communicating with
each other; new ways of looking at functions in the organization.

The fourth plateau occurs when the effort itself gains an independent status and becomes a self-supporting system. At this plateau there
are norms within the organization that support open, direct confronta-

tion of conflict, resolution of conflict without resorting to the power structure unless there is somehow a failure in the process, and a shared commitment to objectives as a consequence of being interdependent. These organizational norms would support the giving and receiving of feedback, openness, experimentation, and day-to-day problem solving.

In this fourth phase we are trying to build procedures into the day-to-day situation which, hopefully, put into concrete terms some of the things we have learned in the earlier phases. For example, when a new project office is started it is probably useful to program some team building early in its life. When there is a new merger within the organization, particular attention can be paid to the merger process. One of the things we have learned is that specific attention should continuously be paid to the processes within the organization: how we make decisions, how we fill key spots, how we communicate with one another, how we decide to reorganize, how we make other important decisions. There is a heavy people involvement in these processes, and, typically, they do not get enough attention. If I am concerned about the quality of staff meetings I attend, I tend to talk about them in the hallways or go home and kick the dog and tell my wife about them. I do not exert effort during the staff meetings to try to change their quality and improve them, because somehow that is not legitimate. "Let's keep personalities out of it. Don't get emotional." These are the kinds of expressions that inhibit me from dealing with the problem.

Development through the four plateaus requires considerable invention because the state of the art of organizational change, in my opinion, is such that one cannot program in advance everything he is going to do within the organization. There are some people who approach organizational change this way. I believe their efforts tend to be mechanical and relatively superficial.

Another important aspect of this effort which I think is particularly consistent with Theory Y formulation is that the direction and pace that the effort takes should be meaningful to the members who are participating in it. The consultant in any particular situation has to get in touch with the needs and concerns of the people involved from *their* point of view, not from *his*.

I have tried to suggest that in many situations in which behavioral scientists are trying to apply their principles the really serious limitations are not within the people or the organizations they are working with, but within themselves—their own skills and ability and courage to act. Theory Y has deeply ingrained in it a profound belief in the abilities, strengths, and motivations of people in general and specifically.

EXHIBIT I

Qualities of TRW Systems Which Have a Direct Bearing on Its Success

1. The individual employee is important, and focus is on providing him the tools and other things that he needs to carry out his assignments.

2. The policies and procedures have been designed to be a platform *from which* the individual operates rather than a set of ground rules *within which* he must confine himself.

3. The work we do ought to be fun (personally rewarding, meaningful, enjoyable), and this has had a direct effect on assignments, among other things.

4. There is a great deal of trust displayed in the individual, a minimum of rules, controls, and forces telling him what to do and how to do it.

5. There is a relative lack of social distance between employees and managers and among the various echelons of management. The accoutrements of rank are not used as barriers between managers and others at lower levels of the organization.

6. A heavy emphasis on quality: Attract the best people, give them excellent working conditions, provide them with challenging assignments, demonstrate that paramount importance is placed on professional and technical excellence.

7. Although there has been continuous and rapid change, the organization as a whole has been relatively stable, providing long-term career opportunities for a high percentage of our key people.

8. In giving responsibility to individuals, we have had a bias toward giving "too much" responsibility rather than being conservative. This has "stretched" the individual and, for those who are capable, it has led to rapid growth and outstanding performance.

9. There is, in a relative sense, less organization "politics" (people ruthlessly working at getting ahead, back-stabbing) and more focus on task. Part of the language is "working the problem."

10. On task issues there is a great deal of direct confrontation rather than "passing the buck," maneuvering, and so on.

11. There is a great deal of delegation downward, so that a large number of persons find themselves assigned to tasks with relatively high responsibility.

12. The management group has been quite experimental in its approach to its task rather than generally traditional.

13. The individual employee enjoys relative freedom to be personally responsible for himself and his job. The job is generally seen as an important one and as making a significant contribution to the technological advances in our society.

14. People who will be markedly affected by decisions feel that they will have the opportunity, to a greater degree than is customary elsewhere, to participate in the decision-making process.

Many times we do not act as if we fully believe or understand that set of formulations.

Next Steps

In TRW Systems, we are now moving in a number of directions, some of which I should like to describe. We are moving more toward day-to-day coaching—on-the-job feedback, if you will—with or without consultants and without calling special meetings, but just as we work together. We are paying continuing attention to process as a way of doing business. We are moving more and more toward using third-party facilitation as a standard operating procedure.

So far there has not been a heavy involvement of the rank and file. The first several years in the effort were specifically biased toward working with key people. These are the ones who have a large effect upon the culture, upon the processes of the organization, upon the tone of the climate. But we are now at a point where we want to get more and more involvement of all the employees within the organization.

I think that the experience of the past several years within TRW Systems has rather clearly demonstrated the potential high leverage of applying some of the behavioral science formulations of people like McGregor, Lewin, and Likert. I think it has also demonstrated that there needs to be much more organizational theory development based upon experience, not upon someone's sitting in a room by himself and thinking about the topic. Some of the statements written about organizational development are to me naive, impractical, unrealistic, and unrelated to organizational problems as they actually exist. Through experiences gained at TRW Systems and many other places, we should be able to develop a more sophisticated understanding of organizational development.

Using Employee Questionnaire Results for Improving Organizations

HOWARD BAUMGARTEL

During the thirty years since the pioneering human-factors research in the Western Electric Company, literally hundreds of interview, observation, and questionnaire studies have been carried out in business, governmental, and military organizations. Often, in the course of these studies, researchers and management personnel have been faced with the problem of how to make productive use of the research findings for benefiting organizations in which the research was carried out.

The use of systematic data on operations—measures of cost, production, sales and nowadays, measures of "human factors"—is one of the key problems in rational administration. How can managers make effective use of information about the functioning of their own organizations?

Ordinarily, internal information on the organization's behavior is used in making routine business decisions. However, we know, for example, that data showing increasing costs do not automatically set in motion the necessary forces to reduce costs. The data must be interpreted and the corrective action must be planned as a consequence.

This article presents the findings of an experiment in which the results of a questionnaire survey of employee perceptions and attitudes were used not only as an aid in decision-making but, essentially, as a planned program of management development and organizational change. The results of this study as well as evidence from other research in applied social psychology indicate that a series of intensive, overlapping group conferences on the problems identified in an employee survey can have markedly beneficial effects on the subject organization. This discovery is one of the exciting new developments in the field of executive management.

Reprinted by permission from author and the *Kansas Business Review* School of Business, University of Kansas, Vol. 12, No. 12, Dec. 1959, pp. 2-6.

This article is a summary of a study conducted when the author was associated with the University of Michigan's Survey Research Center. The study was a part of a long-term research program financed by and carried out in The Detroit Edison Company. Dr. Floyd Mann was the director of the research program.

The process of reporting research findings back into a business organization (or to any other group) has come to be called "feedback" because of the obvious analogy with the feedback principle in the household thermostat and other automatic systems-control devices. By conceptualizing this feedback process it can be better understood as a management tool and perhaps used by businessmen to greater advantage.

Our interest in testing the effectiveness of this survey feedback program as a method of improving organizational functioning stemmed from several sources. First, the frequent failure of the usual industrial supervisory training programs to produce measurable improvement had led to a review of the whole problem of organizational change. (Mann, 1957; Zaleznek, 1951) However, the trial and error experience of human-relations researchers in implementing the results of research in client companies had resulted in the promising but experimentally untested conclusion that an intensive "working through" of survey findings could dramatically improve organizational effectiveness. Second, "information theory" and "general system theory," as developed by electronics engineers, automation theorists, and the like, had emphasized the importance and significance of "feedback" and "servomechanism" processes in the effective functioning of any system. Third, social psychologists had been perennially interested in how more accurate information about the perceptions and attitudes of others influence one's own feelings and motives. Finally, group dynamics researchers had been interested in the effects of the feedback process on group effectiveness and community change in a variety of social settings.

design and execution of this experimental study of a survey feedback program. Experimental designs, while often requiring planning and control beyond the tolerance of many administrators, can provide a conceptual model for thinking about organizational change.

HOW THE STUDY WAS CONDUCTED

The electric light and power company in which this study was carried out had for a number of years been supporting an extensive program of research on human relations, absenteeism, morale and so forth. A collaborative relationship between the company and the Survey Research Center had been established to provide for a mixture of basic and applied research and for consultation. This experimental study was originated and carried out in the course of this company-researcher relationship. The research work was done in the Accounting division of the company.

Careful plans were worked out with officials in the Personnel Planning Department and with the top officials in the company's accounting division to carry out the proposed experiment in the use of survey data to improve organizational functioning. Six accounting departments were included; these departments employed about 60 supervisors and about 640 nonsupervisory personnel. Four of the departments received the "feedback program"—conferences on results of a questionnaire survey—during the year 1951-52 and were called the experimental departments. The other two "control" departments received no special attention from the management or research group other than the regular and routine administrative and management activities characteristic of the normal practices throughout the company. In 1950 before the experiment, and again in 1952 after the program, all supervisors and nonsupervisory personnel filled out lengthy fixed-response questionnaires[1] which covered a wide variety of attitudes and feelings concerning the major aspects of the work situation. Many of the questions specifically referred to certain theoretically important human relations variables and concepts. A comparison of the changes in questionnaire responses in the experimental group with changes in the control group would, in this research design, demonstrate the effects of the feedback program in the four departments.

The material for the feedback program was developed out of the "before" 1950 questionnaire data as well as from an earlier survey carried out in 1948. A booklet was prepared for all supervisors and nonsupervisory employees in each department. The results of the responses to the questionnaire surveys were presented in the four sections of the booklet. The first section presented a comparison of employee responses to a set of morale-type questions asked in both the 1948 and 1950 surveys, thus indicating change over time. The departmental employee and the division employee responses to another set of questions were compared in the second section. The third section of the report referred to the dramatic differences in the way nonsupervisory employees and supervisors responded to an identical set of questions about supervisor-worker relationships. The final section reported exten-

---

1. Respondents indicated by checking which of several alternative answers to questions most suited them. On many attitudinal items, the five-step, Likert-type responses were used, *i.e.* from "very much" to "very little."

sive quotations from employee comments written on the last page of the questionnaire. The booklet gave managers and employees very complete and detailed information about each department and its comparison with the division as a whole as well as how attitudes had changed since 1948.

The most important part of the study was, of course, the actual program of meetings and conferences at which time the survey findings were discussed with company personnel. After a short series of meetings with the top officials in the accounting division and the four department heads, the researcher worked individually with the department heads to plan and execute a conference program. The basic device was the establishment of a relatively undirected series of group discussions of the meaning, implications, and action possibilities of the survey data. Individual conferences with department heads led to lengthy meetings between the department head and his supervisors. In most cases, the researcher had one or more conferences with individual supervisors in addition to his participation in the group meetings. The entire program lasted eight months.

The goal of the researcher was not to tell or interpret the meaning and action implications of the data but rather to facilitate the process of personal and group discovery of important human problems and their solutions. Although the researcher's objective was to conclude the survey feedback program with a discussion meeting of each supervisor with his employees, this did not happen in all cases. Those supervisors who had the most "problems," as in other training efforts, also had the greatest difficulty in benefiting from this program. However, consistent with the voluntary principle, each person was free to choose how far he wanted to go in the program—the researcher acted merely as a staff helper.

THE EXPERIMENTAL RESULTS

Change was measured by a 120-item questionnaire asked in the feedback and nonfeedback departments on the 1950 and 1952 surveys. Of these 120 questions, 61 were asked in identical form on both surveys. Seventeen new questions were asked on the 1952 survey about how various aspects of supervision and the job environment had changed since the previous survey. These 17 questions were called the "perceived change" items. Appropriate tests of statistical significance were used throughout the analysis of comparative changes in order to ascertain the meaningfulness of such changes. Item changes were classified

Table I

Items Which Indicate High Favorable Change in Experimental Departments Compared with Control Departments.

A. Relative differences significant at 1 percent level:

Q 2. What do you think of the job you are on (interest)?

Q 6. How important do you feel your work is?

Q 8. How good is your supervisor at handling people?

Q 21. How does your supervisor give recognition for good work done by the employees in your work group?
(5) Trains for better jobs.
(6) Makes note of it in his reports.

Q 25. From your dealings with your supervisor, how well would you say the following comments fit him?
(4) Is a "leader" of men.
(8) Likeable.

Q 38. How do you feel about the progress you have made in the company up to now (satisfaction)?

B. Relative difference significant between 1 and 5 percent level:

Q 1. How do you feel about the amount of responsibility you have in your job (satisfaction)?

Q 12. How does your supervisor usually treat employees with complaints?

Q 21. How does your supervisor give recognition for good work done by employees in your work group?
(10) Gives privileges.

Q 24. How can you tell what your supervisor thinks of the work you do?
(1) He tells me what he thinks.

Q 25. From your dealings with your supervisor, how well would you say the following comments fit him?
(1) Considerate.
(3) Reasonable in what he expects.
(5) Bossy (inverted).

Q 46. How do you feel your group compares with other groups doing similar work in getting the job done?

C. Relative difference significant between 5 and 10 percent level:

Q 7. Considering your job as a whole, how well do you like it?

Q 21. How does your supervisor give recognition for good work done by the employees in your work group?
(4) Tells his supervisors.

Q 25. From your dealings with your supervisor, how well would you say the following comments fit him?
(7) Is a "driver" (inverted).

Q 26. How often are there group meetings in which employees in your work group can discuss things with the supervisor?

Q 33. Taking all things into consideration, how satisfied are you with your supervisor?

Table II
"Perceived Change" Questionnaire Items Which Indicate High Favorable Change in Experimental Departments Compared with Control Departments.

Question 57. What changes, if any, took place in the following areas since the last survey in May 1950?

A. Differences significant at 1 percent level:
  (2) How your work group compares with other groups in getting the job done.
  (9) How free you feel to talk to your supervisor about job problems.
  (10) How much your supervisor understands the way employees look at and feel about things.
  (13) How well the supervisors in your department get along together.
  (17) How much you understand the way your supervisor sees things.

B. Differences significant at 1-5 percent level:
  (3) How often your supervisor holds meetings with the work group as a whole.
  (5) How often your supervisor praises you or gives you credit for good work.
  (6) How sure you are how you stand with your supervisor.
  (11) How well you feel you know your supervisor.
  (12) How much emphasis your supervisor places on getting out the work.

C. Differences significant at 5-10 percent level:
  (4) How good these meetings are.
  (7) How your supervisor handles suggestions made by the employees.
  (14) How you feel about the amount of information you get on what is going on in the company.
  (15) How your supervisor usually handles complaints.
  (16) How willing your supervisor is to try new ideas.

according to the level of statistical significance. Those at the one percent level of confidence represented the most marked changes (the least likely to have occurred by chance). No significance was attached to those changes which did not attain the 10 percent level of confidence.

Table II shows the "perceived change" items which varied most favorably in the experimental departments in comparison with the non-feedback departments. Here the results showed, among other things, that more employees in the experimental departments felt that:

their group was better at getting the job done
they were freer to take job problems to their supervisors
their supervisors better understood their point of view
their supervisors got along better with each other
they understood better how their supervisor see things

Many of these same questionnaire items and the variables they measure have been found to be related to individual and group productivity, absenteeism, and turnover in other research settings (Katz & Kahn, 1952; Kahn & Katz, 1953).

was supported by the findings. In the experimental departments, 34 per
The prediction of overall positive change in the experimental group
cent of the 61 identical items showed statistically significant "improvement" as measured by the question phrasing. Fifteen of the 17 "perceived change" items showed significant positive change in the feedback
departments as compared with the two control departments. In other
words, the questionnaire results showed marked improvements in the
departments which had experienced the change program.

Table I shows the questionnaire items asked both before and after
the program which changed significantly in the experimental groups as
compared with the control groups. The particular changes are noteworthy. To mention only the most important differences, one notes
that after the program relatively more nonsupervisory employees expressed more interest in their work, felt their work was more important, felt their supervisors were better at "handling" people, felt
supervisors made more specific efforts to give recognition by training
and reports, and felt their supervisors were better "leaders" and more
"likeable." In addition, employees felt more satisfied with their
progress in the company.

CONCLUSIONS

The results of this experimental study lend support to the idea that
an intensive, group discussion procedure for utilizing the results of an
employee questionnaire survey can be an effective tool for introducing
positive change in a business organization. It may be that the effectiveness of this method, in comparison to traditional training courses, is
that *it deals with the system of human relationships as a whole*
(superior and subordinate can change together) and that *it deals with
each manager, supervisor, and employee in the context of his own job,
his own problems, and his own work relationships.*

We have speculated that the following conditions are essential for
such a feedback program to be effective in any organization: (There is
reason to believe that the same principles apply in the use of sales and
production information as well as with data concerning human factors.)

1. The information must be about the organization itself – often
   research findings from other companies do not convince the
   present management.
2. The information must be quantitative and objective – personal
   opinions and impressions are often distorted; there must be some

external point of reference.

3. The information must have some stimulating quality by being:

—new information (A good cost accounting system provides new data on departmental costs.)

—information contrary to common belief (Several studies, for example, have shown that older workers produce more than younger workers.)

—information about things not ordinarily discussed (How many times do personal feelings about the boss ever get talked out in staff meetings?)

4. The information must provide directions for or alternative ways of achieving positive change. (Just knowing that there is high turnover and low "morale" in department X isn't enough; one needs to know what factors created the problem.)

—information about things not ordinarily discussed — how many times do personal feelings about the boss ever get talked out in staff meetings?

The information must provide directions for or alternative ways of achieving positive change — just knowing that there is high turnover and low "morale" in department X isn't enough; one needs to know what factors create the problem.

The results of this study suggest that the creative use of new information for conferences and meetings at all levels of departmental organization may be one of the best and most dynamic avenues to management development and organizational growth.

REFERENCES

Kahn, R. L. and D. Katz, "Leadership Practices in Relation to Productivity and Morale," *Group Dynamics*, ed. D. Cartwright and A. Zander, (Evanston: Row, Peterson, 1953).

Katz, D. and R. L. Kahn, "Some Recent Findings in Human Relations Research in Industry," *Readings in Social Psychology*, eds. G. Swanson, T. Newcomb, and E. Hartley, (New York: Holt, 1952).

Mann, F., "Studying and Creating Change: A Means to Understanding Social Organization," in Industrial Relations Research Association's *Research in Industrial Human Relations*, (New York: Harper & Bros., 1957).

Zaleznek, A., *Foreman Training in a Growing Enterprise*, (Boston: Division of Research, Harvard Graduate School of Business Administration, 1951).

Union Carbide's Patient Schemers

GILBERT BURCK

During quite a few recent years the giant Union Carbide Corp.—it is now second in sales among the nation's chemical companies and twenty-sixth among its industrials—was languishing under a cloud. Between 1959 and 1963 its sales advanced hardly at all, and its earnings actually slumped. Investors who were clamoring to pay $150 a share for its stock in 1959 were scrambling to rid themselves of it at $85 a share in 1962. The whole chemical industry was in a cost-price squeeze during most of this period, but for Union Carbide the squeeze seemed more like a hammerlock. There were reports that top management despaired of its ability to get a firm hold on the company. What, Wall Street asked, was going on up there in that great big expensive new building at 270 Park Avenue?

What was going on was a slow but major upheaval, one whose effects can now be observed almost everywhere in the company, beginning right on the fiftieth floor in the spacious suite of President Birny Mason, Jr. himself. Mason's "office" proper measures roughly twenty-five by forty feet, and through its high glass walls, on a clear day, he can take in Westchester County and Long Island at a single glance. But what makes this arrangement interesting is that three equally spectacular suites occupy the *other* corners of the same floor. Nominally, they are the workrooms of the three executive vice presidents; actually the four suites together are known as the President's Office, and the functions of the four men are substantially the same. They constitute a quadrumvirate in which Mason is first among his peers.

This collective top-management arrangement, which is being adopted by other corporations here and abroad, is in part a recognition of the fact that the boss of any worldwide and diversified organization, in an era of change-by-technology, needs more and more help. But at Union Carbide the concept of the President's Office is more than an attempt to make life easier for its top executive. The corporation has adopted the principle, to a degree practically unique in U.S. business, that management decisions can usually be made better by working groups with diverse views and experience than by individuals. Thus the President's Office is the top working group of a company that is being run on every important level—corporate, divisional, departmental, plant—by similar working groups. Physically, the working groups are small committees; but Mason and his colleagues whenever possible prefer not to think of them as committees. It is not merely that committee rule is an old story in U.S. business; it is that so many committees have been (and are) indecisive and unwieldy, mere discussion groups too underpowered or ill-motivated to get anything done.

Union Carbide's partiality for group decision making evolved during nearly fifteen years of gradual and sometimes stormy change, culminating in a grand scheme that went into effect in September, 1964. The reason for the reorganization was the reason for all such changes: the old organization wasn't working well. The company had been a collection of decentralized, walled in, highly individual operations that almost automatically put their welfare ahead of the corporation's. The new organization was designed to make the divisions almost automatically put the corporate welfare first. The working-group system, Mason says, is doing that; it has already developed company-wide agreement about corporate goals and the way to achieve them, and is enabling managers to act with uncoerced unity of purpose.

Happily, the last phase of the reorganization has seen a sharp upturn in the company's fortunes. After years of lethargy, sales in 1964 increased 13 percent to $1.9 billion, and earnings 18 percent to $189 million; and the 1965 earnings have been running about 25 percent higher. Since this improvement coincided with the biggest capital-goods boom in history, it is hard to attribute any specific part of it to the reorganization, which in any event will probably show its biggest payoff some time from now. But there is no doubt that Union Carbide, in the past few years, has undergone profound and salutary changes.

The Archconglomerate

Few corporations anywhere, fifteen years ago, seemed more irretrievably disunited than Union Carbide & Carbon Corp., as the parent was called until 1957. A logical combination of five small technically related outfits, the company was put together in 1917 by a group of midwest utility men backed by a wealthy Chicago utility heir named Cornelius Kingsley Garrison Billings. These enterprisers first got control of the original Union Carbide Co., which made calcium carbide in electric furnaces, and gradually they picked up the other four: Electro Metallurgical Co., which used carbon electrodes in making ferroalloys in electric furnaces; Prest-O-Lite, which used calcium carbide to make acetylene for portable lamps; Linde Air Products Co., which used acetylene and made oxygen for oxyacetylene welding; and National Carbon Co., which manufactured electrodes for Union Carbide's furnaces as well as for the electric arc lamps that flared on street corners up to thirty years ago. Technically related these five surely were, but their product diversity did not make for central control.

Then in 1920, in the course of trying to make acetylene from kerosene, Prest-O-Lite and Linde practically created the synthetic organic chemical industry, now known as the petrochemical industry; and the parent company organized a Carbide & Carbon Chemicals subsidiary to exploit the new products. Chemical research constantly got it into new fields and Union Carbide & Carbon's product line grew more diverse than ever. By the late 1930's the corporation was an archexample of the so-called conglomerate company—a huge business in many businesses, selling a wide and disparate line of products. Compared to it, the loosely organized General Motors that Alfred Sloan struggled to put together in the early 1920's was a paragon of simplicity and homogeneity.

Now a conglomerate is notoriously hard to run from on high. Its top managers must of course be familiar with not one but dozens or more of techniques, products, and markets. But they also must rely on and judge division managers whose view of the world at their own level, particularly if they have been there long, is often totally different from the view at the top level. These division managers naturally tend to think primarily of their own divisions. In their anxiety to show immediate handsome profits, they may sacrifice future profits—e.g., by hesitating to spend on research; or in an access of ill-advised farsightedness, by spending too much. Their requests for capital, moreover, must be weighed against the requests of other divisions, as well as against corporate goals. Thus the critical job of spending capital wisely, which is not easy in any company, can be inordinately difficult in a conglomerate.

Right through the 1940's, Union Carbide & Carbon Corp. did not even try to run its subsidiaries closely, but was content to remain a mere holding company, and the hold was not very secure. The fifteen operating companies were practically autonomous, with their own presidents and policies; some even had boards of directors. Secrecy, jealousy, and duplication, not to say multiplication of effort, were the order of the day. No two divisions used the same code for a customer's name; it took days to find out how much Union Carbide sold to, say, U.S. Steel. The corporate staff, which in any large corporation should be a unifying force, offered very little guidance except legal and financial. There was a corporate operating committee, but it did little except review proposed capital outlays; and it consisted mainly of division presidents, who, although they spent much of their time competing for capital funds, rarely criticized one another's programs in a relevant way. So the operating committee didn't really operate at all; it was essentially a group that reported what was going on. The parent company was as obscure as if it had been headquartered in London, and even in Wall Street nobody knew much about it.

Yet for a long time this bunch of variegated dominions worked very well. As chemist to the chemical industry and metallurgist to the metals industries, U.C. & C. could depend on a steady sellers' market to keep it growing at a healthy rate. It was not until World War II that there were signs of trouble. The U.S. Government, in its drive to increase production, put a lot of companies into chemicals; at the same time the war crippled and even eliminated Union Carbide's market organizations. Then at war's end a lot of newcomers stayed in chemicals; and many other newcomers, notably the cash-heavy oil industry, began not only to make chemicals but to cut prices aggressively.

A Long Time To Change

By the late 1940's the time had come for Union Carbide to look to its organization; and between 1949 and 1951 it did absorb its subsidiaries and change itself from a holding to an operating company. But this move by itself meant little. Not until the early 1950's, when a financial man named Morse Dial became president, did the corporation really begin to act like an operating company. One of Dial's first moves was to set up a new four-man capital appropriations committee, which, unlike the old operating committee, would operate from the corporate point of view. Dial staffed it with himself and three division presidents who had been relieved of their operating duties and promoted to corporate vice presidents. Dial also began a policy, now flourishing more than ever, of shifting men from division to division; thus it is getting hard to find a young, up-and-coming Union Carbide man who has made his whole career, or even a large part of it, in a single division. He built up certain staff functions, such as industrial relations. He encouraged

divisions to break down their monolithic structures into vertically integrated product groups, each under a department head. He promoted the
"profit center" technique of identifying business "entities"—i.e., groups
that could be held responsible for their own costs and earnings. But all
this was a slow process. It took five years before the companies even
agreed to use the words Union Carbide on their letterheads, and it was
not until 1963 that they were all designated divisions. "When men are
used to operating as they please," Mason remarks dryly, "they don't
immediately embrace a corporate approach."

Mason knows, for from the early 1950's on he had been Dial's chief
aide in the change. Both by nature and by experience he was eminently
suited to the job. A chemical engineer from Cornell (1931), he had
started working on pilot plants in South Charleston, West Virginia, and
had served in almost every capacity except sales. While in industrial
relations he took a special and abiding interest in personnel administration, management motivation, and other organization problems, not
only because he doubtless grasped their timeliness and importance, but
because they were to his taste. A quiet, handsome man and one given to
understatement, he possesses what one West Virginia employee calls a
"natural, gratifyin' personality," and seems able to impose his ideas on
others easily. His bent, however, is not to impose but to talk over and
try to resolve disagreements and differences.

By 1958, when Mason was elected an executive vice president and
director, the reorganization program had got an adventitious boost in
the form of tougher times. Costs and capital expenditures were rising,
but prices and profits were falling. Dollar volume of chemicals, plastics,
and gases was still growing at a satisfactory rate, from $784 million in
1955 to $900 million in 1958. But volume of carbons was making
relatively little gain, while that of metals declined from $348 million in
1957 to $246 million in 1958, or enough to put total sales on a plateau.
The demand for metals, to be sure, had fallen not because the company's structure was outmoded but because the steel industry was de-
pressed and government stockpiling had ended. But as Mason remarks, a
cost-price squeeze provides a good time to change because change is
then accepted as necessary.

It was also a good time to try new ideas. In late 1959, Mason asked
John Paul Jones (then forty-one), who had come up through industrial
relations and had worked with Mason when he was running the corporate industrial-relations staff, to look into what was being done in the
field of management motivation and to set up a small staff group to
help Union Carbide's managers. Jones concentrated on the work of

behavioral scientists like Rensis Likert, Mason Haire, and the late Douglas McGregor of M.I.T. McGregor's ideas in particular formed the basic "philosophy" of Jones's organization development group, as it was later called. McGregor held that most management organizations are based on traditional authoritarian systems such as that of the military, and that these systems assume that the average man inherently dislikes work and must be directed and coerced by the threat of punishment. Not so, he said; men exercise self-direction in objectives to which they are committed, and not only accept but seek responsibility. Although a large percentage of the race has the capacity to deal with organizational problems, its potential is only partly exploited, and the trouble is not with people but with organizations. McGregor also demonstrated how staff and line collaboration can be vastly improved, and above all how managerial teams can make better decisions than individuals. He predicted that "man's capacity to collaborate with his fellows in the face-to-face group" will eventually enable management to realize the true potential of its human resources.

The Levelers

This notion of commitment to common goals by group discussion and decision making, Mason decided, contained much that could prove useful to Union Carbide. So Jones's organization development group, besides assuming such routine duties as guiding the corporation's "exempt" (professional and managerial) salary program, set up shop as an inside management-consulting service, which, among other things, teaches groups how to function effectively. Jones stresses an attitude he calls "leveling" or "doing away with the phoniness of what passes for communication between people." Once a group levels face to face and discusses problems frankly, he says, it really begins to do things. Periodically, for example, a group of managers representing four of the company's divisions in the Kanawha Valley, West Virginia, get together to exchange views and discuss problems. At first they took up trivial cases, such as improving telephone service, but gradually they got to the things that counted—breaking through division barriers and doing away with redundant jobs and duplicate facilities. Three years ago there were five engineering departments in the valley; today there is one, and the consolidation was not imposed by New York.

Organization development's group programs offer no panacea; as Executive Vice President Kenneth Rush points out, everybody can't be in on everything and know everything, and you can't make a town meeting out of a stock-option plan. O.D. hasn't always been able to get people to agree, and some executives are still indifferent or skeptical. But O.D. finds itself with more work than ever, and even if it never took on another job its residual influence would be immense. Practically everybody of consequence in the company is tolerably familiar with Jones's ideas, and in a company sweating to develop cohesiveness and unity of purpose by group decision making, that is all to the good.

By 1960, Mason knew so much about how the company really worked and had so many notions about how it could work better that he became the logical candidate for the presidency. He was duly elected in July, and spent the best part of the next three years trimming fat, jacking up operations, and making minor organizational changes.

The Centralizers Win Out

In May, 1963, when Mason succeeded Morse Dial as chief executive officer, the cost-price squeeze was if anything getting worse. So he decided that it was now his "direct and primary responsibility to get the form of organization we needed" as soon as possible. But the idea of a basic reorganization stirred up an immense amount of heat, and Mason found himself spending a year discussing the problem. "Everybody had ideas," he puts it somewhat euphemistically, "and they were all different." Some argued stoutly that Union Carbide was too inherently a conglomerate to be managed centrally; the company should go back to the good decentralized life before it was too late. A few even maintained that the divisions should be given more independence than they had ever had. They could cite worthy precedent. The literature and history of corporate management is full of examples of the irresolvable conflicts between the corporate and division management of a conglomerate, and full of reasons why a highly diversified company is naturally a decentralized one.

In the end, however, most of the company's managers agreed that Union Carbide's divisions had more to gain by closer association than by separation, and they came up with a raft of ideas for making an integrated corporation work—what the corporate staff departments should do and how they should be grouped, how to develop a common measuring stick for capital projects, and so on. Mason also interviewed dozens of executives of other large corporations, and spent many an evening and weekend boning up on management theory and practice.

It was soon manifest that the reorganization would be no simple matter of centralizing an excessively decentralized company. The all-important problem of how to organize a large corporation is never solved by choosing between the extremes of decentralization and centralization; it is solved by achieving a kind of balance between them. When Alfred Sloan decided that General Motors could be run best by delegating as much authority as possible to division chiefs close to their problems, he first had to establish a system for making his multiple giant behave as a single company with a single goal. Similarly, the job of centralizing a large and diversified company is essentially one of devising a system that will let the division chiefs manage and yet encourage them to manage in terms of corporate goals.

By early 1964, Mason had most of the material on the proposed reorganization in hand. Preparing for one of his frequent trips abroad, he packed up a case of memos and reports and booked return passage by sea to give himself time and seclusion for working on them. But the main thing he learned on the five-day return voyage was that disagreement in the executive ranks was still so great that even if he could develop a workable plan by himself he would have a hard time getting his managers to accept it.

When Mason got home, he put himself at the head of a study group of six executives from both the corporate staff and the operating divisions and set to work formulating a new organization plan. The six made rapid progress, and within a couple of months Mason decided it was time to get out of New York and concentrate on a final draft. So they repaired to the company's lodge on Wolf Island, one of the so-called Thousand Islands in the St. Lawrence, where they palavered sixteen hours a day for five days, with time out only for meals and coffee breaks.

The group returned to New York with a clear-cut working "Scheme," as it was thenceforth called. Some loose ends had to be tied up, however, and for two months or more Mason talked at length with dozens of key people. Thus it was midsummer of 1964, a year after he decided to accelerate "a new form of organization," before the study group got its propositions on paper, drew up management charts, and began to explain the final version to the managers. Mason may seem to have trouble making up his mind, but there was method in his apparent irresolution. By letting both staff and operating people discuss the reorganization for years, he subtly achieved a broad if not wholly unanimous acceptance of his aims. By the time he got around to holding meetings to explain the final Scheme, most operating executives were voluntarily committed to it, and it was officially put into effect on a single day—September 9, 1964. "The evolution of the Scheme," Mason puts it neatly, "is a demonstration of some of the principles it involves."

Presidents With Two Hats

In management as in cookery, there are very few totally new inventions; the art of both consists of transforming the old recipes by varying them, the more creatively the better. Union Carbide's Scheme depends on few if any radical innovations. In the main it simply takes the best and most appropriate in modern business practice and adapts it to the corporation's needs. The heart of the Scheme is that it defines corporate centralization as its managers' commitment to corporate goals, and it strives to achieve this commitment by encouraging an extraordinary number of managers, at many levels, to take part in making decisions that affect the corporation as a whole.

The President's Office was established as the top policy- and decision-making group; the office happens to be a quadrumvirate because there were three executive vice presidents when the Scheme was adopted. The three still tend to specialize in what they were doing previously—Kenneth Rush in overseas and staff work, William Haile in domestic operations, and Kenneth Hannan in finance—but they are gradually getting out of their grooves, and any one of them can and does stand in for any of the others. Few of the big problems are solved unilaterally; if differences cannot be overcome at once, the decision is postponed till more information is brought in. But inevitably there comes a time in the most agreeable group when the leader has to resolve an issue; appropriately, the title of chief executive officer was not abolished. Mason remains the leader.

A quadrumvirate of Solomons, however, could handle only a small fraction of the decisions needed to keep a huge conglomerate moving ahead successfully. The divisions must do it; and they must make the kinds of decisions that are right for both themselves and Union Carbide as a whole, and make enough of them to keep from swamping the President's Office with unresolved questions. Doubtless the biggest problem in the reorganization was what to do about the function of the chief executive officers of the divisions. These men still rejoiced in the title of division president, partly because it gave them status in dealing with customers, and they were as proud and possessive as all presidents should be. They held down big and complex jobs; the president of the plastics division, for example, was (and is) responsible for making and selling more than $340 million worth of the stuff a year. At eight one chilly morning "somebody" in the Wolf Island group came up with a way of dealing with the president problem. The solution was first to arrange fifteen of the divisions (since reduced to thirteen) into four groups with more or less common marketing problems:

• Group One includes the chemicals, olefins, plastics, and silicone-products divisions. It accounted for about 40 percent of the corporation's 1964 sales of $1.9 billion. (The $1.9 billion includes all sales in the U.S. and Canada plus exports, but not the $400-million sales by foreign subsidiaries.)

• Group Two, accounting for about 32 percent of the $1.9 billion, now includes the carbon products, mining and metals (ferroalloys), Stellite (high-performance alloys), and Linde (air products) divisions.

• Group Three, accounting for some 13 percent of the $1.9 billion, now includes three divisions oriented to the consumer market—consumer products (Prestone, other auto-care products, Glad Wrap, Englander mattresses, Eveready batteries, etc.), fibers and fabrics (e.g., Dynel), and food products (sausage casing and meat wrappings).

• Group Four, accounting for some 15 percent of the $1.9 billion, consists of the two extraterritorial divisions, Union Carbide of Canada and Union Carbide International.

But merely grouping the divisions doesn't necessarily make them more corporation-minded. The significant innovation is that each division president now wears two hats. He sits on the operating committee that coordinates his group, and spends only half his time running his own division and the other half helping with the affairs of the other divisions in the group. This divided responsibility, some felt, would rob the presidents of their drive, but the objection was met by providing each president with a full-time executive vice president, who spends all his time helping run the division. Given such assistance, the presidents seem to be relishing their new responsibilities. Whether their performance as division chiefs will be affected over time remains to be seen.

Each operating committee is headed by a group vice president who is nominally superior to the division presidents. In practice, however, he is a peer and colleague who keeps the lines of communication flowing between his group and the corporate President's Office. Logically enough, the four group vice presidents, together with the quadrumvirate in the President's Office, constitute the capital-projects committee, which passes on all proposed capital expenditures of more than $250,000.

"People Are Peering Down My Throat"

The Scheme seems to be working particularly well at the operating committee level. The committees have a high degree of responsibility; among their duties is to help develop formalized annual plans. Unlike so many business committees, they are working groups and they *are* acting—and acting in the corporate interest. Now that each division president must answer searching questions by his knowledgeable peers, he finds it hard to nurse along some product that isn't paying its way. Until a year or so ago, most proposals to drop unsuccessful products were initiated by the corporate president; today the operating committees are making them.

Simply by coming into agreement with one another, the committees have solved the problem of how to price products that the divisions sell to one another—an old source of fierce interdivisional strife appropriately known as the "transfer problem." Since September, 1964, the President's Office hasn't had a single transfer problem sent up to it. And proposals for capital expenditures are judged much more sagaciously by the people proposing them than they ever were before. "Life is not easier," says "Rod" Johnstone, carbon-products division president, who started as an engineer with the old National Carbon Co. twenty-nine years ago. "Although I'm in full control of my division, people are peering down my throat with meaningful looks. But decisions are better; these days a project doesn't leave the group for the capital-projects committee until it is thoroughly understood."

The operating committees even undertake reorganizations; a year ago William Nicholson, vice president of Group Two, reduced the number of his divisions from six to four. After months of study he consolidated the ore and metals divisions and the mining operations of the nuclear division into one division (mining and metals), and transferred the rest of the nuclear division to Robert A. Charpie, corporate director of technology. The posts of two division presidents and vice presidents, to say nothing of lesser division functions, were abolished. The very people who lost their jobs helped make the decision, but all these were assigned elsewhere. Thus the operating committees seem to be proving Mason's belief that groups with diverse knowledge and experience, particularly when the problems are "ill structured" or hard to define with mathematical precision, can arrive at better conclusions than individuals. "I hated the idea," says William Humes, vice president of Group Three, "but now I believe it."

At a higher level, the Scheme seems to be breaking down barriers between the operating groups, and enlarging and expediting the flow of information between the groups and the President's Office. The four group vice presidents, who spend about half their time on group affairs and the rest working with the President's Office, regularly meet to review salaries and appraise personnel, with the express purpose of moving people to posts where they can perform most effectively, whether or not they end up by moving across division lines. "It used to be that each division hoarded its talent," says Nicholson, "but today we only think of the best names for the job."

A Sweetener At The End Of The Year

All this enables the men in the President's Office to know more about what is going on in the company than their predecessors ever did. Together with the staff department heads and division presidents, they receive the minutes of all operating committees, which are recorded in considerable detail. They are also in continual touch with the group vice presidents, either individually or in the capital-projects committee. Decisions come better and more quickly. The proposal to build a new $100-million petrochemical plant at Taft, Louisiana, for example, involved several divisions. A few years ago the president might have assigned a task force to appraise the project. But the group vice presidents had enough information on tap to enable the capital-projects committee to allocate the money with dispatch and efficiency. "All the divisions talk to each other," exults Kenneth Hannan. "There is comprehension of our over-all problems that never existed before."

Group effort, moreover, is rewarded by a variable compensation plan, approved by the stockholders in early 1965. A sizable number of management, professional, and technical employees receive an extra year-end compensation related to the return on the corporation's capital investment, dividing up a maximum of 15 percent of the excess over a 7 percent return. For 1965 the payments could amount to some $8 million before taxes, and could average some $3,000 per eligible employee.

Union Carbide's staff functions still remain a problem. Companies with homogeneous products like autos or steel can easily build up large general staffs with clearly defined functions, but conglomerates find it hard to create staff functions useful to all divisions. Mason accordingly has not yet worked out a good "linkage" between staff and line. He has assigned a study committee to the problem and is rearranging and redefining staff responsibilities.

Mason's only new staff function, so far, is the development of a company-wide computerized information system. The corporation operates twenty-five computer systems, but they are scattered around in the divisions, and are used mainly for routine data processing. Since there can be no such thing as effective central management in a company as complex as Union Carbide without plenty of relevant information, Mason made the provision of a centralized computer system a basic element in the Scheme. He set up a department, under William Feathers, previously president of both the carbon and the metals divisions, who envisions an information system that would encompass practically every one of the company's activities. To build a centralized information system, Feathers must analyze and ask hundreds of questions about everything the company does, and in the process he seems bound to uncover many a redundancy. The corporation, for example, supports no fewer than sixteen different sales-analysis systems, many of which may be superfluous.

The Age-Old Conflict

As Mason says, the Scheme was not and still is not expected to provide "a final answer to everything." He is only too painfully aware that the problem of running a huge conglomerate, from the Soviet economy on down, is never solved because there is no perfect solution short of developing a new race of men with the accurate memory and analytical capacity of computers and the intuitive judgment of the greatest of managers. The age-old conflict between division and staff managers, particularly in planning for expansion, still exists and doubtless always will exist. The staff will always tend to think of aggregates, trends, and balance; and the divisions will always tend to press their advantages single-mindedly.

But if there is no perfect and final solution to the problem of running a conglomerate, better and better solutions are possible; and Mason observes what to his mind are significant omens. "A few years ago," he says, "discussions in our company raged about whether we were centralizing or decentralizing, whether this or that was something the division or the corporation should do. Just recently I realized that nobody asks this question any more. The big question now is how we should solve this or that problem."